KU-739-231

THE GUINNESS
BOOK OF WORDS

F CUTHBERTSON
17 FODBANK VIEW
DUNFERMLINE
FIFE
KY11 4UA
0383 726243

THE GUINNESS BOOK OF
WORDS

Martin Manser

GUINNESS BOOKS

Editor: Honor Head
Design and Layout: Jean Whitcombe

© Martin H. Manser and Guinness Publishing Ltd, 1988

Published in Great Britain by Guinness Publishing Ltd,
33 London Road, Enfield, Middlesex

All rights reserved. No part of this publication may
be reproduced, stored in a retrieval system, or transmitted
in any form or by any means, electronic, mechanical,
photocopying, recording or otherwise, without prior
permission in writing of the publisher.

Typeset in Rockwell 9/11
by Fakenham Photosetting Ltd, Fakenham, Norfolk
Printed and bound in Great Britain by Adlard & Sons Ltd, Letchworth, Herts.

'Guinness' is a registered trade mark of Guinness Superlatives Ltd

British Library Cataloguing in Publication Data

Manser, Martin H.
   The Guinness book of words.
   1. English language. Words & phrases.
   Etymology
   I. Title
   422

   ISBN 0-85112-884-X

CONTENTS

Summer afternoon—summer afternoon; to me those have always been the two most beautiful words in the English language.
Henry James

INTRODUCTION

Many people are fascinated by words. Word games and puzzles are immensely popular on television and radio, in newspapers and magazines, and now also on teletext. People enjoy finding out the strange origin of a word or phrase and they sometimes complain about what they see as the misuse of words. All this reflects a lively interest in the language.

This book is for such word-buffs. It's full of words—from word records in the familiar Guinness style—through a survey of the wide range of languages from which English has borrowed (do you know where **ketchup**, **yoghurt**, **geyser**, and **yacht** have come from?)—to looking at unusual stories behind some common words and phrases—such as **white elephant**, **bloomers**, and **beyond the pale**.

We often unwittingly use quotations—and misquotations—in speech and writing (**escape by the skin of one's teeth**, **the be-all and end-all**), so that is the next stop on our tour of the language, taking in some familiar—and some less well-known—slogans and graffiti (from **Kilroy was here** to **Queen Elizabeth rules UK**). And finally, to word games; anagrams, doublets, spoonerisms (**You must leave by the next town drain**), puns, tongue-twisters and lots more.

The Guinness Book of Words has been designed for anyone who enjoys delving into the language. It has been written as an informative and entertaining guide to the language; and I hope that something of the intriguing wonder of words will be discovered in the following pages.

Martin H. Manser
1988

The two most beautiful words in the English language are
'Cheque Enclosed'.
Dorothy Parker

1 *World word records*

The ability to speak is believed to be dependent upon physiological changes in the height of the larynx between Homo erectus and Homo sapiens sapiens as developed *c.* 45,000 BC. **The earliest written language** discovered has been on Yangshao culture pottery near Sian in the Shensi province of China found in 1962. This bears proto-characters for the numbers 5, 7, and 8 and has been dated to 5000–4000 BC. **The earliest dated pictographs** are on clay tablets from Nippur, southern Iraq from a level equivalent to Uruk V/V1 and dated in 1979 to *c.* 3400 BC. Tokens or tallies from Tepe Asiab and Ganji-I-Dareh Tepe in Iran have however been dated to 8500 BC. **The earliest known piece of English writing** (*c.* AD 630) is a fragment of Irish uncial script in an ecclesiastical history sold for £75,000 by the Folger Shakespeare Library, Washington DC to the British Rail Pension Fund at Sotheby's, London on 25 June 1985.

Fragments of Roman wooden writing tablets found in the 1970s at Vindolanda near Newcastle-upon-Tyne have been shown to make up the **earliest known substantial written records** in British history. These contain letters and a quotation from the Roman poet Virgil and are dated *c.* AD 100.

The **written language** with the **longest continuous history** is Chinese, extending over more than 6000 years from the Yangshao culture (see above) to the present day.

The rarest speech sound is probably the sound written ř in Czech which occurs in very few languages and is the last sound mastered by Czech children. In the southern Bushman language !xo there is a click articulated with both lips, which is written ☉. The l sound in the Arabic word Allah, in some contexts, is pronounced uniquely in that language. The commonest sound is the vowel a (as in the English father); no language is known to be without it.

If the yardstick of ability to speak with fluency and reasonable accuracy is adhered to, it is doubtful whether any human could maintain fluency in more than 20–25 languages concurrently or achieve fluency in more than 40 in a lifetime. Historically the **greatest linguists** have been proclaimed as Cardinal Mezzofanti (1774–1849) (fluent in 26 or 27), Professor Rask (1787–1832), Sir John Bowring (1792–1872) and Dr Harold Williams of New Zealand (1876–1928), who were all fluent in 28 languages.

The most multi-lingual living person is Georges Henri Schmidt (b. Strasbourg, France, 28 Dec 1914), the Chief of the UN Terminology Section in 1965–71. The 1975 edition of *Who's Who* in the United Nations listed 'only' 19 languages because he was then unable to find time to 'revive' his former fluency in 12 others. Powell Alexander Janulus (b. 1939) has worked with 41 languages in the Provincial Court of British Columbia, Vancouver, Canada.

Britain's great linguist is George Campbell (b. 9 Aug 1912), who is retired from the BBC Overseas Service where he worked with 54 languages.

Language is not an abstract construction of the learned, or of dictionary-makers, but is something arising out of the work, needs, ties, joys, affections, tastes, of long generations of humanity, and has its bases broad and low, close to the ground.

Walt Whitman

Alphabet

The **earliest example of alphabetic writing** has been found at Ugarit (now Ras Sharma), Syria dated to *c.* 1450 BC. It comprised a tablet of 32 cuneiform letters.

The **oldest letter** is 'O', unchanged in shape since its adoption in the Phoenician alphabet *c.* 1300 BC. The **newest letters** added to the English alphabet are 'j' and 'v' which are of post-Shakespearean use *c.* 1630. Formerly they were used only as variants of 'i' and 'u'. There are 65 alphabets now in use.

The **alphabet** with the most letters is Cambodian with 72 and Rotokas in central Bougainville Island has **least** with 11 (just a, b, e, g, i, k, o, p, ř, t and u).

The language with **most distinct consonantal sounds** is that of the Ubykhs in the Caucasus, with 80–85, and that with **least** is Rotokas, which has only 6 consonants. The language with the **most vowels** is Sedang, a central Vietnamese language with 55 distinguishable vowel sounds and that with the **least** is the Caucasian language Abkhazian with two. The record in written English for **consecutive vowels** is 6 in the musical term euouae. The Estonian word jäääärne, meaning the edge of the ice, has the same 4 consecutively. The name of a language in Pará State, Brazil consists solely of 7 vowels—uoiauai. The English word 'latchstring' has 6 consecutive letters which are consonants, but the Georgian word gvprtskvnis (he is feeling us) has 8 separately pronounced consonants.

A selection of words without vowels (including y) currently used in English include:

brrr   used to represent shivering

cwm   a deep basin on a mountain
grr   used to represent the growl of an angry dog
hmm   a sign of hesitation or agreement
psst   used to attract someone's attention
shh   used to request silence
zzz   used to represent snoring or sleep

The **largest permanent letters** in the world are giant 600 ft/183 m letters spelling READYMIX on the ground in the Nullarbor near East Balladonia, Western Australia. These were constructed in December 1971.

The world's **smallest letters** are the 16 letters MOLECULAR DEVICES which have been etched into a salt crystal by an electron beam so that the strokes were only 2 to 3 nm (10^{-9}) wide—the width of 20 hydrogen atoms. This was done by Michael Isaacson at Cornell University, Ithaca, New York in February 1982.

Braille alphabet

a b c d e f g h i j k l m

n o p q r s t u v w x y z

The system of Braille writing used by and for blind people was originally invented in 1824 by the French teacher Louis Braille (1809–52). The full code consists of 63 characters, each made up of one or more embossed dots on a six-position cell.

Greek alphabet

The Greek alphabet consists of twenty-four letters—seven vowels and seventeen consonants. The seven vowels are alpha (short a), epsilon (short e), eta (long e), iota (short i), omicron (short o), upsilon (short u, usually transcribed y), and omega (long o).

Name	Capital	Lower case	English equivalent	Name	Capital	Lower case	English equivalent
Alpha	A	α	a	Nu	N	ν	n
Beta	B	β	b	Xi	Ξ	ξ	x
Gamma	Γ	γ	g	Omicron	O	ο	ō
Delta	Δ	δ	d	Pi	Π	π	p
Epsilon	E	ε	ĕ	Rho	P	ρ	r
Zeta	Z	ζ	z	Sigma	Σ	σ ζ	s
Eta	H	η	ē	Tau	T	τ	t
Theta	Θ	θ	th	Upsilon	Y	υ	u or y
Iota	I	ι	i	Phi	Φ	φ	ph
Kappa	K	κ	k	Chi	X	χ	kh
Lambda	Λ	λ	l	Psi	Ψ	ψ	ps
Mu	M	μ	m	Omega	Ω	ω	o

Greek has no direct equivalent to our c, f, h, j, q, u, v, or w.

Russian alphabet

The Russian alphabet is written in Cyrillic script, so called after St Cyril, the 9th century monk who is reputed to have devised it. It contains thirty-three characters, including five hard and five soft vowels. Five other Cyrillic letters appear only in Bulgarian (one) and Serbian (four).

Capital	Lower case	Name	English equivalent	Capital	Lower case	Name	English equivalent
А	а	ah	ā	Т	т	teh	t
Б	б	beh	b	У	у	oo	oo
В	в	veh	v	Ф	ф	eff	f
Г	г	gheh	g	Х	х	hah	h
Д	д	deh	d	Ц	ц	tseh	ts
Е	е	yeh	ye	Ч	ч	cheh	ch
Ж	ж	zheh	j	Ш	ш	shah	sh
З	з	zeh	z	Щ	щ	shchah	shch
И	и	ee	ee	Ъ	ъ	(hard sign)	—
К	к	kah	k	Ы	ы	yerih	I
П	п	ell	l	Ь	ь	(soft sign)	—
М	м	em	m	Э	э	eh	e
Н	н	en	n	Ю	ю	you	yu
О	о	aw	aw	Я	я	ya	yā
П	п	peh	p				
Р	р	err	r	Е	е	yaw	yo
С	с	ess	s	Й	й	short й	elided 'y'

From *The Guinness Book of Answers*, Guinness Publishing.

The world's main languages

The world's total of languages and dialects is now estimated to be about 5000. The most widely spoken, together with the countries in which they are used, are as follows.

1 **Guóyǔ** (standardized Northern Chinese or Běifānghuà). Alphabetized into Zhùyīn fùhào (37 letters) in 1918 and converted to the Pinyin system of phonetic pronunciation in 1958. Spoken in China (Mainland). Language family: Sino-Tibetan. 709,000,000.

2 **English**. Evolved from an Anglo-Saxon (Old English), Norman-French and Latin amalgam c. 1350. Spoken in Australia, Bahamas, Canada, Sri Lanka, Cyprus, The Gambia, Ghana, Guyana, India (non-constitutional), Ireland, Jamaica, Kenya (official with Swahili), Malaysia, Malta (official with Maltese), New Zealand, Nigeria (official), Pakistan (now only 1 per cent), Sierra Leone (official), Singapore, South Africa (38 per cent of white population), Tanzania (official with Swahili), Trinidad and Tobago, Uganda (official), UK, USA, Zimbabwe and also widely as the second language of educated Europeans and of citizens of the USSR. Language family: Indo-European. 400,000,000.

3 **Great Russian**. The foremost of the official languages used in the USSR and spoken as the first language by 60 per cent of the population. Language family: Indo-European. 250,000,000.

4 **Spanish**. Dates from the 10th century AD; spoken in Argentina, Bolivia, Canary Islands, Chile, Colombia, Costa Rica, Cuba, Dominican Republic, Ecuador, El Salvador, Guatemala, Honduras, Mexico, Nicaragua, Panama, Paraguay, Peru, The Philippines, Puerto Rico, Spain, Uruguay, Venezuela. Language family: Indo-European. 230,000,000.

5 **Hindustani** (a combination of Hindi and Urdu) is foremost of the 845 languages of India of which 15 are 'constitutional'. Hindi (official) is spoken by more than 25 per cent, Urdu by nearly 4 per cent and Hindustani, as such, by 10 per cent. In Pakistan, Hindustani is the third most prevalent language (7½ per cent). Language family: Indo-European. 220,000,000.

=6 **Bengali**. Widely spoken in the Ganges delta area of India and Bangladesh. Language family: Indo-European. 135,000,000.

=6 **Arabic**. Dates from the early 6th century. Spoken in Algeria, Bahrain, Egypt, Iraq (81 per cent), Israel (16 per cent), Jordan, Kuwait, Lebanon, Libya, Maldives, Morocco (65 per cent), Oman, Qatar, Saudi Arabia, Somalia, Sudan (52 per cent), Syria, Tunisia, United Arab Emirates and both Yemens. Language family: Hamito-Semitic. 135,000,000.

=6 **Portuguese**. Distinct from Spanish by 14th century and, unlike it, was more influenced by French than by Arabic. Spoken in Angola, Brazil, Goa, Macao, Mozambique, Portugal, East Timor (Indonesia). Language family: Indo-European. 135,000,000.

9 **German**. Known in written form since the 8th century AD. Spoken in the Federal Republic of Germany (West) and the German Democratic Republic (East), Austria, Liechtenstein, Luxem-

---

Esperanto

Esperanto (meaning 'one who hopes') is probably the world's most successful 'artificial language', one specially created for use as an international medium of communication. Introduced in 1887 by the Polish doctor and philologist Ludwig Lazarus Zamenhof (1859–1917), the language has a relatively simple grammar, with characteristic word endings for nouns, adjectives, and verbs. The vocabulary is derived from word roots found in the European (especially the Romance) languages. The rules of the language's structure and formation were laid down in Fundamento de Esperanto, published in 1905.

Estimates of the number of speakers vary from under 1 million to 15 million; a World Esperanto Congress is held annually and over 30,000 books—including many of the world's literary classics—have been translated into the language.

bourg and Switzerland plus minorities in the USA, USSR, Hungary, Poland, Romania and in formerly colonized German territories in eastern and southern Africa and the Pacific. Language family: Indo-European. 120,000,000.

10 **Japanese**. Earliest inscription (in Chinese characters) dates from the 5th century. Spoken in Japan, Formosa (Taiwan), Hawaii and some formerly colonized Pacific Islands. Unrelated to any other language. 110,000,000.

11 **Malay-Indonesian**. Originated in Northern Sumatra, spoken in Indonesia (form called Bahasa is official), Malaysia, Sabah, Sarawak, Thailand (southernmost parts). Language family: Malayo-Polynesian. 100,000,000.

12 **French**. Developed in 9th century as a result of Frankish influence on Gaulish substratum. Fixed by Académie Française from 17th century. Spoken in France, French Pacific Is., Belgium, Guadeloupe, Haiti, Luxembourg, Martinique, Monaco, Switzerland, the Italian region of Aosta, Canada, USA (Louisiana) and widely in former French colonies in Africa. Language family: Indo-European. 95,000,000.

= 13 **Italian**. Became very distinct from Latin by 10th century. Spoken in Eritrea, Italy, Libya, Switzerland and widely retained in USA among Italian population. Language family: Indo-European. 60,000,000.

= 13 **Punjabi**. One of the 15 constitutional languages of India spoken by the region of that name. Also spoken in parts of Pakistan. 60,000,000.

= 13 **Urdu**. One of the 15 official languages of India. Also spoken in parts of Pakistan and Bangladesh. 60,000,000.

16 **Korean**. Not known to be related to any other tongue. 55,000,000.

= 17 **Cantonese**. A distinctive dialect of Chinese spoken in the Kwang-tung area. Language family: Sino-Tibetan. 50,000,000.

= 17 **Telugu**. Used in south India. Known in a written, grammatic form from the 11th century. Language family: Dravidian. 50,000,000.

= 17 **Tamil**. The second oldest written Indian language. Cave graffiti date from the 3rd century BC. Spoken in Sri Lanka, southern India, and among Tamils in Malaysia. Language family: Dravidian. 50,000,000.

= 17 **Marathi**. A language spoken in west and central India, including Goa and part of Hyderabad and Poona with written origins dating from about AD 500. Language family: Indo-European. 50,000,000.

21 **Javanese**. Closely related to Malay. Serves as the language of 50 per cent of Indonesian population. Language family: Malayo-Polynesian. 45,000,000.

= 22 **Ukrainian (Little Russian)**. Distinction from Great Russian discernible by 11th century, literary zenith late 18th and early 19th century. Banned as written language in Russia 1876–1905. Discouraged since 1931 in USSR. Spoken in Ukrainian SSR, parts of Russian SFSR and Romania. Language family: Indo-European. 40,000,000.

= 22 **Wu**. A dialect in China spoken, but not officially encouraged, in the Yang-tse delta area. Language family: Sino-Tibetan. 40,000,000.

= 22 **Min (Fukien)**. A dialect in China which includes the now discouraged Amoy and Fuchow dialects and Hainanese. Language family: Sino-Tibetan. 40,000,000.

= 22 **Turkish**. Spoken in European and Asian Turkey—a member of the Oghuz division of the Turkic group of languages. 40,000,000.

= 26 **Vietnamese**. Used in the whole of eastern Indo-China. Classified as a Mon-Khmer by some and as a Thai language by other philologists. 35,000,000.

= 26 **Polish**. A western Slavonic language with written records back to the 13th century, 300 years before its emergence as a modern literary language. Spoken in Poland and western USSR and among émigré populations notably in the USA. Language family: Indo-European. 35,000,000.

PRIMITIVE LANGUAGES

There is a popular belief that some languages are 'primitive'—have a simple grammar, not many sounds, and a vocabulary of only a few hundred words. It is thought that because of 'deficiencies' in the language its speakers have to communicate by making gestures; however, every culture has a developed language with a level of complexity that is similar to that of 'civilized' countries. All natural languages have complex grammatical rules and the vocabulary of a language is sufficient for its needs. There will be words for the technological developments found in one culture, whereas another culture without such developments will have no need for such words—compare the number of words for a hole in English with the many words in some Australian aboriginal languages. It takes between three and 14 English words to distinguish the various senses of hole in the Australian aboriginal language, Pintupi, but the distinctions can nonetheless be conveyed:

yarla   a hole in an object
pirti   a hole in the ground
pirnki   a hole formed by a rock shelf
kartalpa   a small hole in the ground
yulpilpa   a shallow hole in which ants live
mutara   a special hole in a spear
nyarrkalpa   a burrow for small animals
pulpa   a rabbit burrow
makarnpa   a goanna burrow
katarta   the hole left by a goanna when it has broken the surface after hibernation.

(From *Cambridge Encyclopedia of Language* by David Crystal, published by Cambridge University Press 1987.)

Words, words, words

The **longest words** are lengthy concatenations and some compound or agglutinative words or nonce words which have been written in the closed-up style of a single word e.g. the 1185 letter name for Tobacco Mosaic Virus, Dahlemense strain which has appeared in the American Chemical Society's *Chemical Abstracts*, the 3641 letter name of the protein bovine glutamate dehydrogenase, the systematic name for deoxyribonucleic acid of the human mitochondria containing 16,569 nucleotide residues and is thus *c.* 207,000 letters long (published in key form in *Nature* on 9 Apr 1981), the 182 letter fricassee of 17 sweet and sour ingredients in Aristophanes' comedy *The Ecclesiazusae* in the 4th century BC. A compound 'word' of 195 Sanskrit characters (which transliterates into 428 letters in the Roman alphabet) describing the region near Kanci, Tamil Nadu, India appears in a 16th century work by Tirumalāmbā, Queen of Vijayanagara.

The longest word in the *Oxford English Dictionary Supplement* is pneumonoultramicroscopicsilicovolcanoconiosis (45 letters), a lung disease contracted by some miners.

The longest word in the *Oxford English Dictionary* is floccipaucinihilipilification (alternatively spelt in hyphenated form with 'n' in seventh place), with 29 letters, meaning 'the action of estimating as worthless', first used in 1741, and later by Sir Walter Scott (1771–1832).

The medical term hepaticocholangiocholecystenterostomies (39 letters) refers to the surgical creation of new communications between gallbladders and hepatic ducts and between intestines and gallbladders. The longest words in common use are disproportionableness and incomprehensibilities (21 letters). Interdenominationalism (22 letters) is found in *Webster's Dictionary* and hence perhaps interdenominationalistically (28 letters) is permissible.

The longest words known to most people are antidisestablishmentarianism (28 letters) 'opposition to the idea that the Church should cease to be formally recognized by the State' and supercalifragilisticexpialidocious (34 letters), made popular by the song in the film *Mary Poppins* (1964).

Finally, a sound of a long fall in James Joyce's novel *Finnegans Wake* had 100 letters: bababadalgharaghtakamminarronnkonnbronntonnerronntuonnthunntrovarrhounawnskawntoohoohoordenenthurnuk.

Come in Charlie Bravo

Phonetic alphabet to clarify individual letters in radio communications. Use of such alphabets dates back to World War I.

A Alpha, B Bravo, C Charlie, D Delta, E Echo, F Foxtrot, G Golf, H Hotel, I India, J Juliet, K Kilo, L Lima, M Mike, N November, O Oscar, P Papa, Q Quebec, R Romeo, S Sierra, T Tango, U Uniform, V Victor, W Whisky, X X-ray, Y Yankee, Z Zulu.

The **longest known abbreviation** is S.K.O.M.K.H.P.K.J.C.D.P.W.B., the initials of the Syarikat Kerjasama Orang-orang Melayu Kerajaan Hilir Perak Kerana Jimat Cermat Dan Pinjam-memin-jam Wang Berhad. This is the Malay name for The Cooperative Company of the Lower State of Perak Government's Malay People for Money Savings and Loans Ltd, in Teluk Anson, Perak, West Malaysia (formerly Malaya). The abbreviation for this abbreviation is Skomk. The 55-letter full name of Los Angeles (El Pueblo de Nuestra Señora la Reina de los Angeles de Porciuncula) is abbreviated to LA or 3.63 per cent of its length.

The **longest acronym** is NIIOMTPLABOPARM-BETZHELBETRABSBOMONIMONKONOTD-TEKHSTROMONT with 56 letters (54 in Cyrillic) in the *Concise Dictionary of Soviet Terminology* meaning: The laboratory for shuttering, reinforcement, concrete and ferroconcrete operations for composite-monolithic and monolithic constructions of the Department of the Technology of Building—assembly operations of the Scientific Research Institute of the Organization for building mechanization and technical aid of the Academy of Building and Architecture of the USSR.

LONGEST WORDS

Japanese[1] Chi-n-chi-ku-ri-n (12 letters) *a very short person (slang).*

Spanish Superextraordinarisimo (22 letters) *extraordinary.*

French Anticonstitutionnellement (25 letters) *anticonstitutionally.*

Croatian Prijestolonasljednikovica (25 letters) *wife of an heir apparent.*

Italian Precipitevolissimevolmente (26 letters) *as fast as possible.*

Portuguese Inconstitucionalissimamente (27 letters) *with the highest degree of unconstitutionality.*

Icelandic Hæstaréttarmálaflutningsmaður (29 letters) *supreme court barrister.*

Russian Ryentgyenoelyektrokardiografichyeskogo (33 Cyrillic letters, transliterating as 38) *of the radioelectrocardiographic.*

Hungarian Megszentségtelenithetetlenségeskedéseltekért (44 letters) *for your unprofaneable actions.*

Turkish[4] Cekoslovakyalılastıramadıklarımızdanmıymıssınız (47 letters) *'are you not of that group of persons that we were said to be unable to Czechoslovakianize?'.*

Dutch[4] Kindercarnavalsoptochtvoorbereidingswerkzaamheden (49 letters) *preparation activities for a children's carnival procession.*

Mohawk[2] Tkanuhstasrihsranuhwe'tsraaksahsrakaratattsrayeri' (50 letters) *the praising of the evil of the liking of the finding of the house is right.*

German[3, 4] Donaudampfschiffahrtselectrizitaetenhauptbetriebswerkbauunterbeamtengesellschaft (80 letters) *The club for subordinate officials of the head office management of the Danube steamboat electrical services (Name of a pre-war club in Vienna).*

Swedish[4] Nordöstersjökustartillerflygspaningssimulatoranläggningsymaterielunderhållsuppföljningssystemdiskussionsinläggsförberedelsearbeten (130 letters) *Preparatory work on the contribution to the discussion on the maintaining system of support of the material of the aviation survey simulator device within the northeast part of the coast artillery of the Baltic.*

---

[1] Patent applications sometimes harbour long compound 'words'. An extreme example is one of 13 kana which transliterates to the 40-letter Kyūkitsūrohekimenfuchakunenryōsekisanryō meaning 'the accumulated amount of fuel condensed on the wall face of the air intake passage'.

[2] Lengthy concatenations are a feature of Mohawk. Above is an example.

[3] The longest dictionary word in everyday usage is Kraftfahrzeugreparaturwerkstätten (33 letters or 34 if the ä is written as ae) meaning motor vehicle repair shops (or service garages).

[4] Agglutinative words are limited only by imagination and are not found in standard dictionaries. The first 100-letter such word was published in 1978, by the late Eric Rosenthal in Afrikaans.

From *The Guinness Book of Records*, Guinness Publishing.

The **most succinct** word is the Fuegian (south-ernmost Argentina and Chile) word 'mamihlapina-tapai' meaning 'looking at each other hoping that either will offer to do something which both parties desire but are unwilling to do'.

The condition of being inebriated has **more synonyms** than any other condition or object. Delacourt Press of New York City, USA has published a selection of 1224 from 2241 compiled by Paul Dickson of Garrett Park, Maryland, USA.

The **most homophonous** sounds in English are air and sol which, according to the researches of Dora Newhouse of Los Angeles, both have 38 homophones. The homonym with the most variant spellings is air with Aire, are, Ayer, Ayr, Ayre, err, e'er, ere, eyre and heir.

Accents were introduced in French in the reign of Louis XIII (1601–43). The **word with most accents** is újjáépítésére, the Hungarian word meaning 'for its reconstruction'. Two runners up each with 5 accents are the French hétérogénéité, meaning heterogeneity and an atoll in the Pacific Ocean 320 miles/516 km east-south-east of Tahiti which is named Héréhérétué.

The **longest sentence** ever to have got past the editor of a major newspaper is one of 1,379 words (counting common hyphenated words as one) in an article written by Albert Sukoff of Berkeley, California, in the *This World* section of the *San Francisco Chronicle* of 16 June 1985.

A sentence of 1,300 words appears in *Absalom, Absalom!* by William Faulkner, and one of 3,153 words with 86 semi-colons and 390 commas occurs in the *History of the Church of God* by Sylvester Hassell of Wilson, North Carolina, USA c. 1884. The Report of the President of Columbia University, 1942–43, contained a sentence of 4,284 words. The first 40,000 words of *The Gates of Paradise* by George Andrzeyevski appear to lack any punctuation. Some authors such as James Joyce (1882–1941) appear to eschew punctuation altogether.

The **most common** 100 words in English, according to one frequency list, are:

the, of, and, to, a, in, that, I, it, was, is, he, for, you, on, with, as, be, had, but, they, at, his, have, not, this, are, or, by, we, she, from, one, all, there, her, were, which, an, so, what, their, if, would, about, no, said, up, when, been, out, them, do, my, more, who, me, like, very, can, has, him, some, into, then, now, think, well, know, time, could, people, its, other, only, it's, will, than, yes, just, because, two, over, don't, get, see, any, much, way, these, how, down, even, first, did, back, got, our, new, go. (From *Computers in English Language Teaching and Research* by John Sinclair, published by Longman 1986.)

The **commonest letter** in English is 'e' and the **commonest initial letter** is 'T'.

In Great Britain and Ireland there are six indigenous tongues: English, Cornish, Scots Gaelic, Welsh, Irish Gaelic and Romany (Gypsy). Mr Edward (Ned) Maddrell (1877–1974) of Glen Chass, Port St Mary, Isle of Man, died as the last islander whose professed tongue was Manx. Cornish, of which there are now some 300 students, came within an ace of extinction. A dictionary was published in 1887, four years before the death of the then last fluent speaker, John Davey. A novel by Melville and Kitty Bennetto, *An Gurun Wosek a Geltya*, was published in November 1984. In the Channel Islands, apart from Jersey and Guernsey normand, there survive words of Sarkese or Sèrtchais in which the Parable of the Sower, as recited by some fishermen, was noted and published by Prince Louis Lucien Bonaparte (1813–91) in 1862.

Vocabulary

How many words are there in English? Estimates vary from half a million to over two million. The answer depends largely on the question of what precisely is meant by a word. For example, should dialectal words and highly technical words be included? And what about words that have the same form but come from different roots—such as *ball* ('round body') and *ball* ('social function for dancing'), *till* ('until'), *till* ('to cultivate and work the land') and *till* ('a cash register'). Moreover, are compounds, such as sitting room, city council—and idiomatic verbs, such as *go at* ('to attack') and *go on* ('to happen')—to be counted as one word or two? The answer to ques-

'When I use a word,' Humpty Dumpty said, in rather a scornful tone, 'It means just what I choose it to mean—neither more nor less.'
'The question is,' said Alice, 'Whether you can make words mean so many different things.'
'The question is,' said Humpty Dumpty, 'which is to be master—that's all.'

Lewis Carroll, *Through the Looking-Glass*

tions about the size of the vocabulary of English is that it probably contains between one and two million words, though of course the number is changing as new words are constantly being added to the language.

Words are traditionally divided into **word classes**, commonly known as parts of speech. Traditionally, eight such categories have been recognized:

nouns   man, chalk, love
adjectives   clever, each, seven
verbs   come, set, become
pronouns   he, they, which
prepositions   in, above, towards
adverbs   (sometimes regarded as something of a catch-all class) today, fast, sometimes
conjunctions   and, when
interjections   ah, ouch, hurrah.

Some words can belong to more than one word class, for example, round:

adjective   big round eyes
preposition   The wall went right round the house.
adverb   The hands on the clock go round.
verb   to round a corner
noun   in the next round of negotiations.

The English language is constantly changing. **New words** are continually being introduced into the language, and existing words take on new meanings. Here is a selection of words that have recently become established in the language.

BUSINESS AND FINANCE
Big Bang the radical reorganization of the London Stock Exchange in 1986.
Buyout the purchase of a business company, often by a group of managers: *a management buyout.*
Golden hello a large sum of money paid to an employee on joining a company.

Greenmail the business strategy of buying many shares in another company.
Insider trading the illegal buying and selling of shares by people who possess knowledge of the business companies for which they work.
Intrapreneur a person who begins or manages a new business within an already established business company.
Rate-capping the limitation by central government on the level of rates that a local authority can levy.

NEW TECHNOLOGY
Cellular telephone a mobile telephonic communication based on a network of transmitters, each of which serves a small area.
Compact disc a digitally recorded disc that is read by a laser beam.
Desktop publishing an office system made up of a personal computer, software, and a laser printer, used to produce printed text and graphics.
Email electronic mail.
Hacker a person who, by means of a personal computer, breaks into the computer system of a government, business company, etc.
Interface a common boundary between different systems; point of contact or communication.
Mouse a hand-held device used to control the cursor on the screen of a visual display unit.

Neither is a dictionary a bad book to read. There is no cant in it, no excess of explanation, and it is full of suggestion—the raw material of possible poems and histories.

Ralph Waldo Emerson

Definitions from Johnson's *Dictionary of the English Language*:

Cricket   A sport, at which the contenders drive a ball with sticks in opposition to each other.

Lexicographer   A writer of dictionaries, a harmless drudge.

Oats   A grain, which in England is generally given to horses, but in Scotland supports the people.

Patron   Commonly A wretch who supports with insolence, and is paid with flattery.

Cynical definitions were the art of the US writer Ambrose Bierce (1842–?1914), in his *Devil's Dictionary* (1911):

Acquaintance   A person whom we know well enough to borrow from but not well enough to lend to.

Alliance   In international politics, the union of two thieves who have their hands so deeply inserted into each other's pocket that they cannot safely plunder a third.

Bore   A person who talks when you wish him to listen.

History   An account, mostly false, of events mostly unimportant which are brought about by rulers, mostly knaves, and soldiers mostly fools.

Peace   In international affairs, a period of cheating between two periods of fighting.

Personal stereo a very small cassette tape-recorder designed to be carried on one's person, used with lightweight headphones.

State-of-the-art of the most recent level of technical achievement, knowledge, etc.

User-friendly easy to use or understand.

Viewdata an electronic system that enables computer-based data to be available via a visual display unit or an adapted television set.

WYSIWYG what you see is what you get; the exact reproduction on a printer of graphics displayed on the screen of a visual display unit.

GENERAL

AIDS acquired immune deficiency syndrome.

Bar code a printed code found on shop-bought goods that consists of an arrangement of numbers and parallel vertical lines and can be read by a light pen, wand, or scanner.

Contraflow a system of two-way traffic on one carriageway of a motorway, especially when road works are being carried out on the other carriageway.

DBS direct broadcasting (by) satellite.

Demi-veg having a diet that is mainly vegetarian but also sometimes including animal produce and fish.

Designer (adjective) (of clothes and other manufactured goods) produced by a well-known business company that has a reputation for fashionable designs: *designer jeans*.

E number a number (prefixed by the letter E) designating a particular food additive as recognized by the EEC; used on food labels.

Flagship the most important single item in a group of products, projects, etc.: *the flagship of the government's legislative programme*.

Foodie a person with an enthusiastic interest in good food.

GCSE General Certificate of Secondary Education; British secondary-school examination.

Gender-bender a person who adopts the behaviour, clothes, etc., of someone of the opposite sex.

Genetic fingerprinting the technique of identifying people by their unique genetic (DNA) make-up.

Glasnost the increased openness in East-West relations and in Soviet internal policies under Mikhail Gorbachev.

Green associated with improving the environment and the conserving of natural resources: *the green party*; *the green vote*.

Maglev type of high-speed train that is powered

by a linear motor and is raised by magnetic levitation along a guiding track.

Number crunching the processing of a large amount of numerical data using a computer.

Perestroika the restructuring or economic and social reform programme in the Soviet Union under Mikhail Gorbachev.

Sloane Ranger a fashionable upper-class young woman.

Star wars a system of artificial satellites which have lasers that are used to destroy enemy missiles in space; popular name of strategic defense initiative.

Street credibility good standing in terms of popular youth culture.

Yuppie a young fashionable urban professional person working in a well-paid job.

Dictionaries

I am not yet so lost in lexicography as to forget that words are the daughters of earth, and that things are the sons of Heaven.

Samuel Johnson

'The dictionary is the most successful and significant book about language. In Britain, its success is shown by the fact that over 90 per cent of households possess at least one, making the dictionary far more popular than cookery books (about 70 per cent) and indeed significantly more widespread than the Bible (which was to be found in 80 per cent of households in England in 1983, according to the Bible Society).' (Robert Ilson, University College London).

The dictionary is our most well-known and authoritative book of words. Dictionaries list words in alphabetical order, and provide information on spelling, pronunciation, grammatical part of speech, meaning, usage, and history.

● As early as the 5th century BC the Greeks compiled lists of difficult words in the works of such authors as Homer.

● In the 7th century AD explanations of difficult words were written between the lines of Latin manuscripts. Later, these glosses were collected as lists.

● The first bilingual list, a French-English glossary, was printed in England by William Caxton in 1480.

● The earliest English *dictionary*—a systematic list—was compiled by Robert Cawdrey and his son Thomas and published in 1604 under the title *A Table Alphabeticall, Contayning and Teaching the True Writing and Understanding of Hard Usuall English Wordes.*

● The first attempt to cover the whole range of English vocabulary was Nathan Bailey in his Universal Etymological Dictionary (1721).

● Samuel Johnson's great Dictionary, published in 1755 is famous for its definitions—see pg. 18—and illustrative quotations. The dictionary ran to four editions in Johnson's lifetime.

● Noah Webster's *An American Dictionary of the English Language* took over 20 years to compile and was published in 1828. It was the most influential of all American dictionaries.

● Significant foreign dictionaries include: *Vocabolario della Crusca*, with extensive literary quotations, compiled by the Italian Accademia della Crusca (1612); the famous 'official' French dictionary *Dictionnaire de la langue française* of the language-legislating Académie Française (first Edition, 1694); the 15-volume *Grand diction-*

> *Dictionaries are like watches: the worst is better than none, and the best cannot be expected to go quite true.*
>
> Samuel Johnson

naire universel due XIXe siècle, by Pierre Larousse, issued in fortnightly parts between 1866 and 1876; and the monumental German *Deutsches Wörterbuch*, started in 1854 by Jacob and Wilhelm Grimm and completed in 1971.

● Publication of Webster's *Third New International Dictionary* in 1961 caused a storm of protest e.g. about *ain't* as 'used orally in most parts of the U.S. by many cultivated speakers'.

● The largest English language dictionary is the 12-volume Royal quarto *The Oxford English Dictionary* of 15,487 pages published between 1884 and 1928 with a first supplement of 963 pages in 1933. Of the 4-volume supplement, edited by R. W. Burchfield, the final (Se–Z) volume and the Bibliography were published in 1986. The work contains 414,825 words, 1,827,306 illustrative quotations and reputedly 227,779,589 letters and figures, 63.8 times more than the Bible.

● The development of the use of computers, under the guidance of such lexicographers as Laurence Urdang, is ushering in a new era in lexicography. Computers are used for example in compiling concordances, alphabetical listings of words in contexts of actual usage, that guide the dictionary compiler in formulating definitions and illustrative examples.

The most beautiful words in the language

melody	silken	champagne
velvet	willow	dusk
gossamer	mellow	beloved
crystal	lullaby	sleep
autumn	dawn	echo
peace	shimmer	magic
tranquil	silver	sorrow
twilight	marigold	love
murmur	golden	mist
caress	dream	darling
mellifluous	harmony	laughter
whisper	blossom	

(From *Beyond the Tingle Quotient* by Godfrey Smith. Published by Weidenfeld and Nicolson.)

2 *The English language*

The three Germanic dialects on which English is based are descended from the Indo-Germanic or Aryan family of languages, spoken since *c.* 3000 BC by the nomads of the Great Lowland Plain of Europe, which stretches from the Aral Sea in the Soviet Union to the Rhine in West Germany. Now only fragments of Old Lithuanian contain what is left of this ancestral tongue.

Of the three inherited Germanic dialects, the first was Jutish, brought into England in AD 449 from Jutland. This was followed 40 years later by Saxon, brought from Holstein, and Anglian, which came from the still later incursions from the area of Schleswig-Holstein.

These three dialects were superimposed on the 1000-year-old indigenous Celtic tongue, along with what Latin had survived in the towns from nearly 15 generations of Roman occupation (AD 43–410). The next major event in the history of the English language was the first of many Viking invasions, beginning in 793, from Denmark and Norway. Norse and Danish left permanent influences on the Anglo-Frisian Old English, though Norse never survived as a separate tongue in England beyond 1035, the year of the death of King Canute (Cnut), who had then reigned for 19 years over England, 16 years over Denmark and 7 years over Norway.

The Scandinavian influence now receded before Norman French, though Norse still struggled on in remote parts of Scotland until about 1630 and in the Shetland Islands until *c.* 1750. The Normans were, however, themselves really Vikings, who in five generations had become converts to the Latin culture and language of northern France.

For three centuries after the Norman conquest of 1066 by William I, descendant of Rollo the Viking, England lived under a trilingual system. The mother tongue of all the first 13 Kings and Queens, from William I (1066–1087) until as late as Richard II (1377–99), was Norman. English became the language of court proceedings only during the reign of Edward III, in October 1362, and the language for teaching in the Universities of Oxford and Cambridge in *c.* 1380.

English did not really crystallize as an amalgam of Anglo-Saxon and Latin root forms until the 14th century, when William Langland (*c.* 1300–*c.* 1400), and Geoffrey Chaucer (*c.* 1340–1400) were the pioneers of a literary tradition, which culminated in William Shakespeare, who died in 1616, just four years before the sailing of the Mayflower.

In this chapter we explore the various languages from which English has 'borrowed' words. Over the centuries, the vocabulary of English has been continually enriched by an influx of words from

If you go up into the mountains you are likely to come across a spring. This source of water coming from the ground, the origin of a gentle brook or stream, is later joined by other streams and becomes a faster-flowing river until, swelling with the power of several rivers, the rushing currents surge into the sea.

The US writer Ralph Waldo Emerson used this picture of rivers and the sea when he described the English language as 'the sea which receives tributaries from every region under heaven'.

many languages. This has happened mainly through the invasion and consequent settlement by foreign peoples—as with the Norman conquerors in the 11th century—when new terms were gradually assimilated into the mother tongue. It has also occurred through a long heritage of trading and colonial links with many countries. Words have been borrowed to aid communication and integration with other nations and have gradually become part of the language. Today English is fast becoming a universal language. Yet it must be remembered that its rich and diverse vocabulary is a product of many different countries and tongues.

The following pages show the wide range of languages from which English has taken words. The dates show the approximate time of the introduction of the word into English, dated by century.

The shortened squash

When the European settlers came to North America in the early 17th century, the most widespread American Indian language was Algonquian, but this had not yet been written down. The colonists therefore found it difficult to spell and pronounce Indian words. Sometimes they shortened the Indian word, such as the marrow *squash*, from the original *asquatasquash*. Similarly, *opossum* became shortened to *possum*, and early spellings of *raccoon* included *arocoun* and *raugrougheun*.

Sometimes the settlers attempted to pronounce parts of the American Indian words as English words that were already known to them—for example, *wejack* (or *otchig* or *otcheck*) for *woodchuck*, the North American marmot.

Some of the American Indian words also have remarkable origins. For example, *powwow* originally meant a medicine man or sorcerer. Later the word came to stand for a conjuring ceremony and in due course a council or conference.

Yiddishisms

The large influx of almost 3 million Jews into America between 1880 and 1910 led to a significant influence on the (American) English language. The Jews spoke Yiddish, a blend of Old German and Hebrew, that originated 1000 years ago amongst the Jews of central and Eastern Europe. Amongst the well-known Yiddish words that have entered the general English language is *chutzpah*, 'impudence'. As William and Mary Morris describe *chutzpah*: 'a lad with real *chutzpah* is one who would kill both his parents and then demand leniency of the court on the ground that he is an orphan'.

Other Yiddishisms are: *kosher*, 'legitimate, proper, or authentic', *schlemiel*, 'unfortunate bungler', *schlepp*, 'to drag or pull', and *schmaltz*, (literally 'melted fat') 'excessive sentimentality'.

The influence of Yiddish is also seen in several idiomatic expressions, including *I'm telling you!*, *I need it like a hole in the (or my) head!*, and *I should worry!*

Aussie talk

It is 200 years since the settlement of Australia began: a colony of convicts was established just north of Botany Bay in 1788. A great deal of Australian English grew out of the different dialects of England, Scotland, Ireland, and Wales, as well as from the native Australian (Aboriginal) words. Some of the native Australian words have entered the international English vocabulary, as the accompanying list shows. Others are almost unknown outside Australia, for example *bombora*, 'a dangerous submerged reef' and *humpy*, 'a primitive hut'.

The formation of words by shortening, often with the ending *-ie* or *-o*, is a feature of Australian English, for example *wharfie*, 'a wharf labourer', *garbo* 'a garbage collector', *arvo* 'afternoon', *sickie* 'a day taken off work for a real or invented illness', and *smoko* 'a break from work, for tea, to smoke a cigarette, etc.'

Australian English is also noted for its vivid phrases such as *come the raw prawn* 'to attempt to deceive someone' and *have a shingle short* 'to be unintelligent'.

AFRICA
African languages
C 16 banana, guinea
C 17 yam
C 18 banjo, chimpanzee, cola, mumbo-jumbo, okra
C 19 raffia, voodoo
C 20 tango, zombie
Afrikaans
C 18 kraal
C 19 aardvark, commando, spoor, trek, veld
C 20 apartheid

NORTH AMERICA
American Indian languages
C 17 hickory, moccasin, moose, papoose, opossum, powwow, raccoon, squaw, terrapin, tomahawk, woodchuck
C 18 pecan, totem
C 19 chipmunk, tepee
Eskimo
C 18 kayak
C 19 igloo
C 20 anorak

CENTRAL AMERICA
Nahuatl
C 17 avocado, chilli, chocolate, tomato
C 19 coyote

Caribbean
C 16 cannibal, canoe, hammock, hurricane, maize, potato, tobacco
C 17 barbecue

SOUTH AMERICA
South American languages
C 16 guava, iguana, toucan
C 17 coca, condor, guano, jaguar, llama
C 18 jacaranda, pampas, poncho, tapioca
C 19 piranha

ASIA
Chinese
C 11 silk
C 16 typhoon
C 17 soya, tea
C 18 kaolin
C 19 kowtow, tycoon
Japanese
C 17 sake (drink), shogun
C 19 geisha, harakiri, judo, kimono, rickshaw, samurai
C 20 kamikaze, karate
Malay
C 16 bamboo, sago
C 17 amok, cockatoo, compound (buildings), gong, orang-utan
C 18 caddy, kapok, ketchup
C 19 batik, sarong

Tibetan
C 19 polo, yak
Hindi
C 17 bungalow, chintz, coolie, cot, dungarees, juggernaut, kedgeree, pundit, tom-tom
C 18 bandana, chit, jungle, shampoo
C 19 bangle, chutney, dinghy, gymkhana, loot, thug
Malayalam
C 17 teak

Tamil
C 16 curry
C 17 catamaran, cheroot, pariah
C 18 corundum, mulligatawny

AUSTRALASIA
Native Australian languages
C 18 dingo, wombat
C 19 billabong, boomerang, budgerigar, waddy, wallaby
C 20 didgeridoo
Maori
C 19 kiwi, moa
Tahitian
C 18 tattoo
Tongan
C 18 taboo

Arabic numbers

The Arabs were known for their great knowledge of science during the Middle Ages. The English words *algebra*, *cipher*, and *zero* are all mathematical terms that have originated from the Arabic language. Further, words such as *alcohol* and *alkali* are evidence of the Arabs' keen interest in chemistry. They were also famous for their knowledge of astronomy; *zenith*, and probably *almanac* have likewise entered the English language from the Arabian language.

1066 and all that

The Norman conquest of 1066 exerted a greater influence on English than any previous event. It has been estimated that between 10,000 and 12,000 words were introduced by the Normans into English. To cite an instance, words describing government, law, and administration are French in origin, for example *advise*, *command*, *court*, *govern*, and *parliament*.

Amongst the thousands of other terms introduced, the Normans brought the terms for the flesh of animals to be eaten as food. Words such as *beef*, *mutton*, and *veal* entered the language in the early Middle Ages, meaning not only the flesh of a *cow*, *sheep*, and *calf*, but also the animals themselves. The sense of these words narrowed in about the 18th century, when the words of French origin were restricted to the flesh of the animal eaten as food.

NEAR EAST

Arabic
C 13 mattress
C 14 algebra, alkali, cipher, cotton, syrup
C 16 alcohol, arsenal, assassin, magazine, monsoon, sash, tariff
C 17 alcove, harem, sofa, zero
C 18 carafe, ghoul

Hebrew
C 11 rabbi
C 13 amen
C 14 behemoth, jubilee, shibboleth
C 17 seraph
C 19 kosher
C 20 kibbutz

Persian
C 14 taffeta
C 16 bazaar, caravan
C 17 shawl, sherbet

Turkish
C 16 caviar, kaftan
C 17 jackal, kiosk, tulip
C 19 bosh (nonsense), kismet, yoghurt

EUROPE

Irish Gaelic
C 16 brat, brogue, shamrock
C 17 galore, leprechaun, Tory
C 18 shillelagh, whisky
C 19 blarney, colleen, smithereens

Scottish Gaelic
C 14 bard, clan, loch
C 15 cairn
C 16 plaid, slogan
C 19 sporran, spree

Welsh
C 14 flannel
C 16 coracle
C 17 flummery
C 19 cwm, eisteddfod
C 20 corgi

Czech
C 16 howitzer, pistol
C 20 robot

Dutch
C 14 dock, kit, splinter
C 15 deck
C 16 frolic, landscape, split, wagon, yacht
C 17 brandy, cruise, easel, keelhaul, sloop, tattoo
C 18 roster, sleigh
C 19 boss, coleslaw, dope, waffle

French
Thousands of words from French have entered the English language. This list represents a small sample of such words.
C 12 baron, crown, justice, mercy, prison, religion, saint, treasure, war
C 13 anguish, battle, beef, chapel, courtesy, feast, govern, manor, marriage, parliament, vessel
C 14 carpenter, liberty, navy, pleasure, venue
C 15 kestrel, serviette
C 16 grotesque, pioneer, police, valet, volley
C 17 brunette, contour, group, prestige, reprimand, role, soup
C 18 avalanche, bouquet, brochure, casserole, elite, envelope, meringue, ricochet, souvenir, terrain, vaudeville

English, Franglais, ...

In this chapter we are describing the importing of words into English from other languages. Yet this traffic is in fact two-way: many English words are exported to other languages also. For instance, many English words have been introduced into French, which has raised the hackles of some French scholars. This blend of French and English, known as Franglais, includes such words as: *le camping, le drugstore, le hamburger, le marketing, le parking, le snob, le weekend*.

Many other languages, such as German, Japanese, and Swedish have taken over numerous English words. Sometimes, however, the words in the borrowing language do not have exactly the same meaning as in the original language. For example, in German, *Flirt* does not mean a person that flirts, but the act or instance of flirtation, and *ein Smoking* is not the act of smoking a cigarette, pipe, etc., but what we would call a smoking-*jacket*.

War words

The World Wars brought many new terms into use that have since become part of the English language. Such words from German include: *blitz*, from *blitzkrieg*, the word first used of Hitler's attack on Poland in 1939; *ersatz*, to describe an artificial substance used to replace a natural one that had become scarce during the war; and *flak*, for anti-aircraft fire, and later, intense criticism or nagging, deriving from *Flieger, Abwehr Kanone*, 'an anti-aircraft gun'.

C 19 beret, café, cigarette, communism, gourmet, masseur, mirage, suede, surveillance
C 20 camouflage, compere, fuselage, garage, limousine

German
C 17 cobalt, spanner, zinc
C 18 nickel, quartz, waltz
C 19 dachshund, delicatessen, edelweiss, hinterland, kindergarten, lager, poodle, poltergeist, seminar
C 20 blitz, flak, frankfurter, hamburger, snorkel

Hungarian
C 15 hussar
C 16 coach
C 19 goulash, paprika

Icelandic
C 18 geyser

Italian
C 15 cameo
C 16 bandit, canto, carnival, gondola, infantry, macaroni, parapet, squadron, violin

C 17 allegro, balcony, cartoon, granite, incognito, regatta, solo, stiletto, umbrella, volcano
C 18 casino, duet, extravaganza, lava, malaria, portfolio, soprano, torso
C 19 fiasco, piano, replica, spaghetti, studio, vendetta
C 20 fascism, pizza

Polish
C 19 mazurka

Portuguese
C 16 caste, marmalade, molasses
C 17 albatross, dodo
C 18 palaver
C 19 cobra

Russian
C 17 steppe, tsar
C 18 balalaika, mammoth
C 19 samovar, tundra, vodka
C 20 cosmonaut, intelligentsia

Spanish
C 16 armadillo, cask, corral, embargo, galleon, mosquito, potato, renegade, savanna, tornado

C 17 alligator, cargo, cockroach, junta, plaza, siesta
C 18 bolero, cigar, stevedore
C 19 alfalfa, bonanza, canyon, chaparral, guerrilla, lasso, patio, rodeo, silo

Norse
C 12 anger, crook, skill
C 13 awe, leg, ransack, rotten, sky, they, ugly, window
C 14 egg, freckles

Norwegian
C 17 fjord, lemming
C 19 floe, ski
C 20 slalom

Finnish
C 20 sauna

Swedish
C 18 tungsten
C 20 ombudsman

The Italian connection

Many Italian words entered English during the Renaissance, when Italian culture was considered fashionable. Architectural terms such as *balcony, cupola, portico,* and *stucco* and musical terms such as *allegro, duet, madrigal,* and *sonata* are all Italian in origin. Many terms denoting Italian food have more recently entered the language, for example *espresso* (literally, 'pressed out as by steam'), *minestrone* ('to serve'), *pasta, ravioli,* and *vermicelli* (literally, 'little worms').

The conquistadores

The early English explorers clashed with the Spanish adventurers and conquerors (the *conquistadores*) in the 16th century. The Spanish terms used to describe the new surroundings filtered back to Europe, and eventually into English. Examples are: *alligator, canyon,* and *potato*. The Spanish conquest of Mexico led to many terms being taken into American English and used by the American cowboys, for example *bronco, lasso, ranch, rodeo,* and *stampede*. Indeed, overall, American English has borrowed more words from Spanish than from any other language.

Television—a mixed medium

C. P. Scott, the editor of the *Manchester Guardian* is reported to have once said, 'Television? No good will come of this device. The word is half Greek and half Latin.' *Television* comes from Greek *tele* 'far' + Latin *visio* 'sight'. Other examples of such combinations include: *heliport* from Greek *heli* + Latin *port* and *speedometer* from Latin *speed* + Greek *metron*. Such combinations are instances of an older process than some would like to admit; the joining of elements from different languages has been occurring since ancient times. The word *ostrich*, for example, is a combination of the Latin *avis* and the Greek *strouthion*. The word entered the English language during the 13th century.

Greek
Thousands of words from Greek have entered the English language. This list represents a small sample of such words.
C 7–C 11 angel, apostle, martyr, psalm
C 13 hypocrisy
C 14 allegory, character, cycle
C 16 alphabet, atom, chorus, cynic, emphasis, idea, rhythm, theory

C 17 cosmos, drama, pathos, museum
C 18 automatic
C 19 myth
C 20 moussaka

Latin
Thousands of words from Latin have entered the English language. This list represents a small sample of such words.
C 7–C 11 altar, candle, fever, disciple

C 13 hospitality, perfect, tribe
C 14 community, divine, essence, literature, moral, pagan, tradition
C 15 education, invention, public
C 16 accommodate, area, circus, estimate, manufacture, refrigerate, vacuum
C 17 album, candidate, dictator, focus, lens, series
C 18 alibi propaganda, via
C 19 omnibus, referendum

TALKING LIKE A DUTCH UNCLE

The word Dutch occurs in numerous expressions, many of which have pejorative overtones. Such expressions include:

double Dutch 'gibberish'
Dutch auction 'an auction in which the price is lowered until a buyer is found'
Dutch cap 'a contraceptive device for women; diaphragm'
Dutch courage '(false) courage inspired by drinking alcohol'
Dutch treat 'a meal or entertainment in which those present pay for themselves'
Dutch uncle 'a person who criticizes people strongly and frankly'
or I'm a Dutchman, used to show that one is completely certain of what one just said.

It seems that these *Dutch* expressions result mainly from the trading rivalry between Britain and Netherlands in the 17th century.

Other nationalities have not, however, suffered similar linguistic abuse. How many of the following missing nationalities are you familiar with? Answers on page 30.

1	_____ chequers	11	_____ pastry
2	_____ ink	12	_____ mummy
3	_____ delight	13	_____ violet
4	_____ windows	14	_____ goulash
5	_____ measles	15	_____ twins
6	_____ lantern	16	_____ carpet
7	_____ stew	17	_____ rum
8	_____ mist	18	_____ roll
9	_____ omelette	19	_____ rarebit
10	_____ roulette	20	_____ cross

American English and British English

You would certainly notice the difference between American English and British English if an American and a Briton arranged to meet 'on the first floor' of a building. The British person would be waiting one storey above the entrance, while the American would be waiting at the level of the ground, what the British call 'the ground floor'. Some of the differences between American and British English are seen in their different spelling, vocabulary, and grammar.

SPELLING
- American English favours *-er*, British English *re*: *centre, fibre, theatre*.
- American English has *-or*, where British English has *-our*: *colour, labour, vigour*.
- American English prefers *-se*, where British English has *-ce*: *defence, offence, pretence*.
- British English distinguishes *license* and *practise* (verbs) and *licence, practice* (nouns), in American English both the noun and verb are commonly spelt *license* or *practice*.
- In American English, the final *-l* is not usually doubled in an unstressed syllable: American English *traveling*, British English *travelling*.
- American English favours *-e-*, British English *-oe-* or *-ae-* in some technical words *oesophagus, anaesthetize* (American: *esophagus, anesthetize*).

Many words have slightly different meanings in American and British English. In American English, *homely* means 'plain or unattractive', in British English, 'pleasant or familiar; domestic'. In American English *mean* stands for 'bad-tempered or nasty', in British English it stands for 'stingy'.

Finally, there are also many differences between American and British grammar: American *back of*, British *behind*; American English *do something over*, British English *do something again*; American English *Monday through Wednesday*, British English *Monday to Wednesday*. Americans also differ in the use of some tenses and the verb *to have*, e.g. American English *Do you have a computer?*, British English *Have you got a computer?*

Britain and America are 'one people divided by a common language'.

George Bernard Shaw

Here is a selection of differences between British and American English. British English in bold type.

aeroplane airplane
aluminium aluminum
anticlockwise counterclockwise
anywhere anyplace
autumn fall
bath bathtub
bill check
biscuit cookie
bonnet (on a car) hood
boot (in a car) trunk
braces suspenders
call box telephone booth
candy floss cotton candy
car auto, automobile
caretaker janitor
chemist druggist, drug store
cheque check
chips French fries
crisps (potato) chips
cornflour cornstarch
crotchet quarter note
cupboard closet
current account checking account
curtains drapes
dialling code area code
draughts checkers
drawing-pin thumbtack
dual carriageway divided highway
dummy (baby) pacifier
dustbin garbage can, trashcan
engaged (of a telephone line) busy
engine driver engineer
estate agent real-estate agent, realtor

ex-directory (of a telephone number) unlisted
ex-serviceman veteran
fire brigade fire department
flat apartment
goods train freight train
got gotten
grey gray
grill broil
hair grip bobby pin
high street main street
hoarding billboard
holiday vacation
ill sick
jug pitcher
to lay (a table) to set
lift elevator
lodger roomer
lorry truck
market garden truck farm
maths math
milometer odometer
mince ground meat
minim half note
motorway expressway, freeway
nappy diaper
notice board bulletin board
noughts and crosses tick-tack-toe
number plate license plate
off-licence liquor store
oven cloth pot holder
paraffin kerosene
parting (in the hair) part

pavement sidewalk
pelmet valance
petrol gas, gasoline
post mail
postcode zip code
pram baby carriage
railway railroad
removal man moving man
return (ticket) round-trip ticket
rise (in salary) raise
roundabout traffic circle
saloon sedan
shop store
shop assistant salesclerk
silencer (on a car) muffler
single (ticket) one-way ticket
somewhere someplace
spring onion scallion
stalls (in a theatre) orchestra
standard lamp floor lamp
sweets candy
tap faucet
terraced house row house
tin can
torch flashlight
tramp hobo
treacle molasses
trousers pants
underground subway
underpants shorts
waistcoat vest
windscreen windshield
zip zipper

A passing phrase?

As we have seen in this chapter, English has imported a large number of words from other languages. There are also a large number of expressions—mainly from Latin and French—that are felt to be foreign. English speakers in many cases try to pronounce these according to the phrase's language of origin.

Latin

ab initio   from the beginning

ad hoc   for a specific purpose

ad infinitum   endlessly

ad nauseam   to an excessive degree

alma mater   one's school, college, university, etc.

alter ego   very close friend; another aspect of one's personality

a priori   (reasoning) from cause to effect; with no reference to experience

bona fide   genuine; made in good faith

ceteris paribus   other things being equal

curriculum vitae   outline of a person's professional, etc., qualifications

de facto   in actual fact

deus ex machina   unexpected intervention of a power or event that resolves a seemingly impossible situation

dramatis personae   list of characters in a literary work

ex cathedra   with papal authority

ex officio   by virtue of the office

habeas corpus   writ requiring the appearance of a person before a court

homo sapiens   the human race regarded as a species

in absentia   in (a person's) absence

in loco parentis   in the place of the parent

in memoriam   in memory of

in vitro   outside the living body; in an artificial environment

ipso facto   in the fact itself

locus classicus   most authoritative source or passage (of a subject)

modus operandi   method of working

modus vivendi   way of living; practical compromise

mutatis mutandis   with the necessary changes having been made

non compos mentis   insane

non sequitur   something that does not logically follow from what has gone before

per annum   annually

per capita   for each person

per se   by itself; intrinsically

persona non grata   person unacceptable to others

post mortem   examination of a corpse to discover the cause of death

prima facie   at first sight

primus unter pares   first among equals

pro forma   (of an invoice) issued before the goods are sent

pro rata   in proportion

pro tem   for the time being

quid pro quo   thing given as compensation

status quo   existing status of things

sub judice   under consideration (and therefore not to be disclosed publicly)

sui generis   of its own kind

terra firma   dry or solid ground

ultra vires   beyond one's legal power

vice versa   the other way round

viva voce   oral examination

French

agent provocateur   person employed to tempt others to commit criminal acts

aide-mémoire   aid to the memory

à la carte   ordered as separate items on the menu

ancien régime   old order of things

après ski   (of) social activity after skiing

à propos   (of) with reference (to)

art nouveau   decorative style of the late 19th century

au fait   well-versed

au fond   basically

belles lettres   literary writings and essays

bête noire   person or thing strongly disliked

billet doux   love letter

carte blanche   complete authority given to someone

cause célèbre   notorious incident or legal case

chargé d'affaires   temporary or minor diplomat

cordon bleu   (cook) of the highest distinction in cookery

coup de grâce   finishing stroke

coup d'état   violent or sudden change in government

crème de la crème   the very best

cri de coeur   heartfelt appeal

cul de sac   no through road

déjà vu   feeling of having previously experienced something

de rigueur   required by custom, fashion, etc.

double entendre   expression that has two meanings, one of which is indecent

eminence grise   person who exercises great authority without actually holding office

en bloc   taken all together

en masse   as a body or group

enfant terrible   person who causes embarrassment by behaving unconventionally

en passant   by the way

en route   on the way

entente cordiale   informal international agreement

entre nous between us; confidentially

esprit de corps spirit of loyalty and devotion among members of a group

fait accompli thing that has already been done and beyond alteration

faux pas social blunder

femme fatale alluring or seductive woman

force majeure unforeseen event that excuses the fulfilment of a contract

hors d'oeuvre savoury dish served as an appetizer to a meal

je ne sais quoi indescribable quality

joie de vivre feeling of lively enjoyment of life

laisser (or: *laissez*) *faire* doctrine of non-interference by the government

ménage à trois relationship in which a married couple and the lover of one of the couple live together

mot juste exactly appropriate word

noblesse oblige obligation of honourable and responsible behaviour of those in high positions

nom de plume pseudonym

nouveau riche person who has recently acquired wealth

objet d'art small artistic article

par excellence above all others; having the finest possible qualities

pièce de résistance most impressive item

pied-à-terre accommodation kept for occasional use

raison d'être justifying purpose or reason

savoir faire ability to act appropriately and with self-assurance in any circumstances

son et lumière entertainment at night with light, sound, and historical narrative

table d'hôte set meal in a hotel served at standard time and price

tour de force display of great skill

trompe l'oeil painting (style) in which a three-dimensional effect is achieved by optical illusion

vis-à-vis concerning

vol au vent small pastry with savoury filling

volte face complete reversal of opinion

Foreign abbreviations

A number of abbreviations in general use have their origins in French (F) or Latin (L), for example:

AD anno Domini (L), used in numbering years from the date of the birth of Christ

AH anno Hegirae (L), used in the Muslim system of dating, numbered from the Hegira, the flight of Mohammed from Mecca

a.m. ante meridiem (L) in the morning

e.g. exempli gratia (L) for example

etc. et cetera (L) and so on

i.e. id est (L) that is

N.B. nota bene (L) note well

nem. con. nemine contradicente (L) unanimously

no. numéro (F) number

p.m. post meridiem (L) in the afternoon

p.p. per procurationem (L) used by the signer of a letter who is not its writer

R.S.V.P. répondez s'il vous plaît (F) please reply, used at the end of an invitation

viz. videlicet (L) namely

Dutch Uncle Answers
1 *Chinese* chequers 2 *Indian* ink 3 *Turkish* delight 4 *French* windows 5 *German* measles 6 *Chinese* lantern 7 *Irish* stew 8 *Scotch* mist 9 *Spanish* omelette 10 *Russian* roulette 11 *Danish* pastry 12 *Egyptian* mummy 13 *African* violet 14 *Hungarian* goulash 15 *Siamese* twins 16 *Persian* carpet 17 *Jamaica* rum 18 *Swiss* roll 19 *Welsh* rarebit 20 *Maltese* cross

3 Words with a story

A large number of picturesque expressions are in common use—such as describing something as a **white elephant**, saying that a room is so small that there is **no room to swing a cat in it**, hearing a story that **warms the cockles of your heart**, and gaining an achievement that puts a **feather in your cap** as you **nail your colours to the mast**. Some such idiomatic expressions derive quite simply from literal uses, for example the **ball is now in your court** from tennis and to **pull out all the stops**, from the musical instrument, the organ. Others are born of a lively, and sometimes surprising, background story, such as **curry favour** and **between the devil and the deep blue sea**. In this chapter we explore the origin of a selection of these common idiomatic phrases and also some words—such as **adder**, **gamut**, and **nice** that have an unusual story behind them.

Animal spirits

A large number of idiomatic expressions feature mammals, animals, etc.:

To **have bats in one's belfry** is sometimes used to describe a person who is slightly mad or eccentric. It is thought to have been first used by Ambrose Bierce in the early 20th century. The phrase alludes to the bats that inhabit a belfry or bell-tower and which, on hearing the ringing of the bells, fly about wildly, as the thoughts of a mad person are thought to fly around in the mind.

An eager beaver is a person who is keen to volunteer or be involved in something. The beaver is used as a comparison because it is such an industrious creature. Ample evidence of this is seen in the way beavers build up many layers of mud, stone, and timber in order to construct their dams.

The origin of the phrase **the bee's knees** may lie in the fact that bees carry pollen in sacs which are located on their legs. If people regard themselves as the bee's knees, then they think that they are clever or superior in some way. **To make a beeline** is to travel in a straight line in the way that bees are supposed to do when they are returning to their hive with the nectar collected from flowers.

To **let the cat out of the bag** probably originated in the market places of England many years ago. Traders would try to deceive unwary customers by putting a cat in a bag, claiming to would-be purchasers that it was a pig. Buyers would then make a purchase without close inspection only to let a cat out of the bag and realize that they had been tricked.

The cat in **no room to swing a cat** is probably a cat o' nine tails, a whip used for flogging rebellious sailors. The expression may refer to the cramped conditions on board ship which were hardly large enough to carry out the punishment successfully. Because of this, the flogging took place on deck.

It's raining cats and dogs is a very old expression which is linked with the ancient beliefs of sailors and in Norse mythology that cats were associated with heavy rain and dogs with storms and the wind. Thus raining cats and dogs came to be associated with severe rainstorms.

The expression **a cock and bull story** alludes to stories in which animals converse with one another. It probably dates from Aesop's Fables. Nowadays the expression refers to a long rambling story that is unlikely to be believed.

To **shed crocodile tears** derives from the loud sighing and moaning noises attributed to a crocodile luring its victims. When the crocodile is devouring its prey, it is said to shed tears—false tears or feigned sorrow.

As the crow flies means 'in a straight line', for the

crow always flies the shortest distance between two points.

If you are living in **cloud cuckoo land** then you are living an imaginary fantasy world that bears little resemblance to reality. The phrase comes from a comedy called *The Birds*, written by the 5th century BC Athenian dramatist Aristophanes. In this play the birds built an imaginary city in the air, a sort of cloud cuckoo land.

A dog in a manger comes from one of Aesop's Fables. A dog lay in a manger and growled at the animals who came to eat the hay even though it did not want to eat the hay itself. A dog-in-the-manger attitude is seen in those who selfishly deny others the pleasure of things they themselves cannot use. Anyone who is **in the doghouse** is in disgrace: the phrase alludes to a disobedient dog that is sent out to his kennel as a punishment.

Top dog and **under dog** may allude to timber cutting. In the days before electric saws, logs were placed over pits. One man, the top dog, would stand above the pit with one end of the saw and his partner would stand in the pit holding the other end of the saw. This man in the pit was the unfortunate under dog who would get covered with sawdust.

Donkey's years may well be a variation of donkey's ears. Donkey's ears are of course very long, hence the meaning of the phrase, 'a long time'.

Lame duck is from an old American hunting maxim 'Never waste powder on a dead duck'.

The expression seems to be the origin of the phrase a lame duck, often nowadays applied to an organization or business company that cannot function properly because of financial problems. The expression was also applied to American congressmen who failed to stand for re-election or who were defeated in November polls. They would, however, remain in office as 'lame ducks' until the following March, retaining some power and able to cause trouble if they so desired.

To **get someone's goat**, meaning 'to annoy or irritate someone', is a metaphor which derives from the racecourse. A goat was sometimes stabled with an excitable racehorse in order to keep it calm before a race. If the goat was stolen or removed, it could have disastrous consequences for the horse's owner.

To **kill the goose that laid the golden egg** is an expression from one of Aesop's Fables which tells the story of a man who had a goose that laid golden eggs. In his greed he killed the goose to try and obtain all the eggs at once.

To **go the whole hog** may refer to the purchase of the whole of a pig in preference to parts of it. Some authorities suggest that since hog was slang for shilling, to go the whole hog meant to spend a whole shilling at once.

Don't look a gift-horse in the mouth is an ancient saying referring to the way that a horse's age is calculated, by looking at its teeth. The expression is now used to mean that you should not try to find fault with a gift that is offered, rather you should accept it gladly. **A dark horse** is a racehorse whose ability to win races is unknown. The metaphor is used to describe someone whose character or abilities are not widely known and may be underrated but who may surprise everyone in actual achievements.

To **buy a pig in a poke** means to buy something before you have had the opportunity of seeing its true value. The expression derives from the old practice of trying to trick potential customers at a market into buying a cat instead of a pig tied up in a bag (poke). (See also *let the cat out of the bag*.)

To **play possum** alludes to the opossum, a North American mammal, that pretends to be dead or unconscious to avoid being captured or threatened by other animals.

To **cry wolf** comes from the fable by Aesop

about a young shepherd boy. To amuse himself, he shouts 'wolf', and the villagers come running up the hillside to protect the sheep from the supposed wolves. When, one day, a wolf really does appear, he cries out, but nobody takes any notice of him and consequently all the sheep are attacked and killed.

Body language

A large number of idiomatic expressions mention a part of the body, from **falling head over heels in love**, through **not seeing eye to eye** with someone, having a **heart-to-heart** talk, **pulling someone's leg** and finally **putting one's foot down**. Some expressions link an actual action of the body with a figurative meaning: **shrug one's shoulders**, to show indifference to something; **raise one's eyebrows**, to express disapproval, doubt or scepticism; **hold one's tongue**, not to say anything; and **twist someone's arm**, to persuade someone to do something.

To **chance one's arm** is an expression which may have had its origin in the military circles. It meant losing a stripe or badge from the uniform sleeve if the risk that was to be taken involved breaking the rules of the establishment.

To **get one's back up** refers originally to the way that the hackles on a cat's back rise up when it sees a dog. If someone gets your back up you may react in a very hostile manner.

A bone to pick with someone also alludes to the animal kingdom. In this case the bone is probably being fought over by two dogs. Having a bone to pick with someone means that you are annoyed with him or her and prepared for a confrontation.

The phrase **make no bones about it** may come from the days when soup was the staple diet of many people. If the soup contained no bones, it was thought to be palatable and easy to eat. If it contained bones, however, complaints were made. Thus the expression came to stand for something that could be said or done straightforwardly or plainly.

To **make a clean breast** of something alludes to the ancient religious rite of marking a sinner's breast with ashes to indicate the sins that he or she had committed. To make a clean breast of something was therefore to confess, wash yourself clean, and be purified from your sins.

To **keep one's ear to the ground** means to be aware of what's going on around you. The expression may derive from a supposed tracking system used by the American Indians where they listened with their ears to the ground.

The wool in **to pull the wool over someone's eyes** actually means 'hair' and it alludes to the days when gentlemen wore wigs. Pulling the wool over someone's eyes meant that he could not see what was going on around him, hence the current meaning to deceive or trick someone.

Neither hide nor hair is an expression from hunting. If huntsmen have seen neither hide nor hair of an animal, they have had an unsuccessful day and caught nothing. So to have seen neither hide nor hair of someone means that you have not detected any traces of that person's presence.

To **bite the hand that feeds** one is to insult or be ungrateful towards someone to whom one should be thankful. The origin of this phrase is uncertain but it is possible that the 18th-century political theorist Edmund Burke may have been one of the first to use the expression. In an essay published posthumously he wrote: 'And having looked to government for bread, on the very first scarcity they will turn and bite the hand that fed them.'

To **bury one's head in the sand** comes from the alleged habit of an ostrich burying its head in the sand when it is in danger, believing that, as it cannot itself see, so others cannot see it. It is doubtful, however, whether the bird actually buries its head but it does bend its head close to the ground when listening for approaching predators.

The warmed **cockles of the heart** are not, as popularly believed, the shellfish of cockles and mussels but rather the ventricles (chambers) of the heart and so, one's inner feelings that are warmed by a success story or kind deed.

To **show a leg** is commonly thought to have been originally a naval expression and a shortened form of show a leg or a purser's stocking. It derives from the time when women were allowed on board ship and the order to show a leg was given first thing in the morning to identify that a woman was asleep in the bunk and therefore, unlike the men, who had to get up, allowed to lie in.

There are various theories of the origin of **to pay through the nose**. One suggestion is that during the 9th century the Danes inflicted a type of poll tax on the Irish and that the punishment for failing to pay this tax was a slit nose. Other authorities suggest that the derivation lies in the slang word, rhino, meaning 'money', which is similar to the Greek word rhinos meaning 'nose'. A further explanation links the pain of paying too much to being 'bled' for money, and so to a nosebleed.

One explanation of the expressions **thumbs-down, thumbs-up** is the ancient Roman practice of spectators sparing the life of a defeated gladiator by giving the thumbs-up sign. Less popular gladiators whom the crowd wanted killed would be given the thumbs-down. Thus the modern senses of thumbs-up meaning permission to 'go ahead' with a plan or other good news and thumbs-down being bad news or 'rejection'.

Long in the tooth means 'getting old'. It originally referred to horses' teeth, as horses' gums recede with age, so making the teeth appear longer. In the expression **give one's eyeteeth**, the eyeteeth are the valuable canine teeth in the jaws, hence the expression I'd give my eyeteeth for ..., showing that you are prepared to sacrifice them in order to gain the desired object.

Off the cuff

Many expressions contain words that refer to items of clothing, footwear, or headgear.

Below the belt means someone has behaved unfairly. The phrase comes from the Queensberry rules (see also page 54) for boxing which were established in 1867 by the Marquis of Queensberry. In these rules it is stated that an attack below the belt is regarded as foul play.

The expression **best bib and tucker** was first used in the late 16th century. If a couple were dressing up for a special occasion the man may have worn a bib-front to his shirt to keep it clean, and the woman may have worn a tucker—a piece of fine material such as muslin or lace to adorn the top part of her dress. Hence the term best bib and tucker to mean one's best outfit.

In the expression **to boot** the boot has nothing to do with the object of footwear, but comes from the Old English word bōt meaning 'remedy' or 'advantage'. The sense has developed to mean 'in addition' as in 'The journey was long and tedious, and uncomfortable to boot'.

A feather in one's cap is an achievement of

which one can justifiably feel proud. The feather in question is probably that of an American Indian brave who, after a battle, was given a feather for his head-dress for every warrior that he had killed. However, it may also refer to the plume of a heron that was worn in the caps of the Knights of the Garter, and thus signified the highest possible honour.

Speaking **off the cuff**, or without preparation, may derive from the practice of a speaker writing down all the points that he wishes to mention in his speech on the cuff of his shirt sleeve.

The word gauntlet comes from the French gant meaning 'glove'. A gauntlet was a heavy leather or steel glove originally worn as part of a suit of armour. To **throw down the gauntlet** was to issue a challenge to fight to the death; if the challenge was accepted, the opponent would pick up the thrown glove or gauntlet. The gauntlet in **run the gauntlet** 'to endure an unpleasant ordeal in which many people criticize one', is of a different origin. This gauntlet derives from the Swedish gatlopp, from gata, 'way' and lop, 'course'. A gatlopp consisted of two lines of men who stood facing each other and would strike out at the person—a victim of military punishment—who ran between them.

Kid gloves are made of kid leather which is the softest leather available. Hence the idea that something **handled with kid gloves** is to be treated with the utmost tact and discretion.

There are various explanations of the origin **knocked into a cocked hat**. One suggestion is that the cocked hat was a hat with three corners, popular in the 18th century, made by folding down the edges of a round hat. Hence its original meaning: 'to change completely' which gradually developed into 'to defeat completely'. The change in meaning may perhaps be traced to a game known as 'three-cornered hat' where three skittles were set up in a triangle; when all the skittles had been bowled and only these three remained, the game was described as knocked into a cocked hat, or no longer of any real worth.

The phrase to **wear one's heart on one's sleeve** is spoken by Iago in Act 1, Scene 1 of Shakespeare's *Othello*: 'But I will wear my heart upon my sleeve.' Some authorities add that in Roman times a soldier would wear the name of his sweetheart embroidered on his sleeve and during the Middle Ages, when chivalry was fashionable, the custom once again became popular. Soldiers would wear a token gift from their lady; a ribbon or brooch being a sign of his allegiance.

Tools and weapons

The significance of tools and weapons throughout the history of mankind has left its mark on the language in many expressions.

The expression to **have an axe to grind** is attributed to a story called *Too Much For Your Whistle* by Benjamin Franklin. In the story the young Franklin is asked by a stranger to demonstrate how his father's grindstone worked. Franklin obliged and the man put his axe on the grindstone as the boy turned the wheel. The man praised the boy for the swiftness of the machine, but when the axe was sharp he merely laughed and walked away. The man had known all along how the grindstone worked and merely wanted to fool and deceive Franklin. The expression is now in general use and means to have an interest, especially a selfish one, in helping someone or something. The phrase is usually found in the negative: I've no particular axe to grind.

The phrase **kick the bucket** is used informally and, slightly disrespectfully, to describe someone's death. There are two theories as to the origin of the phrase. One suggests that when pigs were slaughtered on reaching the market, and hung on a bucket beam for prospective buyers to view, they would kick the bucket beam. Other authorities suggest that the bucket does not refer to a beam, but rather to a bucket which someone committing suicide stands on and then kicks away after tying the noose.

Bite the bullet is said to have arisen during the 19th century. At that time there were no anaesthetics available with which to treat soldiers on the battlefield. Instead doctors would give the wounded man a bullet to bite on, to help relieve some of the pain of the operation.

A brave soldier would always **stick to his guns** and never flee from an approaching enemy. The phrase now means 'stand fast for what you believe'. The expression **son of a gun** has its origins in the time when women were permitted to live on naval ships. The description was originally applied to boys born during the long sea voyages and conceived near one of the ship's cannons. The phrase, originally one of contempt, has lost its derogatory connotations and is used more as a term of affection.

Bury the hatchet comes from the American Indian custom of burying tomahawks and other weapons as a sign that hostilities between the American Indians and the Whites had ended. Nowadays the expression is used to refer to coming to peaceful terms with an opponent.

The phrase **lock, stock and barrel** means 'the whole or everything': the burglars cleared the whole house out, lock, stock, and barrel. The lock, stock and barrel are originally the three main parts that make up a gun.

To **put the screws on someone** is to compel someone forcefully and alludes to thumbscrews which at one time were common instruments of torture. The screws could be gradually tightened to crush the thumb slowly and cause the victim excruciating pain.

The whole shooting match means the whole lot. The expression probably dates back to the time of the American frontier when large crowds of people must have assembled to watch gunfights or shooting matches.

A **parting shot** was originally a Parthian shot. The Parthians were an ancient people of southwest Asia and were renowned for shooting arrows while fleeing from their enemies. Thus someone's parting shot today is a hostile retort or gesture made while departing.

To **call a spade a spade**, or to speak in a direct and plain manner, is thought to originate in the Latin proverb 'Ficus ficus, ligonem ligonem vocat'. The identity of the poet is unknown but both Menander and Plutarch are possibilities.

There are several theories of the origin of **get down to brass tacks** meaning 'to start discussing the important fundamental facts of a matter'. One interesting idea is that brass tacks were nailed onto a shop counter and used to measure material by the yard. In this way the measurements could be calculated quickly and efficiently. Another theory is that brass tacks may be rhyming slang for 'facts'.

On tenterhooks alludes to a process whereby cloth, and particularly canvas, is stretched. The material is placed on a tenter frame and held taut by tenterhooks. If someone is on tenterhooks he or she is tense and anxious.

To **blaze a trail** comes from the days when explorers would mark out a trail by scratching off part of the bark of a tree, leaving bare wood that was known as a blaze. In that way the trail could be easily followed when it was used again. Nowadays the idiomatic expression and the derived noun, trailblazer, are used figuratively for pioneering.

A sporting chance

Many idiomatic expressions come from the language of sport and games.

On the ball, meaning 'alert' or 'quick to react', originated from ball games in which the players must watch the ball carefully and be constantly ready to accept it if it is passed to them. The expression to **keep one's eye on the ball** expresses the same idea. The **ball is in your court** comes from the game of tennis.

To **get to first base** comes from baseball. To get to first base is to reach the first of the four stations when scoring a run and, figuratively, to achieve the first stage in a series of objectives. **Off base** means 'out of order, in error, or unprepared'.

To **hedge one's bets** is to play safely in the money market by making several smaller bets in order to protect oneself from a great loss on a larger stake. The phrase originated from card games where players may actually have placed a hedge or barrier around their bets. Figuratively,

the expression means not to commit yourself to a single definite course of action.

Above board, meaning 'free from all traces of deception and fraud', comes from the difficulty of cheating at cards or gambling when your hands are above the table (or board).

To **have a card up one's sleeve** originated in the practice of playing card games where a player cheated by concealing an ace or another winning card up his or her sleeve. Magicians, when performing tricks, might also hide a card or other object in the sleeve of their coat or shirt. Thus to have a card up one's sleeve now means that you are keeping a secret or something in reserve which is not known to your opponent but will be revealed at the most opportune moment. Other expressions from games with cards include: **play one's cards right**, 'to handle things well'; **put one's cards on the table**, 'to declare your intentions' and **hold all the cards**, 'to be in a position in which you can dictate the conditions'.

On the cards is an expression which may have its origins in fortune-telling. Predictions about the future, what is likely or on the cards, may be made from reading special cards.

Loaded dice comes from gambling, where certain players may cheat by loading the dice. To do this, a heavy substance such as lead is put into the dice to ensure that it only lands on certain numbers. This obviously gives one player an unfair advantage, as is seen in the expression the dice are loaded against him. Dice is also used in the expression **no dice**. In the game of dice when one player is unable to throw a winning combination of numbers, he may be said to have no dice or no luck.

The die is cast were words apparently first used by Julius Caesar in 49 BC, when he crossed the Rubicon in order to march towards Rome. His words in Latin are, it is reputed, 'Jacta alea est'. He had made an irrevocable decision. When the die is cast in a game of dice, a player must accept whatever luck has been allotted by the fall of the dice.

At the start of a race a gun is fired to signal that the athletes may begin. If an athlete **jumps the gun** he leaves his blocks before the gun has been fired. The idiom is used in an extended sense to mean 'to act too hastily'.

No holds barred derives from wrestling: any

form of gripping or holding is allowed. Figuratively, the expression means that free use can be made of any methods in an argument, competition, etc., without any regard for the usual conventions of honour or fairness. The phrase is often used in front of a noun: a no-holds-barred attack.

To **have a good innings** comes from the game of cricket, and is typically found in contemporary usage to describe the long length of someone's life especially when that person has just died. An innings is the turn of one side (or batsman) to bat: to have a good innings is one in which many runs are scored. Other expressions that derive from cricket include **off one's own bat** 'by oneself, without seeking the help, advice, etc., of another person'; **be bowled over** 'to be taken by surprise' and **catch someone out** 'to catch someone doing wrong'.

To **ride roughshod** over someone means 'to treat someone harshly or insensitively'. The phrase originates from the practice of fitting horse-shoes with the heads of the nails jutting out in order to prevent the animal from slipping. Moreover, the shoes fitted to horses in battle sometimes had sharp projections, in order to inflict the greatest injury upon those in whose path they ran. In each instance the horse was said to have been roughshod.

A living language is like a man suffering incessantly from small haemorrhages, and what it needs above all else is constant transactions of new blood from other tongues. The day the gates go up, that day it begins to die.

H. L. Mencken

The idiom **follow suit** refers to the practice in many card games where a player must follow suit when playing his or her hand, i.e. lay a card of the same suit as that which has just been laid by the preceding player. Other expressions that allude to the suit of playing-cards include **play one's trump card** 'to play a card from the suit chosen as trumps', hence figuratively 'to use your strongest resource, argument, etc.' and **come or turn up trumps** 'to bring about a happy conclusion, especially when this is unexpected'.

To **throw in the towel/sponge**, meaning 'to give up or surrender', originates in boxing. If any object is thrown into the ring by a fighter's second while the fight is in progress, then that fighter is disqualified—hence the action of throwing in the towel by a second is a sign of defeat.

Home from home

A number of articles of furniture, implements used in cooking and other items used in the home have interesting origins.

The expression to **get out of bed on the wrong side** is based on the superstition that getting out of bed on the left side is unlucky. Similarly, if the left foot touches the floor before the right foot, this is also supposed to be unlucky. The superstition arose from the fact that the left side was traditionally the inferior or 'bad' side. The expression is now used to describe someone who is grumpy or bad-tempered.

Can't hold a candle to goes back to the times before there was electricity when candles were used after dark as the only source of light. If a master needed light, he would employ an apprentice to hold the candle for him. Thus if someone was not fit to hold the candle or one person couldn't hold a candle to another, he was very inferior to the other.

One explanation of the phrase **the game is not worth the candle** alludes to the lighting of gambling games by candle. If a player was losing money the game to him was not even worth the price of the candle.

The cupboard of **cupboard love** refers to a place where food and other supplies are stored. If you are showing cupboard love then you are hoping selfishly or greedily to gain something material for yourself in return for a show of affection.

Out of the frying pan and into the fire is an ancient expression which describes a situation where, by trying to avoid one problem, a person may find himself or herself in even more trouble and worse off than before. As the Greeks said: 'Out of the smoke and into the flame'.

An Englishman's home is his castle is an expression which comes from the *Third Institute*, a work by the lawyer Sir Edward Coke: 'For a man's house is his castle, et domus sua cuique est tutissimum refugium (and his own home is to each person the safest refuge)'.

People who live in glass houses should not throw stones means 'people with their own faults or problems should not criticize the same faults in others'. An early appearance of the phrase is seen in Chaucer's *Troilus and Criseyde*: 'And forthi, who that hath an hed of verre,/Fro cast of stones war hym in the werre.' In this example it is not a glasshouse but a head of glass that Chaucer uses as the metaphor. The sense, however, remains the same as in the modern version.

In **strike while the iron is hot** the iron is not a domestic iron but rather a blacksmith's iron. When the blacksmith hammers the horseshoes into shape, the iron must be very hot to bring about the required form. The expression means 'to act at the most opportune moment in order to achieve the best results'.

A **flash in the pan** refers to a flash in the lock-pan of a flintlock musket. Instead of firing when the trigger was pulled, there was only a temporary flash which failed to explode the charge. The promising beginnings came to nothing in reality.

There are several theories of the origin of **take down a peg**. Many authorities derive the phrase from 18th-century nautical jargon. Then a ship's flag was raised and lowered by pegs, the higher the peg, the higher the honour. Other authorities suggest that the pegs are those of a guitar or violin and hold the ends of the strings, so enabling the instrument to be tuned to the right notes. The former explanation seems more likely, however, given the contemporary meaning of 'to humble a conceited person'.

From pillar to post refers to an old game dating back to medieval times, which was called court tennis, rather like our squash. The original expression was from post to pillar because of a certain volley which would strike a post and then a pillar.

The **pot calling the kettle black** has two possible explanations of its origin. Firstly, the pot and the kettle were both black from standing so long on a burning stove. Or, secondly, the pot was black and on seeing its reflection in the shiny surface of the kettle, assumed that the kettle must also be black. The source may be Cervantes' *Don Quixote* which in one version reads: 'The pot calls the kettle black'.

For **go to pot**, 'to go to ruin', various explanations put differing items in the pot: old used items of metal or gold, food put into a pot for stewing, or a dead person's ashes into an urn.

To **turn the tables** may allude to certain board-games such as chess or draughts, where the table was turned around, so reversing the roles of winner and loser. Another explanation is that the phrase arose in the days when table tops had two surfaces—a smooth one for eating on, and a rough one for working on. In order to give someone a cold reception, the work surface would be turned uppermost.

Make a meal of it

Several expressions relating to food have unusual stories behind them.

The original apple of the **apple of one's eye** was the pupil of the eye, so called because of the round shape of both of these objects. Moreover, in Old English, æppel stood for both apple and eye. The apple of one's eye is something precious, as is the power of sight.

The most likely explanation of **apple-pie order** is that it is an alteration of the French nappe plié meaning 'folded linen', implying that tidy laundry is one of the hallmarks of an ordered household. This is also the origin of the expression **apple-pie bed**, in which the sheets and blankets are folded in such a way that a person cannot get into it.

To **upset the apple cart** is an old expression that probably derives from the taking of apples to market along rocky and pitted lanes. The cart would only need to get a wheel stuck and its whole load would tumble onto the road. Nowadays the meaning of the phrase is 'to disrupt a carefully made plan or arrangement'.

Butter wouldn't melt in someone's mouth is often said of a child who looks innocent but who in reality is full of mischief. The idiom may have arisen because these supposedly gentle people are not at all 'hot-blooded', so even the smallest portion of butter would not melt in their mouths.

To **curry favour** has nothing to do with the curry that we eat. The phrase derives from the Middle English curry favel. Curry means 'to groom a horse' (still found in modern English currycomb). Favel is from the Old French word fauvel and was the name of a horse which personified cunning and deception in a 14th-century satirical poem, *Roman de Fauvel*. Thus to curry favel (or favour) is to try to ingratiate oneself by insincere means.

A **nest egg** is an egg made of china or porcelain which a farmer puts in the nest of his hens to encourage them to lay more eggs. The metaphor is now used of savings that are set aside for the accumulation of interest.

Sour grapes comes from one of Aesop's Fables. A fox is sitting beneath a beautiful bunch of grapes hanging from a vine. He is desperate to reach them and tries many times, but in the end he gives up, muttering to himself that they are probably extremely sour. Thus the expression sour grapes is used to describe the bitterness felt when pretending not to want something that cannot be obtained.

Grist (corn) sent to the mill was welcome because it helped to keep the windmill or watermill in business, hence **grist to the mill**. The full phrase, all's grist that comes to the mill, has been shortened today but it retains the meaning of 'all contributions are welcome and can be made use of'.

A **red herring** was originally a herring that had been cured in such a way that it had a very powerful smell. It was used in hunting to draw the hounds away from the foxes' trail. When the red herring was pulled along the ground, it left a much stronger scent for the dogs to follow. The dogs would therefore be thrown off the scent and would go in the wrong direction, hence the contemporary meaning of something that misleads.

In medieval times **humble pie** was actually a numble pie or, due to a mistaken word division, an umble pie. It was made of the heart, liver, and entrails of the deer known as the numbles. This was consumed by the servants while the lord of the manor feasted on the choicest cut of venison. Umble was gradually confused with humble, and to eat humble pie now means 'to be (made to be more) apologetic or respectful by admitting that you have done wrong'.

Worth one's salt means 'worth your pay'. It originates from a practice in the Roman Empire where soldiers were originally paid partly in money and partly in salt. In time, this latter amount became an allowance to buy salt, and gradually the Latin salarium ('of salt') came to stand for payment for services undertaken—hence also our present-day salary.

In the money

'Money isn't everything,' runs the proverb, and yet we all know its importance. The following idiomatic expressions are associated with money—its speculation and spending powers...

Go for broke is an expression that comes originally in gambling. If a player puts all his money on a single game or perhaps a final hand of cards, he is going for broke; if he loses then he is broke, he has nothing.

Cash on the nail alludes to the medieval custom of traders setting up a pillar ('nail') in front of their market stall. Customers placed their money on this pole and their change was returned in the same way, thus ensuring that all business was performed promptly, honestly, and openly.

When a player finishes a game of cards or dice, he exchanges the chips that he has won for money. The phrase **cash in one's chips** is used today to mean 'to die'. **When the chips are down** means that a critical point has been reached in a situation. In gambling, it refers to the stage when bets have been made and money has been parted with, but the outcome of the game remains to be seen.

One explanation of the origin of **to make (both) ends meet** is that it was a book-keeping term of the 19th century. Accounts—assets and liabilities—had to be mete or 'equal'. Some authorities add that the phrase also refers to the balancing of accounts at the beginning and end of a year.

The penny drops is sometimes said to a person

Words—so innocent and powerless as they are, as standing in a dictionary, how potent for good and evil they become, in the hands of one who knows how to combine them!

Nathaniel Hawthorne

who finally understands a joke or explanation. It originates from the coin machines that moved into action when a large British old penny was dropped into place. Another expression that refers to this coin before decimalization is **to spend a penny**, to urinate, from the practice of having to put an old penny in the slot of a door of a public convenience in order to gain entry.

Pin money is a small amount of money, formerly a woman's allowance of money or money for her own personal use. A number of different theories account for this expression. Before pins were mass-produced in the 19th century, they were very expensive and it may have been that pin money was an amount set aside to buy pins. It is said that wives would ask their husbands for pin money at the beginning of each year and then buy as many as they could afford at the market. When the price of pins went down, the allowance was used to buy other items, but the expression pin money remained in use.

To **give someone short shrift** comes from the Middle Ages when a prisoner who was about to be executed would be allowed a short time of confession with the priest. The word shrift comes from the Old English word scrifan meaning 'to hear confession'. Short shrift was the brief time that a condemned person had to make confession and receive absolution before going to the gallows. Today, to give short shrift means 'to treat someone or something impatiently and unsympathetically'.

The expression **be sold down the river** arose during the time of the US slave trade when slaves were taken by boat down the Mississippi river to the deep South, to go to the squalid and harsh conditions of the sugar and cotton plantations. Nowadays the expression is used by people who feel that their leaders have betrayed their interests.

Your number's up

Among the picturesque expressions containing numbers are the following:

A.1. is an abbreviation originally used by the insurance company Lloyd's of London to describe a ship that is in perfect condition. The letter describes the state of the hull; the number the state of the equipment. Nowadays the expression refers to an excellent health or condition.

Back to square one comes from various board-games where, at certain times, a player may have to return to square one to begin all over again. It is now used to mean to go back to the beginning.

To **play second fiddle** refers to the violinist in an orchestra who is subordinate to the first violinist. To play second fiddle is therefore to occupy a less important position.

Hit for six comes from the score in the game of cricket, when a batsman strikes the ball that goes over the boundary line without touching the ground. Figuratively it means to have a serious, sometimes harmful effect on: 'Being made redundant really hit him for six'.

All at sixes and sevens is an idiom which originated in a dice-game. At one time a six and a seven could be thrown on dice. This early use of the phrase is used in Chaucer's *Troilus and Criseyde*: 'But manly sette the world on six and sevene', where the plea is to press on even if the odds are against you. The sense in which the phrase is used today to mean 'disorganized' obviously arose from the fact that a player wishing to take such high risks in trying to throw such numbers must be foolish, and hence confused.

The phrase, **seventh heaven**, which describes a state of great happiness, originated in various theories of astronomy and literature: the seventh heaven was the highest sphere and was therefore considered to stand for the state of greatest bliss.

There are various explanations of the origin of **nine-day wonder**. Some suggest that it refers to kittens or puppies who are blind for the first nine days of their life and thus in a mysterious world of wonder, after which everything becomes mundane and ordinary. Another suggestion is that the phrase arose from an ancient Roman custom. After a terrible storm or other natural occurrence would come a nine-day period of religious fervour in order to ward off this supposedly bad omen.

Dressed to the nines may be an alteration of a version of dressed to the eyes, possibly as ... to then eyne, the letter n of then being moved to eyne to give our modern nine. Other authorities point to the fact that the number ten is considered to be the ultimate point of perfection and therefore if someone is dressed to the nines they must look extremely smart.

The most likely origin of **a baker's dozen** lies in the baking industry of 15th-century England. A baker would cook thirteen, not twelve loaves in every batch of twelve to ensure that the total order met with standard weight regulations. Bakers knew that prosecutions could well result if their bread was found to be below the regulation weight. Hence the expression a baker's dozen, meaning thirteen.

During the 18th century the tin and copper mines in Cornwall were often troubled by bad flooding. Steam-powered engines were then used to pump water from the mine shafts. The mine owners had to pay premiums to the inventors for the savings which the pumps made. It was calculated that when the pumps were performing at their peak, they were ejecting nineteen thousand gallons of water for every twelve bushels of coal used; in other words, **nineteen to the dozen**. In contemporary usage the expression means talking 'at full speed' or incessantly.

True colours

Colour terms feature in many idiomatic expressions.

Anyone who is called the **black sheep** of the family is thought by the others to be the 'odd one out', the one who brings disgrace to the family. The black sheep is the outcast of any flock, perhaps because its dark colouring frightens the other white sheep. The black fleece is also of no use to the shepherd because it cannot be sold for wool.

A **bolt from the blue** is used to refer to something that comes as an unexpected or surprising shock. The blue is the blue of the sky and the bolt is a thunderbolt. The phrase refers to the speed and often unexpected onset of a thunderstorm.

Once in a blue moon means 'very rarely'. In reality of course, the moon is never actually blue although, occasionally, because of certain atmospheric conditions, it may indeed appear to be blue. The saying is very old; in 1528 it appeared in print in a work, by an unknown author, called *Rede Me and Be Not Wroth*: 'Yf they say the mone is blewe / We must believe that it is true.' Blue has traditionally been associated with the emotions of gloom, depression, or fear. In the

context **to scream blue murder**, the colour expresses fear or panic: to scream or cry blue murder is to shout or protest noisily. The word murder was used in the past as an outcry or a shout of alarm.

Someone who is good at gardening may be said to have **green fingers**. The idiom may have arisen from the fact that keen gardeners often have green stains on their hands from handling so many different plants. In American English, the idiom is to have a green thumb.

Grey matter is a term used to describe someone's brain or level of intelligence. The matter is in fact nerve tissue, present not only in the brain but also in the spinal cord, and has a brownish-grey colouring.

To **catch someone red-handed** is 'to find or capture someone while he or she is committing a crime or doing something wrong'. The expression alludes to the discovery of a murderer so soon after committing the crime that blood is still on his hands.

Paint the town red is a phrase which dates back to the 19th century and probably originated in the US frontier. It may allude to the fact that the red-light district of a town, associated with brothels, may be extended to the whole town after a person has consumed a large amount of alcohol and is somewhat out of control. Today the phrase is used to mean 'to enjoy a lively time at public places of entertainment'.

A **red-letter day** is a day of happiness or celebration. The expression derives from calendars issued by religious organizations that have the days of religious festivals and saint's days printed in red, the other days being printed in black.

In bull-fights in Spain, the bull-fighter or matador uses a red cape to make the bull attack. There is a belief that anything red will be maddening to a bull—so something that is like **a red rag to a bull** is extremely likely to bring about a violent angry reaction.

Red tape describes formal, especially bureaucratic business or administrative procedures. The term derives from the former use of a reddish colour tape to tie up bundles of official documents.

Born with a silver spoon in one's mouth is used of someone who is a member of a wealthy family. The expression probably comes from an old custom whereby godparents would present their godchild with a silver spoon at the christening.

A **white elephant** describes something that is costly but of no use. The term comes from an ancient custom of the kings of Thailand. When a white elephant was born the king would make it his property immediately because it was such a rare creature. The king did not keep such elephants for long, however—if a courtier or servant displeased him, he would give them a white elephant as a gift, knowing that the animal would be so expensive to keep that it would eventually ruin its owner.

A **white feather** has traditionally been a symbol of cowardice. The metaphor probably originated in the sport of cock fighting. If a bird had white feathers it was thought to be of an inferior breed and therefore a poor fighter.

All at sea

A number of everyday expressions come from the language of ships, boats, and sailing.

Not to touch something with a bargepole is used to express a strong dislike of something or someone and hence the desire to keep at a distance. It seems that the phrase (also ten-foot pole instead of bargepole) was originally used literally; figurative applications of the expression date back to the mid-19th century.

On one's beam ends is an old nautical expression: the beams were the horizontal timbers of a wooden sailing ship and supported the whole structure. If a ship was on its beam ends these planks would be vertical instead of horizontal, and the ship would be nearly capsizing. Today if you are on your beam ends, you are out of money and out of luck—in a desperate position indeed.

The nautical meaning of to **give a wide berth** is to keep a safe distance away from a danger, such as another ship. In general use the expression is used to mean to avoid coming too close to someone or something, especially in order to retain your own peace of mind, health, etc.

The boards of **to go by the board** were the sides of a ship. If the ship was in a heavy storm there was a possibility that parts of the ship, such as the mast, would go by the boards, that is, go over the side (go overboard) and be destroyed. Metaphorically, if an idea or plan goes by the board then it is abandoned.

To **paddle one's own canoe** is to make your own decisions, relying only on your own efforts. Since there is only room for one person in a canoe each person is responsible for himself or herself.

To **nail one's colours to the mast** is to state your position, principles, etc., clearly. The colours meant the ship's flag and if this was nailed to the mast then it could not easily be removed. This signified that the crew were willing to show their allegiance openly and were not willing to take down the flags and so surrender their ship.

To **sail under false colours** is to pretend to have a certain character in order to gain a benefit. The expression originated with pirates who would fly a false flag so that they could sail in waters alongside other ships and remain undetected.

In the doldrums comes from an area of ocean near the equator called the doldrums, where the conditions are very calm. The climate is affected by the south trade winds that leave dark clouds but only a very light breeze. In the past, sailing ships were unable to move far in this area and were often stranded for long periods of time. The word doldrum originated in the 19th century; it probably comes from the Old English word dol meaning 'dull' and may be connected to the word tantrum. Nowadays the expression stands for an inactive or depressed state.

The cut of one's jib refers to the jib on a sailing

'Then you should say what you mean,' the March Hare went on. 'I do,' Alice hastily replied; 'at least—at least I mean what I say—that's the same thing, you know.'

'Not the same thing a bit!' said the Hatter. 'Why, you might just as well say that "I see what I eat" is the same thing as "I eat what I see!"'

Lewis Carroll, *Alice in Wonderland*

ship, the triangular sail at the front of the ship and therefore the first sail to be seen as the ship came into view. Each country had a slightly different cut to its jib sail. The French and Spanish ships usually had their jibs cut higher than the British sails. Thus the jib sail indicated whether the approaching ship was likely to be hostile or friendly. In general usage if you judge people by the cut of their jib, your judgment is based on their general appearance.

Davy Jones' locker, the bottom of the sea, was regarded as the grave of those who have drowned or been buried at sea. Nobody knows precisely who Davy Jones was and what exactly was stored in his locker but there are numerous theories. One interesting suggestion is that Davy Jones was the landlord of a 16th-century London public house that provided the base for a press-gang operation. The lockers behind the pub may well have stored some unwilling sailors as well as quantities of alcohol. Another theory states that Davy Jones was a pirate who made his victims walk the plank, Davy Jones' locker being the watery grave where they met their end. The idiom may have connections with a West Indian word duppy meaning 'devil'. It is also possible that Jones is an altered form of the biblical Jonah thrown overboard and swallowed by a great fish.

Tell it to the marines is used to express disbelief at something that has just been said. The phrase derives from the fact that at one time marines were regarded as stupid by regular sailors and therefore likely to believe anything they were told, even something that was obviously foolish.

To **take the wind out of someone's sails** is a clear description of deflating someone's lofty opinion of himself or herself. The expression alludes to a manoeuvre performed during a naval battle in which a ship would sail into a position where it would shelter its enemy from the wind, so deflat-ing the opponent's sails. The enemy's ship would therefore be an easy and accessible target. Another expression with wind is **sail too close to the wind**, 'to behave just—and only just—within the rules'.

Ship-shape and Bristol fashion is a phrase derived from the days when Bristol was an important and efficient port. It was from Bristol that John Cabot sailed in the 15th century to explore the New World. To survive on long dangerous journeys meant that the ships and equipment had to be in perfect working order, and the port of Bristol had a great reputation as an efficient port.

To **spoil the ship for a ha'porth of tar** means to risk losing something valuable for the sake of a little further expenditure. Surprisingly this idiom has in fact nothing to do with ships. The word ship in this phrase is actually sheep, pronounced as ship in some dialects. The phrase alludes to treating the sores of a wounded sheep with tar. If this task was neglected then the sheep would be spoilt or would die.

Music to your ears

Several idiomatic expressions relating to music and sound have interesting derivations.

To **climb/jump on the bandwagon** comes from the time when campaigners, political or otherwise, would advertise their cause by riding around a town on a horse-drawn wagon. They would often have a band playing on this wagon in order to attract as much attention as possible, hence the term bandwagon. Local dignitaries and other supporters who backed the campaign would climb or jump up on to the bandwagon, sometimes, it must be admitted, in order to gain an advantage for themselves. When some climbed on the bandwagon, others would naturally follow, thinking that this was the fashionable thing to do. Today the phrase is chiefly used of people who join a scheme when they see that by doing so they will reap benefits for themselves.

To **ring the changes** alludes to bell-ringing and, in particular, change-ringing. This is when the bells are rung in a certain sequence. With a number of bells (from three to twelve) the number of changes or sequences that can be rung is very great. In general use, the expression ring the changes means to change the choice that is made within a selection of available things.

Hue and cry is a phrase which dates back to the Middle Ages, when it referred to the pursuit of a suspected criminal with loud cries in order to raise the alarm. Under the law of the land it was considered an offence if a person, on hearing the cry, failed to pursue the criminal. The original Anglo-French words were hu et cri, hu being a shout of warning. Nowadays the expression means a loud public outcry.

To be **drummed out** means to be banished or expelled. The expression refers to the army custom, whereby if an officer was forced to leave his regiment because of dishonourable behaviour, the dismissal took place accompanied by the steady beat of drums.

The expression **face the music** may be connected to the idiom be drummed out. As the soldier was dismissed, he had to face the music in the form of his fellow soldiers beating their drums. Other authorities, however, suggest that the expression refers to actors or entertainers at the beginning of a stage performance: as soon as the curtain is opened to the audience, the orchestra is revealed and the performers must indeed face the music.

A **swan song** is the last performance or work of an artist. It derives from the belief—found for example in poetry by Shakespeare and Coleridge—that swans sing a most beautiful song just before they die. This is in fact untrue but the romantic idea and the expression still survive.

The stops in **to pull out all the stops** are organ stops. These control the pipes which give the organ its great range of tones. To pull out all the stops is to use the organ to its fullest capacity, so achieving maximum volume of sound. In general usage, therefore, the expression means to use all the available resources to their fullest extent. Also from a keyboard instrument comes the expression to **soft-pedal**, to decrease the level of activity that has been used in the fulfilling of a purpose.

A word is not a crystal, transparent and unchanged; it is the skin of a living thought and may vary greatly in color and content according to the circumstances and time in which it is used.

Oliver Wendell Holmes, Jr.

Talk of the devil

Several expressions in modern usage refer to heaven and hell.

On the side of the angels originates from a speech made by the former British Prime Minister Benjamin Disraeli in 1864: 'Is man an ape or an angel? I, my Lord, I am on the side of the angels.' The phrase has come to mean 'on the side which believes in that which is right'. The allusion was to a popular version of Darwin's theory of evolution, that the human race is descended from the monkey. The expression is nowadays used to mean that someone has good moral opinions or intentions even if that person has not actually achieved much.

The devil to pay has in fact nothing to do with Satan. It was a phrase used at sea to describe a type of repair done on sailing ships. The original full expression was there's the devil to pay and no hot pitch. The word *pay* actually derives from an Old French word *peier* meaning 'to cover with hot pitch'. The devil was the name given to the seam on the hull of the ship that had to be paid or sealed to stop water from coming in. If there was no tar or pitch available then the crew were obviously in great difficulties. Hence the modern meaning of the expression, 'trouble is to be expected as a result of some action'. **Between the devil and the deep blue sea** is also a nautical expression. The devil here may also be the seam on a ship's hull as just described—or it may be a heavy plank (known as the gunwale or gunnel) on the side of a ship that was used to support the guns. For whatever meaning—the seam or the plank—to be situated between the devil and the deep blue sea meant that a sailor was in a very precarious position. In modern usage the expression is used to mean to be faced with the choice of two equally undesirable alternatives.

Let the devil take the hindmost is an abbreviated form of each/every man for himself and the devil take the hindmost, meaning that everyone follows his own interests regardless of other people. The expression first appeared in the play *Philaster* by Sir Francis Beaumont and John Fletcher. Medieval superstition held that those who were to become followers of the devil had to spend a certain time in an evil establishment in Toledo, Spain. Prospective disciples had to perform various tasks to show that they were suitable for the devil's work. One of these tasks involved running along an underground passageway; whoever was left behind in this race—the hindmost—became the devil's slave.

The exact origins of **talk of the devil** are unknown but the original form of the proverb, which dates back at least as far as the 17th century, was 'talk of the devil and he's sure to appear'. Today the phrase is used to refer to someone who unexpectedly appears when you have just been speaking of him.

The devil's advocate in Latin is advocatus diaboli. This is the name for an official of the Roman Catholic church who opposes the advocatus dei (God's advocate), during a debate on whether a candidate is suitable for canonization. In modern usage the expression is used to refer to someone who supports an opposing view, especially for the sake of argument.

Hell-bent for something means 'determined to proceed with a course of action even though it may have disastrous consequences'. One of the earliest uses of this phrase has been traced back to the time of the US frontier where, in 1840, a man named Edward Kent was standing for election as Governor of the state of Maine. The slogan with which he won the campaign was 'hell-bent for Kent'.

A–Z of words

The way we speak has sometimes led to changes in the actual words we use. For example, in Middle English an **adder** was a *naddre*. The words were run together so that it was thought of as an adder, the first sound of the original word being wrongly attributed to the preceding indefinite article. Other examples of this 'wrong' shortening include **apron**—originally a *napron* (like our modern day napkin) and **umpire**—originally a *noumpere*. The process happened the other way round as well: **a newt** is a 'mistaken' version of *an ewt*, and a **nickname** a 'mistaken' version of *an ekename*.

We are familiar with the word **aftermath**—commonly used to refer to the period immediately following a disaster such as a war, flood, or earthquake. But what is the *math* that comes afterwards? Originally, a math was a mowing or harvesting of grass, and so an aftermath was the grass cut after the first crop had been harvested, in other words a second crop of grass. The figurative sense in which the word is used today dates back to the 17th century.

Auspices comes from two Latin words, *Aris* means 'bird', and *spicere* means 'to see'. Soothsayers or prophets of ancient Rome foretold the future by means of watching the directions of birds in flight. **Under the auspices** therefore originally meant 'under the omens'.

Bandy is used in the expression **to bandy words** about meaning 'to quarrel'. It comes from a Middle French word *bander*, meaning 'to hit the ball back and forth'. Bandy was thus an early form of tennis. The expression is therefore quite apt—from the sporting exchange of a ball to the angry exchange of words.

In the 12th century the Old English word for **buxom** (buhsum) meant 'compliant, obliging, or obedient'. Coming from Old English *būgan* 'to bend or yield', it applied to both men and women. In the 16th century several meanings developed, 'yielding' (as in Milton's 'Winnows the buxom air'—*Paradise Lost*), this meaning eventually dying out; 'lively; blithe', which also died out; and finally 'plump and comely', the only sense that is still current.

In Roman times *candidatus* meant 'clothed in white'. The word was applied to someone seeking office: a **candidate**. The white toga symbolized the fact that the candidates motives were to be pure and unsullied. From this word, candidus, 'white' developed the sense of 'honest' and 'frank', these meanings conveyed by the modern word **candid**.

The word **chortle** was invented by Lewis Carroll in 1872, in *Through the Looking-Glass*: '"O frabjous day! Callooh! Callay!" He chortled in his joy.' Probably a blend of chuckle and snort, the word has come to mean 'to laugh with happiness and amusement'.

Dismal was formerly a noun used in medieval times to describe a list of 24 unlucky days during the year. The word derives from the medieval Latin phrase *dies mali*, meaning 'evil days'. Today dismal is an adjective which means sad or depressing.

A **forlorn hope** is one that will most probably not be realized. The expression derives from the Dutch *verloren hoop* 'lost troop', used to describe a small group of assault troops that were sent in advance of the main forces. They were seen as expendable, as they had little chance of coming back alive.

The word **gamut**, meaning 'whole range', was originally a musical term. A combination of *gamma* and *ut*, gamut was the lowest note in the musical scale established by the 11th-century Italian monk and musical theorist Guido d'Arezzo. Ut was the first note, the others being re, mi, fa, sol, lai, and si. The notes were named after the first words of each line of a Latin hymn to St John the Baptist and have their equivalent today in doh, ray, me, fah, soh, lah, te.

Gossip derives from an Old English word *godsibb*, 'godparent', *sibb* meaning 'kin' or 'kinsman'. The term came to be used of any women friends who attended the mother at the time of the birth of her child, and from there it came to mean simply 'acquaintance'. By the end of the 16th century gossip had come to describe the idle chatter indulged in by friends or acquaintances.

Hustings, used to refer to the campaigning at an election, was (until 1872) the name given to the platform on which parliamentary candidates were nominated and from which they delivered speeches. In Old English *hūsting* meant a deliberation assembly, the word deriving ultimately from the Old Norse *hūsthung*, from *hūs*, house and *thing*, 'assembly'.

In Old English, a **knave** was simply a boy or male servant—compare modern German *Knabe*—but in the 13th century the word acquired the sense of 'deceitful fellow', thus gaining negative connotations. The older sense of knave

Words should be an intense pleasure just as leather should be to a shoemaker.

Evelyn Waugh

is sometimes referred to when the word is used for the picture-card with the lowest value, commonly, jack.

Other words that were at one time neutral or positive but now have negative or derogatory applications include:
- crafty, formerly 'strong, skilful', now 'cunning'
- idiot, formerly 'an ignorant person; private person', now 'someone who is foolish'
- lewd, formerly 'lay; unlearned, ignorant', now 'lascivious; obscene'
- notorious, formerly 'well-known', now 'well-known for something undesirable'
- pedant, formerly 'schoolmaster', now 'someone over-concerned with tiny, especially academic details'
- villain, formerly 'farm labourer', now 'rascal'
- vulgar, formerly 'ordinary; belonging to the common people', now 'indecent'.

The device that generates a high intensity beam of light or other electromagnetic radiation is known as a **laser**. This word derives from the initials of the words light amplifications by stimulated emission of radiation and is therefore an example of an acronym, a word formed in this way. Other examples of acronyms include:

AIDS from acquired immune deficiency syndrome

Nato from North Atlantic Treaty Organization

OPEC from Organization of Petroleum Exporting Countries

radar from radio detecting and ranging

SALT from Strategic Arms Limitation Talks

sonar from sound navigation ranging

A poet **laureate** is one who is appointed to the British court post and made a lifetime officer of the royal household. The word actually comes from the Latin laurea, and arose because of the custom in ancient Rome of crowning important citizens with a laurel wreath in recognition of their outstanding public or intellectual achievements or contributions. The expressions **rest on one's laurels**, 'to enjoy with satisfaction the distinction, fame, etc., already achieved and not attempt to gain more', and **look to one's laurels**, 'to ensure that a favoured position is retained by preventing others from doing better', also allude to this same custom.

When the Authorized (King James) version of the Bible says, 'I have given every green herb for **meat**' (Genesis 1: 30), it is referring to different kinds of food, not just the flesh of animals. The word has undergone a narrowing of meaning from 'all food' to 'the flesh of animals'. (The older sense of 'food in general' is preserved in the expressions meat and drink and sweetmeat.)

A popular explanation of the word **midwife** is that this woman acts as a 'middle' person between mother and baby. The word in fact, however, derives from the Old English word mid meaning 'with', compare German mit, and wif meaning 'woman'. A midwife attends, or is with, a woman during the birth of her child.

There can be few words whose meaning has changed as much as the word **nice**. Used in contemporary English with the sense 'pleasant or agreeable', nice goes back to the Latin nescius 'ignorant'. The word developed via Old French nice, 'silly; simple', to first appearing in English in the 13th century with the meaning 'foolish'. The meaning developed over the centuries, acquiring in the 14th century the sense 'wanton or lascivious', in the 15th century the sense 'shy' and in the 16th century the sense 'showing fine distinction'— preserved, for example, in the phrase a nice distinction. It was as late as the 18th century that nice adopted its main contemporary sense.

Pandemonium, now meaning a state of utter chaos and confusion, was coined by the 17th-century English poet John Milton in his work *Paradise Lost*. He used it as a name for the capital of hell where all the evil spirits met for their council. Milton wrote in Book 1: 'A solemn council forthwith to be held At Pandœmonium, the high capital of Satan and his peers.' The word is a joining of pan with daimōn, the Greek word for demon.

Paraphernalia, meaning 'a large number of miscellaneous objects', derives from the Greek *parapherna*, the goods a bride brought to her marriage that were over and above (*para*, 'beside') the dowry (*phernē*, 'dowry'). So a married woman's paraphernalia were the articles that she could legally claim as her own.

Posh, meaning smart or fashionable, is popularly believed to date back to the days of long sea voyages to the Far East. The cooler and more expensive accommodation was on the ship's port side outward and starboard side on the homeward journey. This booking procedure became shortened to POSH by the shipping companies—port outward, starboard home.

The origin of the word **punch**, which describes the alcoholic drink often served at parties, is the Hindi word *pā̃c*, meaning 'five', derived ultimately from the Sanskrit word *pañca*, meaning 'five'. The 'five' in question refers to the traditional five ingredients of punch: alcohol (either wine or spirit), water or milk, sugar, spice, and lemon juice.

One possible explanation of the origin of **quiz** lies in late 18th-century Dublin. It is said that a theatre manager, James Daly, bet to a friend that he could introduce a new word into the language within a day. Daly, so the story goes, then proceeded to have the word *quiz* chalked on walls throughout the city. This curious word was an immediate topic of conversation and so Daly won his bet and the language gained a new word.

Robot comes from the Czech *robota* 'work' and came into the language after being used as part of the title of a play by the Czech playwright Karel Čapek. The play was entitled *R.U.R.* (Rossum's Universal Robots). It was written in 1920 and first performed in English in London in 1923.

The word **scapegoat**, for someone who is made to take the blame for others' faults, was coined by the English Protestant William Tyndale as a blend of the words *escape* and *goat*. Tyndale intended the words to be a translation of the Hebrew *'azāzēl*, probably the name of an evil spirit, which was confused with *'ēz 'ōzēl*, 'the goat that escapes' (Leviticus 16: 8). In the Old Testament, goats were symbolically burdened with the sins of the Israelites and then sent away into the wilderness—hence the name scapegoat.

The word **shambles** derives from Old English sceamel, a table or stool used by meat vendors in the market place. The popularity of the street name The Shambles still found today in places such as York, bears witness to the days when whole streets would be filled with butchers selling their wares on trestle tables. A shambles then came to mean an impromptu scene of slaughter. Characteristically such scenes would be chaotic—hence the modern meaning of the word.

The word **silly** has not always been used as an expression of disapproval. In Old English a silly person was one who was 'blessed' or 'innocent'. This came to have marked negative associations, leading to the meaning 'simple; unworldly'. The development of the meaning continued over the centuries, resulting in the present meaning of 'foolish'. It is interesting that the parallel German has not undergone such a sense development: modern German *selig* still means 'blessed'.

The origin of the word **sirloin** is from the Middle French word surlonge; sur meaning 'above' and *longe* meaning 'loin'. The alteration of *sur* to *sir* is popularly believed to have come about as a result of the action of a British monarch in investing the cut of meat with a knighthood, using the words, 'Arise, Sir Loin'.

Smog is a joining of the words smoke and fog, and is known as a blend (or portmanteau word)—a word formed from the joining of two others. Other examples of blends include:

bit (binary + digit)
brunch (breakfast + lunch)
electrocute (electro + execute)
franglais (français + anglais)
heliport (helicopter + airport)
monergy (money + energy)
motel (motor + hotel)
telex (from teleprinter + exchange)
transistor (transfer + resistor)

Teetotal was apparently coined in 1833 by the English advocate of total abstinence from alcohol, Mr Richard Turner (died 1846). He was one of the founder members of the first Total Abstinence Society, formed on 22 March 1832. The word teetotal seems to have been coined from the desire to emphasize the importance of the word *total:* T-*total* (compare *D-day*).

In Old English, a **wasp** was a *waps*, the final letters being reversed. This process of two sounds changing places is known as metathesis. Similarly, in Old English **bird** was *bridd*, and **third** *thridda* (compare the modern German dritt-).

The use of the word **ye**, found in such expressions as Ye Olde Tea Shoppe, arose from a misunderstanding. The y of *ye* was originally in Old English the single letter þ (known as thorn), equivalent to our modern th. As time went on, this unfamiliar letter was often wrongly written as a *y*, to give ye. In fact this word was never pronounced as 'yee'; ye simply represents a misspelling of our commonplace word, the.

Similes

Similes are as old as the hills and are used by most people almost instinctively. A simile is a figure of speech that compares two supposedly similar objects or describes a similar property that two different objects each possess. Here are some of the similes most frequently heard today and explanations of how some of them came about.

as bald as a coot
as black as coal
as blind as a bat
as bright as a button
as busy as a bee
as clean as a whistle
as clear as a bell
as cold as ice
as common as muck
as cool as a cucumber
as dead as the dodo
as dead as a doornail
as deaf as a post
as drunk as a lord
as dry as a bone
as dull as ditchwater
as fat as a pig
as fit as a fiddle
as flat as a pancake
as free as a bird

A gruntled burglar

One of the ways in which new words are created is by removing a prefix or suffix—for example, *edit* comes from *editor*, *burgle* from *burglar*, *televise* from *television*. This process is known as back formation.

Some back formations are created by removing what is commonly thought to be a prefix or suffix—e.g. *gruntled*, from *disgruntled*, *ept* from *inept*, *couth* from *uncouth*, *kemp* from *unkemp*, often for humorous effect.

---

as good as gold
as guilty as sin
as hard as nails
as heavy as lead
as keen as mustard
as large as life
as light as a feather
as like as two peas
as mad as a hatter/a March hare
as old as the hills
as plain as a pikestaff
as playful as a kitten
as pleased as Punch
as poor as a churchmouse
as proud as a peacock
as pure as the driven snow
as quick as lightning
as quiet as a mouse
as regular as clockwork
as right as rain
as round as a barrel
as safe as houses
as sharp as a needle
as sick as a dog/parrot
as sly as a fox
as snug as a bug in a rug
as sober as a judge
as sound as a bell
as stiff as a poker
as strong as an ox
as sure as eggs is eggs
as sweet as honey
as thick as two short planks
as thin as a rake
as tough as old boots
as ugly as sin
as white as a sheet

As bald as a coot. The coot is a European bird that lives in water. It has dark plumage and a distinctive white patch on its forehead that extends from the bill and so gives the bird the appearance of being bald. The saying as bald as a coot is used of a man who has lost all the hair on his head.

As clean as a whistle. The modern-day whistle is made of metal but in the past whistles were made of wood, particularly a reed, like those used in wind instruments such as the clarinet or oboe. In order to get a clear sound the whistle had to be free from dust and other impurities.

Hence our modern expression as clean as a whistle, clean or empty.

As dead as the dodo. A dodo is an extinct species of flightless bird that once inhabited the island of Mauritius in the Indian Ocean. Larger than swans and with a heavier body, the birds became extinct by about the 18th century. Thus now if something is said to be as dead as the dodo it is completely out of date or no longer in existence.

As dead as a doornail. For a long time the doornail in this phrase was believed to be the metal plate against which a door knocker banged. This was understandably 'dead' from so many years of being hit. However, the doornail is now thought to refer to an actual nail, used to provide a fastening for a door by turning over the point of the nail. The bending of the nail's point makes the joint secure and the nail 'dead'.

As drunk as a lord. Someone who is as drunk as a lord is extremely drunk. The simile dates at least from the 18th century: the days when drunkenness was regarded as a characteristic of the aristocracy.

As fit as a fiddle. Today this phrase is used to mean 'in very good health and physical condition'. The expression may derive from the belief, said to be in the 17th or 18th century, that fiddles were regarded as beautiful instruments.

This quality of beauty was applied, it seems, to humans: 'to have one's face made of a fiddle' meant that you were very attractive.

As mad as a hatter. The Mad Hatter is a popular figure in Lewis Carroll's *Alice's Adventures in Wonderland* (1865), yet the phrase has been in circulation longer than that. There is much discussion of the origin of this expression. Some believe that the original phrasing was as mad as an atter, *atter* being the Old English for 'poison'—compare *adder*, the poisonous snake. The sting of the adder was thought to cause madness. Others hold that the simile originated in the hat trade; constant inhaling of the mercury used in making felt hats caused a severe twitching that was interpreted by some as madness.

As mad as a March hare. The March hare also appears at the tea party in *Alice's Adventures in Wonderland*. The explanation of this expression may be, it is said, that hares are more lively and prone to odd behaviour in March. Other authorities believe that March hare is an alteration of marsh hare—hares that live in marshes supposedly act very strangely because of the damp environment.

As plain as a pikestaff. Today this simile means 'obvious' or 'easy to recognize', a pikestaff being the staff on which a traveller carried his pack over his shoulder. Such a staff would in time become worn—plain or smooth from constant use. An alternative explanation is that the pikestaff—the wooden pole of the medieval weapon, the pike—was very long and so easily seen.

As sure as eggs is eggs. This expression, used to mean 'definitely' or 'certainly', is an alteration of the 17th-century mathematical statement as sure as x is x.

Throwing out a challenge

Some words have two meanings that seem to be directly opposite to or contradict each other. For example, the old word *cleave* can mean 'to split' (*The tree was cleft in two by the lightning*) and also 'to adhere or cling loyally to' (*'Therefore shall a man leave his father and mother, and shall cleave unto his wife: and they shall be one flesh'*, Genesis 2:24).

Other examples are:

- *scan* 'to look through something quickly' and 'to look at something very closely'
- *ravel* 'to tangle or become entangled' and 'to disentangle'
- *throw out* 'to suggest, especially casually': (*throw out a few ideas for discussion*) and 'to reject' (*The committee threw out all the advisory board's suggestions*).
- *quite* 'fairly' (*The meal was quite nice*) and 'completely' (*It's quite impossible to talk to him*).

Collective nouns

Collective nouns have been in the English language for hundreds of years and were compiled into lists as early as the 15th century in such works as *The Book of St Albans* (1486), compiled by Dame Juliana Berners. These terms were popular during the Middle Ages because of the importance of hunting as a primary means of food supply. The many books on courtly behaviour produced during the 15th century also stressed the importance of these collective nouns; to know the correct terms was a sign of culture and good breeding. Some group nouns arose and became popular through alliteration or onomatopoeia; a gaggle of geese, for example, others arose because of certain characteristics inherent in that particular species of animal; a leap of leopards or a sloth of bears. Many of these terms are now unknown to all but the historical linguist, a few such as a flock of sheep and a swarm of bees remain in everyday use.

An interesting party game is to ask for ideas for collections for groups of, for example, civil servants, directors, joggers, secretaries, students, teachers, etc.

a brood of hens	a fall of woodcock	a peep of chickens
a cast of hawks	a flock of sheep	a plague of locusts
a cete of badgers	a flush of mallards	a pride of lions
a charm of goldfinches	a gaggle of geese	a rout of wolves
a clowder of cats	a gam of whales	a school of porpoises
a congregation of plovers	a gang of elks	a shrewdness of apes
a covert of coots	a kindle of kittens	a skulk of foxes
a covey of partridges	a leap of leopards	a singular of boars
a deceit of lapwings	a murder of crows	a sloth of bears
a dray of squirrels	a murmuration of starlings	a swarm of bees
a drove of cattle	a nye of pheasants	a troop of monkeys
a dule of doves	a parliament of owls	a watch of nightingales
an exaltation of larks		

4 Name into word

The English language is full of words and expressions that come from names of real people (e.g. *cardigan*, *dahlia*, *Parkinson's disease*), literary, biblical, or mythological names (e.g. *Scrooge*, *Job's comforters*, *herculean*), and names of places (e.g. *cos lettuce*, *balaclava*, *astrakhan*). This chapter presents words derived from personal names (eponyms) and words derived from place-names (toponyms), each grouped according to subject area.

Dress sense

The words of many articles of clothing derive from the names of people.

Bloomers, the women's undergarment with full loose legs gathered at the knee, are named after the US feminist Amelia Jenks *Bloomer* (1818–94), the original garment known as bloomers consisted of a loose-fitting tunic, a short knee-length skirt, and billowing trousers gathered at the ankle. The costume was the source of great controversy at the time of its introduction (1851), chiefly because it was thought that trousers should be worn only by men. Later bloomers came to be used to refer to the trousers in the costume, then to knee-length knickerbockers and still later to the present garments, referred to in informal, humorous usage.

Cardigan, the knitted jacket fastened with buttons, is named after the British cavalry officer James Thomas Brudenell, 7th Earl of *Cardigan* (1797–1868). The cardigan was first worn by British soldiers in the severe cold of the Crimean winter. The Earl of Cardigan led the ill-fated Charge of the Light Brigade in the Crimean War (1854), near the village of Balaclava (source of the name of the woollen head-covering).

Jacky Howe (in Australian English) is a sleeveless shirt, as worn by sheep-shearers. Named after

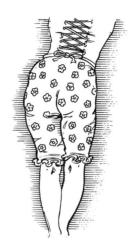

the world sheep-shearing champion John (*Jacky*) *Howe* (1855–1922).

Knickerbockers, short, baggy breeches gathered at the knee is a word derived from Dietrich *Knickerbocker*, the pseudonym of the US author Washington Irving (1783–1859). The name *Knickerbocker* came to represent the typical, solid Dutch burgher, a descendant of the original Dutch settlers in New York. It is said that *knickerbocker* came to be used to describe the baggy breeches as they were regarded as the traditional garment of the Dutch settlers in the USA.

Leotard, the close-fitting one-piece garment worn by acrobats, ballet dancers, etc. is named after the French acrobat Jules *Léotard* (1842–70), who designed and introduced the original costume for the circus. Léotard was one of France's most renowned acrobats, known as 'That Daring Young Man on the Flying Trapeze' from a contemporary song, and he perfected the aerial somersault and starred in circuses in Paris and London.

Levis, a trademark for a type of jeans, comes from the name of *Levi* Strauss (1830–1902), a Bavarian immigrant to the USA and a San Francisco clothing merchant during the Gold Rush. Rivets were added to the corners of pockets produced in the mid-1870s, apparently so that the pockets would not tear when loaded with samples of ore.

Mackintosh, a raincoat, especially one made of rubberized cloth, was so-called after the Scottish chemist Charles *Macintosh* (1760–1843). Another Scotsman, James Syme first invented the process of making waterproof fabrics (1823), but it was Macintosh (spelt without a *k*), who refined the process and patented it. Macintosh founded a company in Glasgow and the first mackintoshes were sold in 1830.

Raglan, a coat with sleeves that extend to the collar without shoulder seams is named after the British Field Marshal Fitzroy James Henry Somerset, 1st Baron *Raglan* (1788–1855), who served in the Napoleonic Wars. He was wounded at the Battle of Waterloo and had to have his arm amputated, after which he is reputed to have said, 'I say, bring back my arm—the ring my wife gave me is on the finger!' He later became Secretary to the Duke of Wellington, and then Commander-in-Chief of the British forces in the Crimean War, his tactics at the Battle of Balaclava being heavily criticized.

Several articles of footwear and headgear are also named after people. There are a number of different theories of the origin of **bowler**, a stiff narrow-brimmed felt hat with a rounded crown. It is possible that it is named after *Bowler*, a family of 19th-century hatters, while some suggest that the family name was in fact *Beaulieu*. Others point to the shape of the hat as an explanation of its name: it is like a stiff bowl and can be bowled along easily.

Busby, today, is the tall bearskin fur hat worn by soldiers. In the 18th century, however, a busby was a bushy wig. Traditionally, the word is thought to have been named after the London headmaster Dr Richard *Busby* (1606–95), but it is not certain that Busby himself wore a bushy wig: his hair may possibly have just naturally stood upright.

Havelock, a cloth cover for a soldier's cap with a long flap that reaches down the back, is named after the English general Sir Henry *Havelock* (1795–1857). He probably did not invent the cloth cover that is named after him, but it was the havelock which he produced for his soldiers that became widely known.

Plimsoll, the light rubber-soled canvas shoe, is named after the English leader of shipping reform Samuel *Plimsoll* (1824–98). The shoe is so named because the upper edge of the rubber was thought to resemble the *Plimsoll line*, the set of markings on the side of a ship that show the levels to which the ship may be safely loaded. As Member of Parliament Plimsoll was concerned for the overloading of ships and the general safety of maritime transport. Following his demands, a bill that provided for a thorough inspection of ships became law in 1876, and use of the Plimsoll line was adopted that same year.

Stetson, a wide-brimmed high-crowned felt hat, is so-called after its designer, the US hat-maker John Batterson *Stetson* (1830–1906).

Tam-o'-shanter, the Scottish brimless cap, usually with a pom-pom on the top, is named after the hero of the poem *Tam o'Shanter* by the Scottish poet Robert Burns.

Trilby, the soft felt hat with an indented crown, is from *Trilby*, the name of the dramatized version of the novel by the English artist and writer George du Maurier. The heroine, Trilby O'Ferrall, wore such a hat in the novel's original stage version.

Wellington, a waterproof rubber boot that extends to the knee, is named after the British soldier, statesman, and Prime Minister Arthur Wellesley, 1st Duke of *Wellington*, also known as 'The Iron

DO YOU KNOW . . . (*Answers on p. 54*)

1 What word which is used to describe part of an oil rig comes from the name of a hangman?
2 What type of railway travel is named after its US inventor?
3 What regular feature seen on British streets is named after a minister of transport?
4 What everyday writing implement is named after its Hungarian inventor?
5 What personal article is named after a nurse in one of Dickens' novels?

Duke' (1769–1852). Wellington's greatest victory was at Waterloo (1815) where with General Blücher, he defeated Napoleon. A great many articles of clothing were named in honour of Wellington, of which the wellington boot (sometimes referring to a boot that covers the knee) is the best known. The capital of New Zealand, Wellington, is also named after the Duke, 'England's greatest son', as Tennyson described him.

Entertaining expressions

A number of eponyms are found in the world of sports, entertainment, and music, including:

SPORTS

Davis Cup, the men's annual international lawn tennis championship. Named after Dwight Filley *Davis* (1879–1945), the US statesman and sportsman who founded the competition in 1900.

Derby, the flat race for three-year-old colts and fillies run annually at Epsom Downs, Surrey. Probably named after Edward Stanley, 12th Earl of *Derby* (1752–1834), who instituted the horse-race in 1780. The equivalent US race is the Kentucky Derby, founded in 1875.

Jockey, a person who rides a horse, especially professionally in horse-races, derives from *Jockey*, originally the Scottish variant (*Jock*) of the name *Jack*. The name was probably chosen as a nickname for a good rider.

Lonsdale belt, the belt awarded as a trophy to professional boxing champions. Named after Hugh Cecil Lowther, 5th Earl of *Lonsdale* (1857–1944), who originated the awards.

Queensberry rules, which represent the basis of modern boxing, were formulated under the sponsorship of John Sholto Douglas, the 8th Marquess of *Queensberry* (1844–1900). The Queensberry rules established the use of padded gloves, three-minute rounds, and restrictions on the types of blows allowed.

Ryder Cup, the biennial professional match between the USA and Europe, named after Samuel *Ryder* (1859–1936). The Ryder Cup came into being slightly by chance. If Samuel Ryder, a boy from Manchester, had not persuaded his father, a seed merchant, to sell flower seeds in penny packets, he would never have moved south to start his own business at St Albans in Hertford-shire. There, late in life, he took up golf under the skilled and watchful eye of the English professional golfer Abe Mitchell and, whether at Mitchell's suggestion or not, presented a cup for competition between the professionals of the USA and Britain.

St Leger, an annual flat race for three-year-old colts and fillies run at Doncaster, South Yorkshire. Founded in 1776. Named after a leading local sportsman of that period, Lieutenant-General *St Leger*.

Wightman Cup, the annual tennis competition between British and US women's teams. Named after Hazel Hotchkiss *Wightman* (1886–1974), who donated the trophy and was the US national singles champion from 1909–11. Wightman bought the silver cup about 1920, when plans were being made to run a competition similar to the Davis Cup. These attempts were unsuccessful but in 1923 a competition was arranged between the British and US women's teams, which has since been played annually.

CARD GAMES

Faro, a game in which players gamble on the value of the cards that the dealer will turn up. Probably originally from *Pharaoh*, the title of ancient Egyptian rulers. During the history of the game a picture of one of the ruling pharaohs may have been shown on the cards.

Nap, a card game similar to whist. Named after the French Emperor *Napoleon* Bonaparte (1769–1821), but the reason why the card game should be named after the Emperor remains uncertain.

Do you know ... Answers

1 A *derrick*, originally a gallows, from a 17th-century English hangman with the surname *Derrick*.

2 *Pullman*, the luxurious passenger coach, named after its US inventor George Mortimer *Pullman* (1831–97).

3 A *Belisha beacon*, to mark a pedestrian crossing, named after the British politician 1st Baron (Isaac) Leslie Hore-*Belisha* (1893–1957), minister of transport 1934–37.

4 A *Biro* (a trademark for a type of ballpoint pen), named after its inventor László Biró (1900–85).

5 A *gamp* (large umbrella), named after Mrs Sarah *Gamp*, known for her large loosely tied umbrella in *Martin Chuzzlewit*.

Yarborough, a hand in bridge or whist in which none of the cards is higher than a nine. Named after Charles Anderson Worsley, 2nd Earl of *Yarborough* (died 1897). Apparently, Lord Yarborough once bet 1000 to 1 against the dealing of such a hand. (The real mathematical figure has in fact been worked out as 1827 to 1 against.)

MUSIC

Köchel number, a serial number in a catalogue of the works of the Austrian composer Mozart. Named after Ludwig von *Köchel* (1800–77), the Austrian botanist and cataloguer.

Moog synthesizer, a trademark for a type of synthesizer. Named after its designer, the US physicist, engineer, and electrician Robert Arthur *Moog* (born 1934).

Saxophone, a keyed brass instrument with a single-reed mouthpiece—often used for jazz and dance music. Named after Adolphe *Sax* (1814–94), the Belgian musical-instrument maker who invented it.

Sousaphone, a large brass instrument that encircles the player with a forward-facing bell. Named after John Philip *Sousa* (1854–1932), the US bandmaster and composer who invented it. In 1892 Sousa, 'The March King', formed his own band which toured the world, so winning him great renown. Among the popular marches that he composed are 'Liberty Bell', 'The Stars and Stripes Forever', and 'The Washington Post'.

TOYS AND PUZZLES

Golliwog, a soft-cloth black-faced children's doll with black hair that protrudes around its head. From the name *Golliwog*, an animated doll in children's books by the US writer Bertha Upton (died 1912), and the US illustrator and portrait painter Florence Upton (died 1922).

Rubik's cube, a puzzle consisting of a small cube, each face of which has nine coloured squares that turn round a central square. Named after Erno *Rubik* (born 1944), the Hungarian designer, sculptor, and architect who invented it. Rubik's original aim was to help his students understand three-dimensional design. The cube became known at a mathematical congress in Finland in 1978, and in the following years solving the puzzle—turning the squares on the cube so that the whole of each face shows only one colour—fast became a worldwide craze.

Teddy bear, the soft stuffed toy bear. Named after the US president Theodore (nickname *Teddy*) Roosevelt (1858–1919). Known as a hunter of bears, Roosevelt is said once to have saved the life of a brown bear cub. The story was then illustrated in a cartoon in the *Washington Post*, and stuffed toy bears became known as *teddy bears*.

Wendy house, a small model house for children to play in. Named after the house built for *Wendy*, the girl in the play *Peter Pan, or the boy who wouldn't grow up* by the Scottish dramatist and novelist Sir James Matthew Barrie.

PRIZES

Oscar, one of several gold statuettes awarded annually by the Academy of Motion Picture Arts and Sciences in the USA for outstanding achievements in the cinema. The trophies, first awarded in 1929, were not called Oscars until 1931, when, so it is said, the Academy's librarian, Margaret Herrick, remarked that the statuettes reminded her of her Uncle *Oscar*. A newspaper reporter who happened to be listening passed this fact on to his readers, and so, the story goes, the word came into the language.

Pulitzer prizes, awarded annually for outstanding achievements in journalism, literature, and music. Named after Joseph *Pulitzer* (1847–1911), the Hungarian-born US newspaper publisher. The prizes were established by Pulitzer's will.

Tony, the medallion awarded annually for an outstanding performance in the US theatre. Named after the US actress Antoinette Perry (1888–1946), known familiarly as *Tony.*

An open book

He sat in the library, looking at the blurb on the paperback atlas, but decided not to borrow it. Consulting the Dewey system, he found the location of Crockford's Clerical Directory *and later browsed through some travel pamphlets.*

The paragraph above contains five eponyms: *blurb, atlas, Dewey, Crockford's,* and *pamphlet.* A number of words associated with books, editing, and publishing derive from names, including: **atlas**, a book of maps, from *Atlas*, the Greek mythological Titan who, as a punishment for attempting to overthrow Zeus, was condemned to hold up the heavens on his shoulders for the remainder of his life. His name came to represent a collection of maps after a drawing of Atlas was included on the title-page of a book of Mercator's maps, published in the late 16th century.

Blurb, the word for a short promotional notice on a book's cover was coined by the US humorist and illustrator Gelett Burgess (1866–1951) to publicize his book *Are You A Bromide?* In the early 20th century the cover of American novels often contained a picture of an attractive young woman. Trying to parody such a style, Burgess drew a picture of a sickly-sweet girl, Miss Belinda *Blurb*; the success of which led to the word becoming associated with such publicity.

Bowdlerize, meaning to remove the words or passages that are considered indecent from a book, is traditionally thought to have derived from the British doctor Thomas *Bowdler* (1754–1825), who in 1818 published his *Family Shakespeare* with modified expressions (and even characters and plots) instead of ones that he regarded as objectionable. Some recent research has, however,

suggested that it was not Thomas Bowdler but his sister, Henrietta (Harriet) Maria, who was the original *bowdlerizer*: an earlier edition of the *Family Shakespeare* was published in 1807.

Comstockery, strict censorship of literary works considered obscene or immoral, is derived from the US campaigner Anthony *Comstock* (1844–1915), who spent a great deal of his life suppressing plays and books that he thought immoral.

Crockford's Clerical Directory is the reference book of the Church of England and its clergy. First published in 1860, it is named after John *Crockford* (1823–65), managing clerk to the first publisher of the directory, serjeant-at-law Edward Cox.

Debrett's Peerage, the directory of the British aristocracy, is named after the London publisher, John *Debrett* (c. 1752–1822), who first issued it.

Dewey Decimal System, a book classification system used in libraries, is named after the US librarian Melvil *Dewey* (1851–1931), who devised his system while working as a librarian at Amherst College, Massachusetts, USA.

Larousse, the French reference books, are named after Pierre Athanase *Larousse* (1818–75), the French grammarian, lexicographer, and encyclopaedist, whose most notable work was the 15-volume *Grand dictionnaire universel du XIXe siècle.*

Pamphlet, an unbound paper-covered printed publication, derives from a 12th-century Latin love poem, 'Pamphilus seu De Amore' (Pamphilus or On Love), *Pamphilus* being a male name. This poem became so popular that it came to be known simply as *Pamphilet*, then *pamflet*, and, later still, *pamphlet*. The additional sense of a brief note on a topic of contemporary interest came into use in the 16th century.

Plantin, a style of typeface, honours the French printer Christophe *Plantin* (c. 1520–89). Other designers of typefaces who have given their names to typestyles include:

John *Baskerville* (1706–75), English writing-master and printer

Giambattista *Bodoni* (1740–1813), Italian printer and punch-cutter

Arthur Eric Rowton *Gill* (1882–1940), British sculptor, engraver, and typographer

Claude *Garamond* (c. 1500–61), French type-cutter and designer.

The following words and expressions are derived from personal names. Can you explain their origin? The answers are on page 59.

1	aphrodisiac	6	Hobson's choice	11	mansard roof
2	diesel	7	Hoover	12	mesmerize
3	draconian	8	Jacuzzi	13	nicotine
4	galvanize	9	juggernaut	14	the real McCoy
5	guillotine	10	lynch	15	tantalize

Food and drink

A person who cultivates a discriminating taste in food and wine is sometimes known as an *epicure*. This word comes from the Greek philosopher *Epicurus* (341–270 BC). A veritable feast of other words associated with food and drink derive from the names of people.

Bartlett pear, a large juicy variety of pear, is named after a merchant of Massachusetts, USA, Enoch *Bartlett* (1779–1860), who distributed the pears in the early 1800s.

Béchamel sauce, a white sauce made from flour, butter, and milk and flavoured with vegetables, is named after Marquis de *Béchamel* (died 1703), a French financier and steward of Louis XIV of France, who, it seems, first concocted it.

Benedictine, a brandy-based liqueur, originally named after St *Benedict* (AD ?480–?547) was first made up in a *Benedictine* monastery in northern France in about 1510. The monastery was destroyed during the French revolution but the formula for making Benedictine was kept safe and the liqueur was later manufactured in a distillery on the site of the former abbey.

Bloody Mary, a cocktail drink consisting mainly of vodka and tomato juice derives from the nickname of Queen *Mary* I of England (1516–58), whose cruelty in persecuting Protestants earned her the description.

Bramley, a variety of large green cooking apple, is probably named after Matthew *Bramley*, an English butcher of Southwell, Nottinghamshire, who first grew the apple in about 1850.

Châteaubriand, a large thick fillet steak, is named after François René Vicomte de *Chateaubriand* (1768–1848), the French writer and statesman.

Garibaldi, a type of biscuit with a layer of cur-rants, is named after Giuseppe *Garibaldi* (1807–82), the Italian soldier and patriot who may perhaps have enjoyed eating such delicacies.

Graham flour, a US term for wholemeal flour, is named after Sylvester *Graham* (1794–1851), the US dietary reformer who supported temperance and campaigned for changes in diets, particularly the use of unbolted wheat flour. Graham is remembered by, for example, *Graham crackers* and *Graham bread*.

Granny Smith, a variety of hard green apples, is named after the Australian gardener Maria Ann *Smith*, known as *Granny Smith* (died 1870), who first grew the apple at Eastwood, Sydney in the 1860s.

Greengage, the greenish or greenish-yellow plum derives from the word *green* and the name *Gage*. The English botanist Sir William *Gage* (1777–1864) introduced this variety of plum from France into England in the mid-1720s.

Loganberry, the large sweet purplish-red berry of a raspberry hybrid, is named after the US judge, James Harvey *Logan* (1841–1928), who developed the plant in his Californian orchard in the early 1880s.

Melba toast, thinly sliced toasted bread, and **peach melba**, the dessert of peaches, ice-cream, and raspberry, **Melba sauce**, are derived from the stage name of the Australian operatic singer Dame Nellie *Melba* (born as Helen Porter Mitchell) (1861–1931).

Negus, a drink of port or sherry, hot water, lemon juice, sugar, and nutmeg is named after, so tradition has it, the English soldier and politician Colonel Francis *Negus* (died 1732).

Pavlova, a meringue cake topped with cream and fruit, is named after the Russian ballerina

Anna *Pavlova* (1885–1931), who popularized ballet throughout the world. During her ballet performances in Australia and New Zealand, chefs made pavlova a popular delicacy.

Praline, a confection of nuts and sugar, is named after the French field marshal César de Choiseul, Count Plessis-*Praslin* (1598–1675). It is said that the count's chef first made this sweet.

Sandwich, the snack of two slices of buttered bread with a filling, is named after the English diplomat John Montagu, 4th Earl of *Sandwich* (1718–92), who was such a compulsive gambler that, preferring not to interrupt his game by leaving the gaming table to eat, would order his valet to bring food to his table. The earl was brought food of cold beef between two slices of bread. Soon the snack became widely known as a *sandwich*.

Flower power

Many flowers, plants, shrubs, and trees are named after people.

Aubrietia, a trailing perennial plant bearing small purple flowers widely grown in rock gardens, is named after Claude *Aubriet* (1665–1742), the French painter of flowers and animals.

Begonia, the genus of succulent herbaceous plants with bright, showy flowers, is named after the French patron of science and royal commissioner in Santo Domingo, Michel *Bégon* (1638–1710), who introduced the plant to France.

Bignonia, a tropical American flowering shrub with trumpet-shaped yellow or red flowers, is named after the court librarian to Louis XIV, Abbé Jean-Paul *Bignon* (1662–1743).

Bougainvillea is a tropical South American woody climbing shrub with bright purple or red bracts covering the flowers. Named after Louis Antoine de *Bougainville* (1729–1811), the French navigator who sighted the Solomon Islands on an expedition that he led round the world (1766–69). The largest island of the Solomon Islands, in Papua New Guinea, is named after him. Naturalists on the expedition named the shrub in Bougainville's honour.

Buddleia, the genus of trees and shrubs with showy yellow or mauve flowers, is named in honour of the British rector and botanist Adam *Buddle* (?1660–1715).

Flowers at the bottom of the garden

What is the origin of the name *gardenia*, for the ornamental tropical shrubs and trees with large, often white flowers? The origin does not lie in the word *garden*, as might be supposed, but with the name of the Scottish-American botanist Alexander *Garden* (1730–91). From his home in Charleston, South Carolina, Garden not only worked as a physician but also collected specimens of various animals and plants: he is said to have discovered several kinds of herbs and snakes. He also engaged in correspondence with the Swedish botanist Linnaeus, desiring that Linnaeus should name a plant after him. In 1760 Garden's wish was fulfilled and Linnaeus named the genus *gardenia* in his honour.

Camellia, the genus of ornamental shrubs, especially *Camellia japonica* with shiny evergreen leaves, is named after the Moravian Jesuit missionary Georg Josef *Kamel* (1661–1706), who described the shrub.

Cattleya, the genus of tropical American orchids grown for their hooded flowers, is named after the English botanist William *Cattley* (died 1832).

Dahlia, the genus of herbaceous perennial plants with tuberous roots and showy flowers, is named in honour of the Swedish botanist Anders *Dahl* (1751–89).

Deutzia, the genus of ornamental shrubs of the saxifrage family, bearing white or pink bell-like flowers, is named after the Dutch botanical patron Jean *Deutz* (c. 1743–c. 1784).

Douglas fir, the very tall evergreen American tree, is named after the Scottish botanist David *Douglas* (1798–1834).

Eschscholtzia, a genus of plants in the poppy family, especially the California poppy (*Eschscholtzia californica*), grown for its yellow and orange flowers, is named after the Russian-born German naturalist Johann Friedrich von *Eschscholtz* (1793–1834).

Forsythia, the genus of ornamental shrubs that

have yellow bell-shaped flowers, is named after the British botanist William *Forsyth* (1737–1804), who may have first brought the shrub from China to Britain.

Freesia, the genus of ornamental fragrant plants of the iris family, is named after the German physician Friedrich Heinrich Theodor *Freese* (died 1876).

Fuchsia, the genus of ornamental shrubs with drooping purple, red, or white flowers, is named after the German botanist and physician Leonhard *Fuchs* (1501–66).

Hyacinth, the plant of the lily family bearing clusters of blue, pink, or white flowers, is named after *Hyacinthus*, a Greek mythological youth.

Iris, a genus of plants with sword-shaped leaves and large showy flowers, is named after *Iris*, the Greek rainbow goddess, because of the flower's different colours.

Lobelia, the genus of herbaceous flowers with clusters of small, showy, lobed flowers, is named after the Flemish botanist and physician Matthias de *Lobel* (1538–1616).

Magnolia, the genus of evergreen or deciduous shrubs and trees bearing big showy flowers, is named after the French botanist Pierre *Magnol* (1638–1715), who devised a system of classifying plants.

Peony, the herb or shrub grown for its large pink, red, or white flowers. Named after *Paion*, the title of *Apollo*, the Greek mythological god of healing and physician of the gods. The plants were once used in medicine.

Poinsettia, the traditional Christmas evergreen plant, named after the US diplomat Joel Roberts *Poinsett* (1779–1851). After education in and wanderings through Europe, Poinsett returned to the USA. President Madison sent him as consul to South America (1809), where, however, he supported the Chilean revolutionaries. Later he was appointed US minister to Mexico (1825). He is said to have sent back to the United States

---

Words and expressions. Answers to quiz

1   From *Aphrodite*, the Greek goddess of love and beauty.

2   Named after the German mechanical engineer Rudolf *Diesel* (1858–1913), who invented the diesel engine in 1892.

3   From *Draco*, the 7th-century BC Athenian law-giver, who was known for the severity of his code of laws (621 BC).

4   Named after the Italian physician Luigi *Galvani* (1737–98).

5   Named after the French physician Joseph Ignace *Guillotin* (1738–1814). Guillotin did not invent this device for beheading people; he advocated its use as a more humanitarian method of capital punishment than the techniques used at the time.

6   From the English liveryman Thomas *Hobson* (1544–1631) who, it is said, did not allow his customers the right to choose a particular horse, insisting that they always have the one nearest the stable door.

7   (Trademark). Named after the US businessman William Henry *Hoover* (1849–1932). Hoover did not invent the vacuum cleaner; it was his firm that first manufactured them.

8   (Trademark). Named after the Italian-born Candido *Jacuzzi* (?1903–86) who created a system of underwater massaging jets of water.

9   *Jagannath*, one of the titles of the Hindu god Vishnu: an idol of this god is carried annually in a huge wheeled vehicle.

10   Probably from William *Lynch* (1742–1820), a US vigilante in Virginia, who administered mob ('lynch') justice. There is greater evidence for this *Lynch* than for the US planter and justice of the peace Charles *Lynch* (1736–96).

11   Named after the French architect François *Mansart* (1598–1666).

12   From the Austrian physician and hypnotist Franz Anton *Mesmer* (1734–1815), who was known for the hypnotic state he could induce in his patients.

13   Named after the French diplomat Jean *Nicot* (1530–1600), who introduced tobacco into France in the 1560s.

14   There are several suggested origins of this phrase, including the US boxer Kid *McCoy* (Norman Selby, 1873–1940); a Chicago livestock trader Joseph *McCoy* (born 1838); a Prohibition rum-runner, Bill *McCoy*; a chief of the *Mackay* clan; and the Scottish whisky dispatcher A. M. *MacKay*.

15   From *Tantalus*, the mythical king of Phrygia who was condemned to stand in water that moved away from him when he tried to drink it and also to stand under branches of fruit which moved away when he tried to eat them.

specimens of the fiery plant (which had already been introduced into the country) and because he was so well known at the time, the plant was named after him.

Rafflesia, the genus of parasitic Asian herbs, is named after its discoverer, the British colonial administrator Sir Thomas Stamford *Raffles* (1781–1826). It was Raffles who in 1819 acquired Singapore for the East India Company and the famous Raffles Hotel in Singapore is named after him. The mottled orange-brown and white parasitic stinking corpse lily (*Rafflesia arnoldii*) has the largest of all blooms in the world. These attach themselves to the cissus vines of the jungle in south-east Asia and measure up to 3 ft/*91 cm* across and ¾ inch/*1.9 cm* thick, and attain a weight of 15 lb/*7 kg*.

Rudbeckia, a genus of flowers with showy flowers that have yellow rays and dark conical centres, is named after the Swedish botanist Olof *Rudbeck* (1630–1702) and his son, also Olof *Rudbeck* (1660–1740).

Sequoia, the giant Californian coniferous trees, the big tree (or Giant Sequoia) or the redwood. Named after the American Indian *Sequoya* (George Guess) (*c.* 1770–1843).

Tradescantia, the genus of flowering plants, often grown as house plants, named in honour of the British traveller and gardener John *Tradescant* (*c.* 1570–1638).

SPELLING BLOOMERS?

The current names of at least two genera in the plant kingdom may have resulted from incorrect spellings. **Wisteria**, the genus of climbing plants with purple hanging flowers is named after the US anatomist Caspar *Wistar* (1761–1818). It seems that it was a mistake on the part of Thomas Nuttal, the curator of the Harvard botanical garden that led to the misspelling of Wistar in the naming of the plant as wisteria.

Cinchona is a genus of South American trees and shrubs. The bark of one of the most important species produces a drug used to treat malaria. The genus Cinchona is named after the Spanish vicereine of Peru, Countess Ana de *Chinchón* (1576–1641). About 1638 the countess suffered from a fever and she could only be restored to health by the powdered bark of a native Peruvian tree. The bark was returned to Spain where it was known as *Peruvian bark* or *Countess bark*. The modern name Cinchona was given by the Swedish botanist Linnaeus in honour of the countess, but he may have misspelt her name; *Cinchona* should perhaps have been known as *Chinchona*.

Animal life

A number of dogs are named after people.

The **Dandie Dinmont** terrier, a breed of dog with short legs and a long rough coat, is named after *Dandie Dinmont*, a farmer who named a pack of such terriers in the novel *Guy Mannering* by the Scottish writer Sir Walter Scott.

Dobermann pinscher, a breed of short-haired short-tailed dog, which is widely used as a guard dog, is named after the German tax collector and dog breeder Ludwig *Dobermann* (1834–94) and the German *Pinscher*, a hunting dog.

Gordon setter, a black-and-tan breed of dog that originated in Scotland, is named after the Scottish nobleman, sportsman and writer Alexander *Gordon* (1743–1827).

The **Jack Russell** terrier, a breed of dog with short legs and a short white, black and tan coat, is named after *Jack Russell* (1795–1883), an English clergyman who developed the breed from the fox terrier.

The **keeshond**, a breed of small dog with fox-like features and a shaggy grey coat, is often used as

Fishy facts . . .

Guppy, a popular aquarium fish, is named after Robert John Lechmere *Guppy* (1836–1916), the Trinidadian naturalist and clergyman who sent some guppy to England in 1868.

John Dory is a yellow food fish with an oval compressed body and spiny dorsal fins. The name *John* may have been selected arbitrarily, and *dory* probably comes from Middle French *dorée*, 'gilded one'. A few authorities also suggest that the fish is named after a *John Dory*, a 16th-century privateer who was the subject of a song that was fashionable at that time.

Molly, a brightly coloured tropical fish, is named after the French statesman Comte Nicolas-François *Mollien* (1758–1850).

---

a barge dog. *Keeshond* comes from Dutch, probably from *Kees*, a nickname for Cornelius—it remains uncertain why the name Cornelius was chosen—and *hond* dog.

The **St Bernard**, the world's heaviest breed of domestic dog, was formerly used to track down travellers lost in blizzards on the Great *St Bernard* Pass between Italy and Switzerland and the Little *St Bernard* Pass between Italy and France. The hospices on these two alpine passes were originally founded by the Italian churchman *St Bernard* of Menthon (923–1008).

The annual British dog show, **Crufts**, is also an eponym. The dog show is named after the British dog breeder and showman Charles *Cruft* (1852–1938).

Some words used in the general description of animals come from names:

Arachnid, an invertebrate insect-like animal with eight legs, such as a spider, scorpion, or mite. The word arachnid comes from *Arachne*, a Greek mythological girl who challenged the goddess Athena to a weaving contest. Athena became jealous and tore up Arachne's decorative tapestry. Arachne tried to hang herself and Athena changed the girl into a spider (Greek, arachnē).

Hermaphrodite, an animal or plant that has both female and male reproductive organs comes from *Hermaphroditos*, the Greek mythological son of Hermes and Aphrodite, the goddess of love. Hermaphroditos spurned the love offered by a nymph, in whose pool he was bathing. Embracing him she prayed to the gods to make them indivisibly one. Answering her prayer, the gods caused the body of both the nymph and Hermaphroditos to grow as one form.

Scientifically speaking

A large number of terms used in science are derived from personal names, often of the person who devised a particular device or system, for example *pasteurize* (as in *pasteurized milk*), from the French chemist and bacteriologist Louis *Pasteur* (1822–95), the *Beaufort* scale, for measuring wind speed, from the English surveyor Sir Francis *Beaufort* (1774–1857), and *Boolean algebra*, from the British mathematician George *Boole* (1815–64).

Many terms associated with scientific measurement are derived from the names of people:

Ampere, unit of electric current, named after the French physicist André Marie *Ampère* (1775–1836).

Baud, unit of measuring the speed of electronic data transmission, from the French inventor and pioneer of telegraphic communication Jean M. E. *Baudot* (1845–1903).

Becquerel, unit of radiation activity, named after the French physicist Antoine-Henri *Becquerel* (1852–1908).

Celsius, the temperature scale, named after the Swedish astronomer and scientist Anders *Celsius* (1701–44).

Coulomb, unit of electric charge, named after the French physicist Charles Augustin de *Coulomb* (1736–1806).

Decibel, logarithmic unit used to compare two levels of power, especially sound intensity, named after the Scottish-born US scientist Alexander Graham *Bell* (1847–1922).

Fahrenheit, the temperature scale, named after the German scientist Gabriel Daniel *Fahrenheit* (1686–1736).

Farad, unit of electrical capacitance, named after the English scientist Michael *Faraday* (1791–1867).

Henry, unit of electric inductance, named after the US physicist Joseph *Henry* (1797–1878).

Hertz, unit of frequency, named after the German physicist Heinrich Rudolph *Hertz* (1857–94).

Joule, unit of work or energy, named after the English physicist James Prescott *Joule* (1818–89).

Kelvin, unit of thermodynamic temperature, named after the Scottish physicist William Thomson Kelvin, 1st Baron *Kelvin* (1824–1907).

Newton, unit of force, named after the British physicist and mathematician Sir Isaac *Newton* (1642–1727).

Ohm, unit of electrical resistance, named after the German physicist Georg Simon *Ohm* (1787–1854).

Siemens, unit of electric conductance, named after the German electrical engineer Ernst Werner von *Siemens* (1816–92).

Tesla, unit of magnetic flux density, named after the Croatian-born US electrician and inventor Nikola *Tesla* (1857–1943).

Volt, unit of electric potential, named after the Italian physicist Count Alessandro *Volta* (1745–1827).

Watt, unit of power, named after the Scottish engineer and inventor James *Watt* (1736–1819).

Murphy's law and Ockham's razor

Several principles or 'laws' are named after people:

Gresham's law in economics. Generally formulated as 'bad money drives out good money'. Named after the English financier Sir Thomas *Gresham* (?1519–79).

Murphy's law. Several variations of this humorous 'rule' exist, especially: 'If anything can go wrong, it will', 'Nothing is as easy as it looks', and 'Everything takes longer than you think it will'. It is uncertain who the original Murphy was; he may have been the mid-20th-century US aviation engineer Captain E. *Murphy*.

Ockham's or **Occam's razor** in philosophy. Generally formulated as 'entities are not to be multiplied unnecessarily': explanations should

---

WHO'S WHAT?

The scientific *Boyle's law* (after the Irish-born British physicist and chemist Robert *Boyle*, 1627–91), *Charles' law* (after the French scientist Jacques Alexandre César *Charles*, 1746–1823), and the *Richter scale*, used to express the magnitude of earthquakes (after the US seismologist Charles Robert *Richter*, 1900–85), may be familiar, but test your knowledge of the following scientific expressions of *name* and *object*. You won't get a *Nobel Prize* (after the Swedish scientist and philanthropist Alfred Bernhard *Nobel*, 1833–96), but see how many blanks you can fill in (answers on page 66):

1 _____ burner
2 Doppler _____ (change in sound, etc., frequencies)
3 Mach _____ (associated with the speed of sound)
4 Halley's _____
5 Petri _____ (for micro-organisms)
6 Cuisenaire _____ (in teaching arithmetic)
7 Fraunhofer _____ (in the spectrum of the sun)
8 Möbius _____
9 _____ counter (to measure radiation)
10 Fibonacci _____ (of numbers)

consist of the simplest necessary elements. Named after the English philosopher and Franciscan friar William of Ockham (*c.* 1285–1349), though these words were not actually written by him.

Pareto principle or **80/20 rule**, for example that *80%* of the value of all business sales will come from *20%* of a firm's customers. Named after the Italian economist and sociologist Vilfredo Frederico *Pareto* (1848–1923).

Parkinson's law. 'Work expands so as to fill the time available for its completion'. Named after the English historian and author Cyril Northcote *Parkinson* (born 1909).

Peter principle. 'In a hierarchy, every employee tends to rise to the level of his incompetence'. Named after the Canadian educator Laurence J. *Peter* (born 1919).

Doctor's description

The language of medicine and psychology has given us many words and expressions derived from names:

BCG, a vaccine that stimulates the body's defence system against tuberculosis. The initials stand for *bacille* (or *bacillus*) *Calmette-Guérin*, from Albert Léon Charles *Calmette* (1863–1933) and Camille *Guérin* (1872–1961), the French bacteriologists who developed it.

Caesarean section (or **Caesarean**), a surgical incision through the walls of the abdomen and womb to deliver a baby. The expression is traditionally thought to derive from the birth of Julius *Caesar* in this way.

Down's syndrome, a congenital condition characterized by mental retardation and physical features such as a broad short skull and short fingers. Named after John Langdon-*Down* (1828–96), the English physician who described it in 1866.

Freudian slip, an unintentional slip of the tongue considered to show an unconscious thought in the speaker's mind, the words spoken being regarded as nearer the truth than the words originally thought of. Named after the Austrian psychiatrist and pioneer of psychoanalysis Sigmund *Freud* (1856–1939).

Hodgkin's disease, a cancerous disease characterized by an enlargement of the lymph

Eponymous record

The largest object to which a human name is attached is the universe itself—in the case of three different cosmological models, known as Friedmanian models, devised in 1922 by the Russian mathematician Aleksandr Aleksandrovitch *Friedman* (1888–1925).

nodes and liver. Named after Thomas *Hodgkin* (1798–1866), the English physician who described it in 1832.

Oedipus complex, the unconscious sexual attraction of a boy to his mother. Named after the Greek mythological *Oedipus*, who killed his father Laius and married his mother.

Pap test (or **Pap smear**), an examination for cancer in which cells in a smear of bodily secretions are examined. Named after its deviser, the Greek-born US anatomist George Nicholas *Papanicolaou* (1883–1962).

Parkinson's disease, a disease characterized by a tremor of the limbs, muscle weakness, and an awkward gait. Named after James *Parkinson* (1775–1824), the British physician who described it in 1817.

Rh (or **rhesus**) **factor**, in blood, a blood protein present in the red cells of most people. Deriving from rhesus monkeys (in whom it was first discovered), the ultimate origin of *rhesus* factor is *Rhesus*, the Greek mythological king of Thrace.

Rorschach test, a psychological test that shows aspects of a person's personality according to that person's interpretation of a series of inkblots. Named after the test's deviser, Swiss psychiatrist Herman *Rorschach* (1884–1922).

Sabin vaccine, a vaccine, which is administered orally, against polio. Named after Albert Bruce *Sabin* (born 1906), the Polish-born US microbiologist who developed the vaccine in 1955.

Salmonella, the bacteria that cause diseases, including food poisoning, in humans. Named after Daniel Elmer *Salmon* (1850–1914), the US veterinary surgeon who identified it.

Syphilis, a venereal disease, comes from the name of a shepherd, *Syphilis*, in a poem published in 1530 with the title *Syphilis sive Morbus*

Gallicus ('Syphilis or the French Disease') by the Italian physician and poet Girolamo Fracastro (1483–1553).

Venereal, used of diseases such as gonorrhoea or syphilis that are spread by sexual intercourse. The word comes from the Latin *venus* 'sexual love', from *Venus*, the Italian goddess of gardens, fertility, and love.

People portraits

A large number of words and expressions that are used to describe human characteristics, pursuits, and concerns are derived from the names of real people or personal names found in the pages of literature.

Achilles' heel, someone's weak spot or fault. The expression comes from Greek mythology, when Thetis, the mother of the warrior Achilles, dipped him into the river Styx to make him invulnerable. Because she was holding his heel when she dipped him, this remained untouched by the water and therefore vulnerable. Achilles was eventually defeated by a poisoned arrow that was shot into his heel.

Bobby, in informal British English, a policeman. Named after the British statesman Sir *Robert* Peel (1788–1850), who founded the Irish Constabulary ('peelers') and later the Metropolitan Police ('bobbies').

Boycott, to refuse to have dealings with a person, organization, etc. comes from the name of the Irish landlord Captain Charles Cunningham *Boycott* (1832–97), who was severely ostracized for refusing to reduce rents.

Cain, **raise Cain**, to behave in a wild manner or to protest noisily, comes from the biblical *Cain*, the brother and murderer of Abel. The expression *raise Cain* probably arose as a euphemism for *raise the devil*.

Casanova, a man who is well known for his amorous adventures, so-called after the Italian adventurer Giovanni Jacopo *Casanova* (1725–98). Among the occupations Casanova pursued were a preacher, musician, diplomat, and librarian.

Chauvinism, an excessive, unreasoned devotion to a cause, comes from the 19th-century French soldier Nicolas *Chauvin*, who was fanatically devoted to Napoleon.

Cinderella, used to describe someone or something that is considered unjustifiably neglected, is from the cruelly treated heroine in the fairy story of this name.

The original **Darby and Joan**, a contented elderly couple, may have been John *Darby* (died 1730), a London printer, and his wife *Joan*.

David and Goliath, two people fighting in a contest, one seemingly weak and insignificant and the other appearing to have considerably greater strength. From the biblical characters, the Old Testament King *David* (c. 1000–962 BC) and *Goliath*, the Philistine giant whom David killed with a stone.

Body talk

Achilles tendon, the fibrous cord that connects the heel-bone to the calf muscles. See Achilles' heel above.

Adam's apple, the visible projection at the front of a man's neck. Traditionally it is thought that the name comes from the belief that a piece of this fruit from the forbidden tree became stuck in *Adam*'s throat. Interestingly, however, the Bible nowhere states that the forbidden fruit was an apple.

Eustachian tube, the canal connecting the throat to the middle ear. Named after Bartolommeo *Eustachio* (?1520–74), the Italian physician who described it.

Fallopian tubes, the two tubes linking the uterus and the ovaries in female mammals. Named after Gabriel *Fallopius* (1523–62), the Italian anatomist who described them.

Graafian follicle, one of the small liquid-filled sacs in the ovary of a mammal containing the developing egg. Named after the Dutch physician and anatomist Regnier de *Graaf* (1641–73).

Delilah, a treacherous seductive woman. From the Old Testament woman *Delilah*, whom the Philistine rulers bribed in order that she would find out the secret of Samson's great strength.

Don Juan, a man who is constantly seeking to seduce women, is from the 14th-century Spanish aristocrat and womanizer *Don Juan* Tenorio.

Doubting Thomas, a sceptic or a person who will not believe until he has seen proof, is from *Thomas*, one of Jesus' disciples, who doubted the resurrection until he had himself seen and felt Jesus' body.

Dunce, a person who is stupid or slow to learn, is originally from the Scottish theologian John *Duns* Scotus (*c.* 1265–1308), whose teachings were mocked in the 16th century. Duns' followers ('Dunsmen' or 'Dunses') were regarded as slow to accept new theological ideas. The scope of the word's meaning later widened to include anyone who was reluctant to accept new ideas and hence someone who was dull.

Friday, man Friday or **girl Friday,** a loyal trustworthy person employed for general tasks, comes from the name of the native servant in the novel *Robinson Crusoe* by Daniel Defoe.

Gerrymander, meaning to manipulate in order to derive an unfair advantage for oneself, comes from the US politician Elbridge *Gerry* (1744–1814). As governor of Massachusetts, Gerry rearranged electoral districts in order to give his own party an advantage. On a map, the newly drawn electoral district was seen to be in the shape of a sala*mander*, and so the word *gerrymander* was coined.

Mrs Grundy, a narrow-minded prudish person, from a character in the play *Speed The Plough* by the English dramatist Thomas Morton.

Herculean, used to describe a task that needs enormous strength or effort, is from *Hercules*, the greatest Greek demigod, who was given twelve supposedly impossible labours to fulfil. In return for performing these tasks, *Hercules* was rewarded with immortality.

Hitler, a person with a ruthless dictatorial manner, from the German dictator Adolf *Hitler* (1889–1945).

Hooligan, a rough lawless youth, is probably named after the Irish criminal Patrick *Hooligan* (or *Houlihan*), who was active in London in the 1890s.

Jekyll and Hyde, a person with two personalities, one good and the other evil, is from the main character in the novel *The Strange Case of Dr Jekyll and Mr Hyde* by the Scottish writer Robert Louis Stevenson.

Jeremiah, someone who is pessimistic or who condemns the society he lives in, from the Old Testament prophet *Jeremiah* who prophesied judgment and doom.

Jezebel, an immoral, shameless woman, is from the notorious biblical *Jezebel*, daughter of the king of Tyre and Sidon, who had God's prophets killed.

Job's comforter, a person who causes distress and discouragement rather than the much-needed sympathy and encouragement, originates from the three friends of the Old Testament *Job*, who bought no comfort to him in his afflictions. **The patience of Job** in the midst of suffering and difficulty has also become proverbial.

Keeping up with the Joneses or trying to maintain the same material living standards as one's neighbours, is from a comic strip by Arthur R. Momand entitled *Keeping Up With The Joneses*, which began in the New York *Globe* in 1913.

Judas, a person who treacherously betrays a friend, is from the biblical traitor *Judas* Iscariot who betrayed Jesus.

Lady Bountiful, a woman who is known for her generous granting of favours or gifts, especially in a patronizing manner, is from the character in the comedy *The Beaux' Stratagem* by the Irish dramatist George Farquhar.

High-quality scarves turn cheap

The origin of the word *tawdry* lies in the name of the 7th-century queen of Northumbria, St *Audrey* (Etheldreda). The fair, which was held annually at Ely in her honour, was famous for its high-quality jewellery and silk scarves, which gradually became known as *St Audrey's laces*. In time, cheap, showy imitation scarves replaced the original high-quality ones. So it was that the word tawdry developed, a shortened version of (Sain)*t Audrey*('s laces), and *tawdry* is now used to describe anything cheap and gaudy.

Luddite, a person who is opposed to industrial or technological innovations. The term comes ultimately from Ned *Ludd*, an 18th-century English labourer who destroyed labour-saving stocking frames at his place of work. The name *Luddite* was later adopted by workers in the early 19th century who tried to destroy new mechanical textile appliances, considering them to be a threat to their jobs.

McCarthyism, an obsessive opposition to those thought to be disloyal or subversive, from the US Republican senator Joseph Raymond *McCarthy* (1909–57), who led political witchhunts against communists and communist sympathizers in the USA in the early 1950s.

Machiavellian, used to describe cunning, unscrupulous, and opportunist methods, from the Italian political theorist Niccolò *Machiavelli* (1469–1527), though his views seem to have been unfairly distorted in the contemporary derogatory connotations of *Machiavellian*.

Martinet, a strict disciplinarian, is from a 17th-century French army officer Jean *Martinet*, who rigorously turned the French army into an efficient military force using harsh discipline.

Masochism, the deriving of pleasure from the experience of self-inflicted pain, is from the Austrian novelist Leopold von Sacher-*Masoch* (1836–95), whose works described this disorder.

Maudlin, used of someone who is tearfully sentimental or foolishly drunk, is from the name of the biblical Mary *Magdalene*, traditionally depicted in paintings as tearfully penitent.

Maverick, a person who does not give his or her allegiance to a particular group, especially a political one, is from the US pioneer Samuel Augustus *Maverick* (1803–70), who did not want to brand his own cattle.

Mentor, a loyal and wise adviser, comes from *Mentor*, the loyal friend of Odysseus and tutor of Odysseus' son, Telemachus, in Homer's *Odyssey*.

Methuselah, as old as Methuselah, very old, alludes to the age of the Old Testament patriarch *Methuselah* who, according to the biblical record, lived 969 years.

Namby-pamby, insipidly sentimental, from a nickname of the English poet *Ambrose Philips* (1674–1749), who wrote what was regarded as weak sentimental verse, the word namby-pamby coming from the poet's first name (*amby*) and the *p* of his surname.

Narcissism, extreme love for oneself, from *Narcissus*, the attractive youth in Greek mythology who fell in love with his own reflection.

Pander, to gratify the desire of others, derives from the noun *pander*, a go-between in love

---

Quiz: Answers

1   *Bunsen* burner, named after the German chemist Robert Wilhelm *Bunsen* (1811–99).
2   Doppler *effect*, named after the Austrian physicist Christian Johann *Doppler* (1803–53).
3   Mach *number*, named after the Austrian physicist and philosopher Ernst *Mach* (1838–1916).
4   Halley's *comet*, named after the British astronomer Edmund *Halley* (1656–1742).
5   Petri *dish*, named after the German bacteriologist Julius R. *Petri* (1852–1921).
6   Cuisenaire *rods* (trademark), named after the Belgian educationalist Emil-Georges *Cuisenaire* (?1891–1976).
7   Fraunhofer *lines*, named after the German physicist and optician Joseph von *Fraunhofer* (1787–1826).
8   Möbius *strip*, named after the German mathematician August Ferdinand *Möbius* (1780–1868).
9   *Geiger* counter, named after the German physicist Hans *Geiger* (1882–1945).
10 Fibonacci *sequence*, named after the Italian mathematician Leonardo *Fibonacci* (c. 1170–c. 1250).

affairs, a procurer, and an exploiter of evil desires, which comes ultimately from the mythical Greek procurer *Pandarus*. Pandarus also features in medieval legends and romances as the procurer of Cressida for Troilus.

Peter Pan, someone who never seems to grow up and who continues to behave in an immature way into adulthood, comes from the character in the play *Peter Pan, or the boy who wouldn't grow up* by the Scottish dramatist and novelist Sir James Matthew Barrie.

Platonic, of a close relationship between a man and woman, but not involving sexual relations, comes from the Greek philosopher *Plato* (*c.* 427–347 BC), who regarded such love as spiritual or intellectual rather than physical.

Quixotic, having impractically romantic, chivalrous and extravagant ideals, comes from the hero Don *Quixote* in the novel *Don Quixote de la Mancha* by the Spanish novelist Miguel de Cervantes Saavedra.

Romeo, a romantic male lover, from the hero in *Romeo and Juliet*, the tragedy by William Shakespeare.

Sadism, the deriving of pleasure from the infliction of pain on others, is from the French soldier and writer Count Donatien Alphonse Françoise de *Sade* (Marquis de Sade) (1740–1814).

Samson, a man of great strength, from *Samson*, the biblical judge of Israel, whose exploits included striking down 1000 men with a donkey's jawbone.

Scrooge, a miserly person, from Ebenezer *Scrooge*, a character in Charles Dickens' story *A Christmas Carol*.

Shylock, a ruthless extortionate money lender, named after the usurer in Shakespeare's *Merchant of Venice*.

Silly-billy, a foolish person. The name may have been originally applied to King *William* IV (1765–1837), who was known for his relaxed attitude towards his royal duties.

Solomon, a very wise person, from *Solomon*, the Old Testament king of Israel, who was famous for his great wisdom and riches.

Stonewall, to behave defensively or obstructively, from the nickname of the US Confederate general in the American Civil War Thomas Jonathan (*Stonewall*) Jackson (1824–63). In the first battle of Bull Run (1861) his troops were said to have been 'standing like a stone wall' against the Federal forces.

Victorian, used to refer to what are regarded as 'good', even prudish, moral values and the virtues of strict discipline and hard work. Named after Queen *Victoria* (1819–1901), during whose reign such standard of morality and behaviour are popularly believed to have existed.

Yankee, in American English, someone from the northern USA, especially New England; in British English someone from the USA, probably from the Dutch name *Jan Kaas*, a disparaging nickname for a Hollander, meaning 'John Cheese'.

Marking time

Four of the days of the week are named after a mythological husband and wife and their two sons:

Tuesday, *Tiu's Day*, *Tiu* being the Anglo-Saxon counterpart of the Norse Tyr, son of Odin, and god of war and the sky.

Wednesday, *Woden's Day*, *Woden* being the Anglo-Saxon counterpart of Odin and the Norse dispenser of victory.

Thursday, *Thor's Day*, *Thor* being the eldest

Slim silhouettes

The origin of the word *silhouette*, an outline of a dark shape on a light background, lies in the French politician Étienne de *Silhouette* (1709–67). Various reasons are given for derivation. As controller-general of France's economy, Silhouette imposed severe tax increases, which were obviously unpopular. The measures were regarded as mean and the expression *à la silhouette* became fashionable. It is possible that this sense of niggardliness was applied to the partial shadow drawings that were popular at that time. Alternative theories suggest that the origin of the incompleteness of the portraits lies in the shortness of Silhouette's period of office—just nine months. It is also possible that Silhouette's hobby was making these outlines.

Hair the wrong way round

The origin of the word *sideburns*, the hair growing down the sides of a man's face, is found by changing round the two parts of the word, to give *burnside*. The word derives from the US General Ambrose Everett *Burnside* (1824–81), who fought for the Union in the US Civil War, and was known for the full side whiskers that joined his moustache. In the course of time, his side whiskers became shorter and, curiously, the order of the two halves of the word became reversed.

son of Odin and the Norse god of the sky and thunder.

Friday, *Frig's Day*, *Frig* (or *Freya*) being the wife of Odin, and the Norse goddess of married lore.

The origins of some of the months lie in personal names:

January, after *Janus*, the two-faced Roman god of doors and archways. He presides over the 'entrance', the beginning of the year.

March, after *Mars*, the Roman god of war and protector of vegetation.

May, after *Maia*, the Roman goddess of spring and fertility.

June, after *Juno*, the Roman goddess of the moon.

July, named after *Julius* Caesar (born 12 July, probably 100 BC). Originally named *Quintilis* 'the fifth month' (the first being March), Julius Caesar named this month after himself.

August, named after *Augustus* Caesar (born Gaius Octavius), the first Roman emperor. Originally named Sextilis 'the sixth month', Augustus wanted a month named in his honour, as Julius Caesar had done (July), so he chose August, the month in which he had gained his greatest victories. Moreover, not wanting to be inferior to Julius Caesar, Augustus made August have 31 days by taking a day away from February. Thus August and July each has 31 days.

Fighting fit

A number of weapons and other items associated with fighting and the military are derived from the names of people:

Bailey bridge, a type of temporary military bridge that can be quickly assembled. Named after Sir Donald *Bailey* (1901–85), the English engineer who invented it.

Bowie knife, a stout hunting knife, with a long curving single-edged blade. Named after the US soldier and adventurer James *Bowie* (1799–1836), who popularized it.

Colt, a trademark for a type of pistol with a single barrel and revolving breech for six bullets. Named after the US engineer Samuel *Colt* (1814–62), who invented it.

Derringer, a small short-barrelled large calibre pistol. Named after the US gunsmith Henry *Deringer* (1786–1868), who invented it. European imitations of his gun—spelt with double *rr* to get round the patent laws—led to the adoption of the spelling *derringer*.

Mauser, a trademark for a type of pistol. Named after the German firearms inventors Peter Paul von *Mauser* (1838–1914) and his older brother Wilhelm (1834–82).

Molotov cocktail, a type of petrol bomb that consists of a bottle filled with petrol or other flammable liquid that is covered by a saturated cloth and ignited as the bottle is thrown. Named after the Soviet statesman Vyacheslav Mikhailovich *Molotov* (Scriabin; 1890–1986).

Pyrrhic victory, a victory that is won at so great a cost that it really amounts to no triumph at all. Named after *Pyrrhus*, King of Epirus (312–272 BC), who won several victories against Rome, especially Asculum (279 BC) in which many of his men were killed.

Quisling, a traitor who collaborates with an invading enemy. Named after the Norwegian politician Vidkun Abraham *Quisling* (1887–1945), who collaborated with the Germans in World War II.

Shrapnel, an explosive projectile that contains bullets or fragments of metal and a charge that is exploded before impact. Named after its inventor, the English artillery officer Henry *Shrapnel* (1761–1842).

Sten gun, the light 9-millimetre submachine-gun used in World War II. Named after the initials of its inventors, the English army officer Major R. V. *S*hepherd and the civil servant H. J. *T*urpin, and the *en* of *En*gland, or *En*field, London. See also *Bren gun*, page 85.

Tommy gun, the lightweight submachine-gun, popularized by Chicago gangsters of the Prohibition Era. Named after the US army officer General John Taliaferro Thompson (so: *Tommy*) (1860–1940), who, with others, invented it.

Names from places

She was a bohemian type, wearing. denim jeans and a turquoise jersey as she sat on the ottoman, eating some Brie and a peach and finishing a bottle of hock.

This sentence contains nine words or expressions that are derived from place-names (toponyms). Some toponyms have an obvious etymology: it is not hard to guess that *Guernsey cows* come from Guernsey or that the *Plymouth Brethren* originated in Plymouth, although you cannot always jump to conclusions—*guinea pigs* do not actually come from Guinea, nor *india ink* from India, and there is nothing Welsh about *welsh rabbit* or French about *French cricket*! Other toponyms are much more obscure: few people would guess the connection between *peaches* and *Persia*, between *copper* and *Cyprus*, or between *cannibals* and the *Caribbean*.

Eat, drink, and be merry

The area of food and drink is one of the richest sources of toponyms. One might enjoy a whole menu composed of the names of food derived from place-names, from the *vichyssoisse* down to the *Stilton*.

DRINKS

The names of many alcoholic drinks reflect the areas that these drinks are associated with.

Amontillado, a deep golden, dry sherry, produced in the Spanish town of *Montilla*, which is south of Cordoba. The word originated in the early 19th century.

Angostura, short for Angostura bitters, a trademark for a type of flavouring used in cocktails and 'pink gin'. The bitters were named in the early 19th century from the town of *Angostura* in Venezuela, the source of the trees from whose bark the bitters are extracted. Although Angostura changed its name to Ciudad Bolívar in 1849 the famous bitters retained their original name.

Armagnac, a superior brandy made in the district of *Armagnac*, which is in the département of Gers in south-west France. The name originated in the mid-19th century.

Asti, short for *Asti Spumante*, sometimes referred to as 'the poor man's champagne'. It is a sparkling white wine made in *Asti*, a town in northern Italy.

Beaujolais, a light fruity red wine, of the burgundy variety, produced in the *Beaujolais* district of central France. The name is from the mid-19th century but it has become familiar in Britain in recent years because of the extraordinary publicity-seeking exploits of British restaurateurs who compete each year to be the first to bring the *Beaujolais nouveau* over from France.

Bordeaux, the name used since the early 16th century for the wine produced in the *Bordeaux* region of southern France. The name is often associated with clarets, but white Bordeaux is also produced.

Bourbon, a US whisky made from corn, with malt and rye. It was first distilled in the late 18th century by Elijah Craig, a Baptist minister living in *Bourbon* County in Kentucky.

Burgundy, a name used from the late 17th century for the wines, both red and white, produced in the *Burgundy* region of France. It is also sometimes applied to red wines of a burgundy type but produced elsewhere: Spanish burgundy, Californian burgundy.

Calvados, an apple brandy made from distilling cider. It is produced in the *Calvados* département of Normandy in northern France and the name dates from the early 20th century.

Champagne, the famous sparkling white wine. It has been applied since the mid-17th century to the wine produced in the *Champagne* province of eastern France, but it is now also applied to similar wines made elsewhere, although the authenticity of, for example, Australian champagne is challenged by the producers of the genuine French article.

Chartreuse, a trademark for a liqueur made from brandy and herbs. The original liqueur, first produced in the late 18th century, is green, but there is also a sweeter yellow variety. It was first made at *La Grande Chartreuse*, just north of Grenoble in France, and the site of the principal monastery of the Carthusian order. The word is also applied to a yellowish green colour.

Chianti, a dry red Italian wine, named from the *Chianti* mountains in Tuscany where it is produced. Chianti is the wine which comes in the round, straw-covered bottles which some people convert into candle holders or table lamps. The name dates from the early 19th century.

Cognac, a name often used synonymously with brandy, but properly applied only to the brandy distilled from wine made from grapes grown at or near *Cognac*, a small town just north of Bordeaux. The word has been used since the late 18th century.

Hock, a name loosely applied to many fine white German wines. The name was first used in the early 17th century as an abbreviation of *hockamore*, the English name for *hochheimer* or Hochheim wine. *Hochheim* is on the River Main and it

French fare

Given France's well-deserved reputation for gastronomic excellence, it is perhaps surprising that there are not more terms for food including the word 'French'. We have 'French dressing', an oil and vinegar salad dressing; 'French toast', bread dipped in beaten egg and milk and then fried; 'French beans', which the French call *haricots verts*; and 'French fries' (chips).

Other phrases are more dubiously connected with France. The English game of 'French cricket' has no genuine French connection. 'French leave', a hasty or secret departure, may be connected with the French practice of leaving receptions without taking formal leave of the host, but the French call it *filer à l'anglaise*. The British habit of linking the French with things they regard as somewhat improper is probably the only good reason for the French in 'French kiss', 'French knickers' and 'French letters'. The latter are also known as *capotes anglaises* by the French.

was from there that the original wine of this type came.

Malmsey, a sweet red wine of the Madeira type. The word has been used in Britain since the 15th century and derives from the medieval Latin *malmasia*, which was used for the Greek town of *Monemvasia* where the wine was first made. The Duke of Clarence, the brother of Richard III, famously died by drowning in a butt of malmsey.

Manhattan, a cocktail made from whisky, vermouth and bitters. It is said to have been invented at the *Manhattan Club* in *Manhattan*, New York City, in the late 19th century.

Marsala, a sweet fortified wine, usually served as a dessert wine. It was first produced around the late 18th to early 19th century in the Sicilian seaport of *Marsala*.

Médoc, a fine French claret which is made in the *Médoc* district in the Gironde, south-west France.

Moselle, a dry white German wine. The name

dates from the late 17th century and comes from the *Moselle* Valley in Germany where the wine is produced.

Pilsener, a light lager-type beer. Although it is often assumed to be a German beer it was named, in the late 19th century, from *Pilsen* (now Plzeň), a city in Czechoslovakia where it was brewed.

Port, a sweet rich fortified wine. The description has been used since the late 17th century for the wine produced at *Oporto* in Portugal, although it is now also used for similar wine produced elsewhere.

Sherry, a fortified Spanish wine, though also applied to similar wines produced elsewhere. The wine comes from *Jerez*, a port near Cadiz, and in the early 16th century it was known as *sherris*, an attempt to pronounce Jerez. As this sounded like a plural word it was later modified to *sherry*.

Tokay, a sweet white wine. The word has been used from the early 18th century for the wine produced near *Tokaj* in north-east Hungary but it is also used for a sweet blend of fortified wines made elsewhere.

SAY CHEESE

Most cheese names are derived from place-names.

Brie, a soft cheese made in the *Brie* district of the Seine-et-Marne département in France from the late 19th century. It has a soft white exterior and a pale yellow interior and is usually sold in segments cut from a flat round cheese.

Camembert, a soft French cheese originally made in the village of *Camembert* in Normandy. It is rather similar to brie but is usually sold as a whole small round cheese in a box. It has been known in Britain since the late 19th century.

Cheddar, a hard cheese, usually yellow, and mild or strong in flavour according to its maturity. It was first made in the Somerset village of *Cheddar* in the mid-17th century, but cheeses made by the same method and carrying the name Cheddar are now made in many different countries.

Cheshire, a hard, rather crumbly mild cheese, white or yellow. It has been made in the county of *Cheshire* since the late 16th century.

Edam, the best known of the Dutch cheeses has been made in *Edam*, near Amsterdam in the Netherlands since the early 19th century. It is a bright-yellow pressed cheese, characteristically made in balls covered with red wax.

Emmenthal, a hard pale yellow cheese with a mild nutty flavour and characterized by the large holes that form in the maturing process. It is made in *Emmenthal* in Switzerland.

Gloucester, usually sold as Double Gloucester, a deep golden cheese similar to Cheddar, made originally in the county of *Gloucestershire*.

Gorgonzola, a blue cheese with a strong flavour and smell. It was originally made in the late 19th century in the Italian village of *Gorgonzola*, near Milan.

Gouda, a hard, mild Dutch cheese, made in *Gouda* near Rotterdam since the late 19th century. It is usually sold in sections cut from a large wheel-shaped cheese.

Gruyère, a Swiss cheese similar to Emmenthal but with smaller holes. It was originally made in *Gruyère* in the canton of Fribourg.

Parmesan, a very hard cheese usually used in cooking or served grated with pasta dishes. The name comes from *Parma* in north Italy where the cheese has been made for hundreds of years; it has been known in Britain from the mid-16th century.

Port Salut, a fairly soft mild cheese. It was originally made in the mid-19th century by Trappist monks at the abbey of Notre Dame de *Port du Salut* near Laval in north-west France.

Roquefort, a strong blue cheese made from sheep's milk. It is made in *Roquefort* in south-west France, where cheese has been made for centuries, although the cheese that we know as Roquefort today was developed in the 18th century.

Stilton, a rich blue cheese, considered by many to be the finest English cheese. *Stilton* is a village in Cambridgeshire and the name has been used since the early 19th century. The cheese in fact is made in Leicestershire but the village was used as a staging post as the cheeses were carried from Leicestershire to London.

FRUIT AND VEGETABLES

Many fruits and vegetables take their names from places, although the connection is not always obvious.

Brazil nut, an oily nut, notoriously hard to crack, it

comes from the *bertholletia excelsa* tree which grows in various parts of South America, including *Brazil*.

Brussels sprouts, vegetables resembling miniature cabbages. The name comes from *Brussels* in Belgium and was not used until the late 18th century, although the vegetables were developed in Belgium in the 14th century.

Cantaloupe, a sweet orange-fleshed variety of musk melon. The name dates from the early 18th century and derives from the former papal villa of *Cantalupo*, north of Rome.

Cherry, the small sweet red fruit of the cherry tree. The name comes from the Old Northern French *cherise* (mistakenly thought of as a plural), derived from the Latin *cerasum*, meaning 'of *Cerasus*, or Kerasous (now Giresun)'. It was from this place in north-east Turkey that the cherry was said to have been introduced into Europe by the gourmet Lucullus in about 100 BC.

Cos lettuce, a long-leaved crisp lettuce. It was introduced into Britain in the late 17th century from the Greek island of *Kos* (Cos).

Currant, a small seedless raisin; also applied to the red and black acid berries of the *Ribes* species. The word is a development of the Middle English *raison of Coraunte*, 'a raisin of *Corinth*', from where the fruit came.

Damson, a small acid purple plum. The name is derived from damascene plum, the 14th century

name for the fruit which originated in *Damascus*.

Peach, a sweet succulent yellow fruit. The name, first used in the 14th century, is derived from the French, which in turn derives from the Latin *persicum malum* meaning 'Persian fruit'.

Quince, a small, hard, apple-like fruit. The name is a development of the Middle English *coyn*, which came via the Middle French form of the Latin *malum Cydonium*, meaning 'fruit of *Cydonia*'. Cydonia was the main city of ancient Crete.

Satsuma, a kind of mandarin orange. They are grown in the province of *Satsuma* on the Japanese island of Kyushu and the name has been used since the late 19th century.

Seville orange, a bitter orange used in making marmalade. They are grown in *Seville* in Spain and have been known in Britain since the 16th century.

Swede, a large yellow-fleshed turnip. The name was originally Swedish turnip, as the vegetable was introduced from *Sweden*.

Tangerine, a small sweet kind of orange. They were exported to Britain from the Moroccan port of *Tangier* in the mid-19th century.

A PIECE OF CAKE

Here is a small selection of the many cakes that are named after places:

Bakewell tart, an open pastry lined with jam and with a filling made of eggs, sugar and ground almonds. It was originally made in the Derbyshire town of *Bakewell* and has been known since the mid-19th century.

Banbury cake, made from puff pastry with a filling of dried fruits. It comes from the Oxfordshire town of *Banbury*.

Bath bun, a small bun made from yeast dough and covered in crystallized sugar. First made in *Bath* in Avon which is named for its Roman baths. They have been made since the mid-18th century.

Battenberg cake, a sponge cake made in pink and yellow squares and coated in marzipan. It is probably named not so much for the region in the old Prussian province of Hesse-Nassau, but for Prince Louis of *Battenberg* who married a granddaughter of Queen Victoria in 1884.

Dundee cake, a rich fruit cake decorated with blanched almonds. From *Dundee* in Scotland.

Eccles cake, a small round cake made of flaky

pastry and currants. From *Eccles*, on the outskirts of Manchester.

Florentine, more of a biscuit than a cake—a flat confection of nuts and crystallized fruits coated with chocolate. It originates in the Italian city of *Florence*.

Genoa cake, a rich currant cake decorated with almonds. There is also a *Genoese sponge*, a sponge cake which is made with melted butter. From Genoa, the port in Italy.

Swiss roll, a flat oblong sponge cake which is spread with jam and rolled up to make a cylindrical cake. The name originated with the popular Lyons teashops which served the cakes and they are probably unknown in *Switzerland*.

... AND MORE FOOD FOR THOUGHT
Other foods whose names come from places include:

Bologna, a large smoked sausage made from beef, veal and pork. The name comes from the Italian town of *Bologna*, where the sausage originated, and it has been known by that name since the late 16th century. In the United States the word is pronounced, and sometimes spelled, *boloney* and the other meaning of this word—'nonsense'—probably derives from the sausage.

Bombay duck, not a duck at all but a small fish which is served dried and salted. The fish is caught off south Asiatic coasts and is locally called the *bummalo*, a name which English sailors probably associated with *Bombay*.

Cayenne, a very hot pepper. The name has been used from the mid-18th century and comes from *Cayenne* in French Guiana. The word is said to be a modification of the Brazilian Tupi word meaning 'capsicum'.

Demerara sugar, light brown crystallized cane sugar. It comes from *Demerara*, a district of Guyana that takes its name from the Demerara River.

Finnan haddock, smoked haddock. The name, and the alternative *finnan haddie*, dates from the early 18th century and probably comes from the Scottish seaport village of *Findon*, near Aberdeen.

Frankfurter, a cooked sausage of beef or beef and pork. The name dates from the late 19th century and comes from the West German city of *Frankfurt*, where the sausage originates.

Hamburger, a patty of minced beef, usually served sandwiched in a split round bun; in the USA the word is also used for raw minced beef. The name dates from the late 19th century and relates to the West German city of *Hamburg*, although people have taken the *ham* to be a reference to the meat of that name—hence 'beefburger'.

Mayonnaise, a sauce made from olive oil, egg yolks, and either lemon juice or vinegar. The French word derives from *sauce mahonnaise*, which refers to *Mahón* in Minorca, where the sauce was invented.

Montelimar, the confection of nuts and sometimes crystallized fruit in a sweet paste which is also called nougat. From the town of *Montélimar* in south-east France where it is manufactured.

Sardine, a very small fish, the young of the pilchard, usually tinned in oil. They were originally caught near the *Sardinian* coast and the name has been in use since the 15th century.

Vichyssoise, a soup made of leeks, potato, chicken, stock, and cream, and usually served chilled. It comes from the town of *Vichy* in central France and the name has been familiar in Britain since the early 20th century.

Welsh rabbit, toasted cheese, or a mixture of melted cheese and beer poured over toast. Known also as **Welsh rarebit**, the name dates from the early 18th century but it is not known whether the dish has any connection with Wales.

Doctor's orders

Words associated with illness and medicine that are derived from place-names include:

Bornholm disease, an acute viral infection, with fever and pain in the ribs. It is named after *Bornholm*, the Danish island in the Baltic where the disease, also known as *epidemic pleurisy* and *devil's grippe*, was first described.

Derbyshire neck, goitre. This abnormality of the thyroid gland can be caused by iodine deficiency and used to be common in *Derbyshire*, a limestone area where natural iodine was inadequate.

Epsom salts, magnesium sulphate used as a laxative. It was originally made from the mineral spring water at *Epsom* in Surrey, but from the late 19th century it has been applied to all magnesium sulphates.

Kaolin, china clay used, combined with morphine, as a remedy for diarrhoea. The name has been used since the early 18th century and derives from *Kao-ling*, a hill in northern China where the substance was first found.

Lassa fever, an acute and often fatal virus disease. It is common to tropical countries but was first reported in *Lassa*, a village in north-eastern Nigeria, which gave its name to the disease in 1970.

Milk of magnesia, an antacid and mild laxative containing magnesium oxide. The words *magnesia* and *magnesium* both derive from the ancient city of *Magnesia* in Asia Minor (now Manisa in western Turkey).

Mongolism, Down's syndrome, a congenital form of mental handicap caused by a chromosome malfunction. The only connection with *Mongolia* is that people with this handicap usually have a broad short skull and slanting eyes and were thought to look Mongolian. The term was used from about 1900 but it is now thought to be offensive and *Down's syndrome* (see page 63) has been used since the early 1960s.

Plaster of paris, a white powder of calcium sulphate which sets hard when mixed with water and is used for plaster casts in the treatment of fractures. The substance was first made from gypsum from Montmartre in *Paris* and has been used since the 15th century.

Rocky Mountain spotted fever, an acute fever of the typhus group characterized by a red or purple rash. It was first discovered in the early 20th century in the *Rocky Mountain* area of Canada and the northern United States.

Seltzer, an effervescent mineral water used as an antacid. The word has been used since the mid-18th century and derives from the German *selterser Wasser* or 'water of Selters'. Nieder-*Selters* is a village near Limburg in West Germany and the mineral water was originally obtained from the springs there.

Focus on furnishings

Words from place-names in the world of interior decor include:

Afghan, applied both to knitted or crocheted coloured wool coverlets and large carpets of deep pile woven in geometric designs. The coverlets were formerly made in *Afghanistan*, but are now usually made elsewhere. The carpets are made, not in Afghanistan, but in the eastern states of the Soviet Union.

Antimacassar, a cover, often crocheted, protecting the backs of chairs. They were designed to keep the upholstery of chairs free from Macassar oil, a popular Victorian hair-oil; the word, dating from the mid-19th century, is a combination of *anti* and *macassar*. The oil came from the Indonesian port of *Macassar* (now Ujung Pandang) in Sulawesi.

Arras, a tapestry or wall hanging. The word has been used from the 15th century and comes from the French town of *Arras* in the Pas de Calais département which was famous, in medieval times, as a centre for the weaving of fine tapestries.

Aubusson, a tapestry carpet. The word has been used since the mid-19th century and was originally applied to the tapestry wall hangings made at *Aubusson* in the Creuse département of France, but later to the elegant and expensive carpets and rugs which are woven to resemble the traditional tapestries.

Axminster, a machine-woven thick pile carpet. They were originally hand-made, in a style similar to oriental carpets, at *Axminster* in Devon from the mid-18th to the early 19th century, and the modern carpets are machine-woven in the same style.

Indian influence

The confusion of the early explorers, who believed that the New World was part of Asia, has led to some confusion over phrases containing the word 'Indian' or 'India'. Some of our 'Indian' toponyms refer to the Indian subcontinent, some to the West Indies, and some to the North American Indians. The fine opaque paper called 'India paper' and the black pigment called 'India ink' refer to the Indian subcontinent, although in fact both were originally made in China. The erasers, now usually called rubbers but formally known as 'india rubbers', take their india from the West Indies.

Phrases relating to American Indians include: 'indian corn', or maize; 'Indian clubs', the exercise clubs which have some resemblance to weapons used by American Indians; 'Indian file', which comes from the American Indian practice of walking through the woods in single file. One disputed term is 'Indian summer', the phrase for unusually mild weather in late autumn, which is usually thought to refer to the climate in parts of the United States which were former Indian territory, but is believed by some to refer to the climate of the Indian subcontinent.

Japan, a decorative lacquer used on furniture and ornaments; to coat with japan. Oriental furnishings were popular in Britain in the late 17th century and the lacquer called *japan* was a home-made imitation of the rare and expensive lacquers that had previously been imported from China and *Japan*.

Morocco, a fine goatskin leather used for upholstery. The leather was first imported from *Morocco* in north Africa in the early 17th century, but the word is also applied to similar kinds of leather made elsewhere.

Ottoman, an upholstered, stuffed seat or couch, usually without a back or arms and sometimes with a hinged seat for storage. They were first used in what was called the *Ottoman* Empire—the Turkish Empire which lasted from the early 14th to the early 20th century—and were popular items of furniture in Victorian times.

Venetian blind, a horizontally slatted window blind that can be adjusted to let in varying amounts of light. The name has been used from the late 18th century and comes from *Venice*, although the blinds probably did not originate from Venice but were introduced into Italy from the Orient.

Wilton, a carpet woven with loops of cut or uncut pile. *Wilton* is a town in Wiltshire that has been famous for carpet making since the 17th century, but the name now usually applies to the method of weaving and does not necessarily mean that the carpet was made in Wilton.

Metals and money

Several words connected with metals and metal currency have interesting derivations from place-names:

Bauxite, a compound of aluminium oxides, hydroxides, and iron, which is the main source of aluminium. It was first discovered in the mid-19th century at Les *Baux* near Arles in southern France.

Copper, a malleable reddish metal. The word has been used from medieval times; the Middle English word *coper* derived from the Late Latin *cuprum*, which in turn derived from the Latin *cyprium*, meaning 'of *Cyprus*'. Cyprus was an important source of copper in ancient times.

Dollar, any of numerous coins; the main currency unit of the United States. At the beginning of the 16th century silver coins were minted from metal mined at St *Joachimsthal* in Bohemia. They were named *joachimsthalers*, which soon became shortened to *thalers*. The names *thaler*, *taler*, and *daler* spread throughout Europe and finally became translated into *dollar* in the New World, where dollars became the official currency at the end of the 18th century.

Florin, used for various gold or silver coins. Gold coins, decorated with the lily that was the emblem of the city, were struck in *Florence* in the mid-13th century. Coins similar to these were made all over Europe and known as *florences*, but *florins* in England. The first gold florins were made in the mid-14th century and had a value of six shillings; in mid-19th century Britain the word was used again for silver coins worth two shillings (10p).

Guinea, the chief English gold coin from 1663 to 1813, worth 20 shillings until 1717 when the value changed to 21 shillings. When the coin was first struck, England was involved in trade with *Guinea* in west Africa and the gold for the coins was originally mined there.

Strontium, a malleable silver metallic element. It takes its name from *Strontian* in the Highland region of Scotland, where the element was first discovered in the early 19th century.

Troy, a system of weights for gold and silver. The Troy system dates back to the 15th century and was first used at the French town of *Troyes* in the Aube département.

Cloak-and-dagger clothes

Clothes often take their names from places, sometimes because they originated there.

The **Aran sweater**, usually made of thick, cream-coloured wool, and knitted in a complex cable pattern, is a traditional product of the *Aran* islands off the west coast of Ireland.

The name **Ascot**, a broad necktie or cravat, has been used in the United States since 1900, and is a reference to the racecourse at *Ascot* Heath near Windsor, scene of the annual Ascot Week, an important event in the British social calendar and an occasion for fashionable dressing.

The name **balaclava**, a knitted helmet covering the head and neck, like the eponyms *cardigan* (page 52) and *raglan* (page 53), originates from the Crimean war; *Balaclava* is a village on the Black Sea, near Sevastopol, where a battle was fought in 1854. The helmet was not worn at the time of the battle but is thought to have been invented some years later and named in view of the extreme cold suffered by the army in the Crimean winters.

Balmoral, the name for a round flat cap with a top projecting all round, was first used in the mid-19th century, soon after Queen Victoria bought *Balmoral* Castle in Scotland (Grampian region). Balmoral also briefly gave its name to boots, pet-

ticoats, and cloaks, but the cap is still in use among some Highland regiments.

Knee-length **Bermuda shorts** were invented at the beginning of the 1950s in the *Bermuda* islands and soon became popular in the United States.

The **bikini**, a woman's scanty two-piece swim-suit, was invented in France in 1947 and named bikini after *Bikini* Atoll in the Marshall Islands in the Pacific. The previous year the USA had used the islands to test atomic bombs and the beach-wear's power to cause a sensation was associated with the power of the weapons.

The word **cravat**, a neck scarf or necktie, has been used since the mid-17th century and comes from the French word *cravate*, meaning 'Croatian', as the scarves were worn by soldiers from *Croatia*, now in northern Yugoslavia.

The word *dungaree*, extended to **dungarees** for a one-piece work garment, often of trousers and bib front was used from the late 17th century for the coarse cloth that the garments were made from, and this word derives from the Hindi *dungri*, the local name for the district in Bombay where the cloth was sold.

The word *duffle*, as in **duffle coat**, a thick hooded woollen coat done up with toggles, or *duffel* has been used since the late 17th century for the cloth from which the coats are made. The cloth came originally from the Belgian town of *Duffel*, near Antwerp.

Eton collar; Eton jacket, a large stiff collar, worn over the jacket; a short jacket with wide lapels. Both names were first used in the 19th century and were worn by boys at *Eton* College, the famous public school near Windsor.

The **Fair Isle sweater**, a knitted woollen sweater with characteristic coloured patterns against a plain background, has been made in *Fair Isle*, one of the Shetland Islands, from the mid-19th century.

The word **fez**, a brimless, flat-topped hat, with a tassel and usually made of red felt, has been used since the early 19th century and comes from the city of *Fez* in Morocco, where they were originally made.

Glengarry, a woollen cap or bonnet, higher at the front than the back, is a word that has been used from the mid-19th century, and comes from *Glengarry*, a valley in the Highland region. It is worn by several Scottish regiments.

Trips down memory lane

Argosy, a large merchant ship. The word comes from the late 16th century and derived from the Italian *ragusea*, meaning 'Ragusan'. *Ragusa*, a port on the Dalmation coast (it has since become Dubrovnik in Yugoslavia), was where the ships were first built.

coach, a large closed four-wheeled carriage; a single-deck bus used for long-distance travel. It has been used from the mid-16th century and derives from the Hungarian word *koksi* (*szekér*), a wagon made at *Kocs* in Hungary.

landau, a four-wheeled carriage with a folding top in two halves so that it can be open, closed, or half-closed. The name has been used from the mid-18th century and comes from the Bavarian town of *Landau* where the carriages were first made.

Limousine, a large and luxurious car. The name, dating from the early 20th century, was originally applied to closed-top cars and came from the French word for a closed carriage *limousine*, which referred to the hooded cloaks traditionally worn in the old French province of *Limousin*.

Sedan, a carrying chair for one person, carried on poles by two people; a saloon car (in United States). The word has been used from the early 17th century and, although it was thought by some to derive from the Latin *sedere* 'to sit', it may possibly have come from the French fortress town of *Sedan* in the Ardennes.

Surrey, a two-seater horse-drawn pleasure carriage. The name comes from the late 19th century and comes from the English county of *Surrey* where the first *Surrey carts* were made; they became popular in the United States where the sun canopy was often fringed, as in the celebrated surrey in the musical *Oklahoma!*

Guernsey, the thick woollen sweater, was traditionally made in France and worn by French sailors but was later taken up by the Channel Island of *Guernsey*.

The name **Homburg**, a man's felt hat with a dented crown, similar to the trilby, comes from the West German spa town of *Homburg*, near Frankfurt. This was a favourite resort of King Edward VII when Prince of Wales and it was he who popularized the hat in Britain in the late 19th century.

The **Inverness** coat, which has a removable cape, has been manufactured in the Scottish town of *Inverness* from the mid-19th century.

The word **jeans**, trousers made from a twilled cotton cloth, comes from the cloth known as *jean* from the late 16th century. This was a shortened form of *jean fustian*, which derived from the French word for *Genoa* in Italy where the cloth was once made.

Although the word **jersey**, a knitted sweater, is now used for any knitted sweater it was originally applied to those made of the knitted fabric also called *jersey* and manufactured on the Channel Island of *Jersey*.

The word **jodhpurs**, riding breeches wide at the hip but tight-fitting from knee to ankle, has been used from the late 19th century and comes from the town of *Jodphur* in the state of Rajasthan in north-west India, where they were worn, rather than made.

Millinery, meaning women's hats and trimmings, comes from the word *milliner*, first used in the early 16th century for sellers of fancy bonnets, ribbons, and accessories from *Milan* in Italy. It later became associated with hat makers and the word *millinery* was used from the late 17th century.

Norfolk jacket, a belted and pleated jacket, originated in the county of *Norfolk* and has been known from the mid-19th century.

Oxford bags, loose-bottomed trousers, come from the university city of *Oxford*, which has also provided the shoes called **Oxfords**, low-cut shoes which lace over the instep.

A **Panama hat** is a lightweight hat made of

Written off

Ordinary type with upright characters is what printers call 'roman' as the first *Roman type* was copied from the writing on Latin inscriptions. It is often distinguished from the sloping type which is called 'italic' because it was invented by a 15th-century *Italian* printer. One might write on 'parchment', originally made from animal skin but now tough paper that resembles skin; the English word derives from the Latin *pergamena*, meaning '*of Pergamum*', the ancient Greek city *Pergamon* (now Bergama in Turkey), where parchment was invented. The envelopes we use may be made of the tough paper called 'manilla', made from the hemp grown in the Philippines and exported from the capital, *Manila*. And perhaps the fruits of our writing might be one of the five-line humorous verses known as 'limericks'; the connection with *Limerick*, the south-west Ireland city and county is uncertain, but the word is said to come from the refrain 'Will you come up to Limerick', sung between comic songs and verse recitations at late 19th-century smoking parties.

natural-coloured straw. The name has been used from the early 19th century although the hats were not, in fact, made in Panama, but in Ecuador; they were, however, worn in and distributed from *Panama*.

The **tuxedo**, a man's evening jacket, popularized in Britain by the Prince of Wales, was introduced into the United States in the late 19th century and was first worn at the exclusive *Tuxedo* Park Country Club near Tuxedo Lake, New York State.

The word **ulster**, a long loose man's overcoat of heavy material, has been used from the late 19th century and comes from the Northern Ireland province of **Ulster**, as the coats were originally made in Belfast.

The animal fair

Various different birds and animals are named after places with which they are associated.

THE CATTLE MARKET
Most breeds of cattle are named after the places where they originated, including:

Aberdeen Angus, black hornless beef cattle. The cattle were bred in Scotland in the early 19th century and were the result of crossing cows from *Aberdeen*shire (now part of Grampian region) with bulls from the neighbouring county of *Angus* (now part of Tayside region).

Alderney, a breed of small dairy cattle. *Alderney* is one of the Channel Islands. While the name originally referred to the particular breed found on the island it is now sometimes used to include all the Channel Island cattle.

Ayrshire, a hardy breed of brown-and-white dairy cattle. They were bred in the mid-19th century in the former county of *Ayrshire* (now part of Strathclyde region) in Scotland, the final result of crossbreeding local Scottish cows with Jersey, and possibly Dutch, cattle.

Charolais, large white beef cattle. Known in Britain from the late 19th century, the cattle come from the *Charolais* region in Burgundy, eastern France.

Friesian, large black-and-white dairy cattle. The cattle came originally from the *Friesland* province of northern Netherlands, but are now bred elsewhere. In the United States the same cattle are known as *Holsteins*.

Guernsey, large fawn-and-white dairy cattle producing particularly rich milk. *Guernsey* is the most westerly of the Channel Islands, and the cattle have been bred there from the early 19th century.

Hereford, hardy red-and-white beef cattle. They were first bred in the former county of *Hereford*shire in the late 18th century but are now reared throughout the world, particularly in the western USA.

Jersey, a breed of small fawn or yellowish dairy cattle producing very rich milk. *Jersey* is the southernmost of the Channel Islands and the famous cattle have been bred there from the early 19th century.

GOING TO THE DOGS

Toponymous breeds of dog include:

Aberdeen terrier, a breed of small dog with short legs, a large head, and a short wiry coat. They take their name from the city of *Aberdeen* in Scotland but they have also been widely known, from the early 19th century, as *Scotch terriers.*

Afghan, a large, slim hunting dog with long silky hair. They have been bred in *Afghanistan* from ancient times but were not known in Britain until the early 20th century.

Airedale, a large black-and-tan terrier with a wiry coat. They were first bred in the valley of the River *Aire* (West Yorkshire) and the name was first used in the late 19th century.

Alsatian, a large, intelligent breed of working dog, used as a police dog, guard dog, and guide dog for blind people. They originate from Germany and were known in Britain as *German shepherd dogs* until 1917 when, because of anti-German feeling aroused by the war, the name was changed to *alsatians* although the dogs had no connection with the disputed province of *Alsace*, now restored to France. The name German shepherd is beginning to come back into use.

Blenheim spaniel, a small red-and-white spaniel.

Blenheim is a village in Bavaria, the site of the battle in 1704 which was a great victory for the first Duke of Marlborough. The spaniels are not named after the Bavarian village but after *Blenheim* Palace in Woodstock, Oxfordshire, built by Vanbrugh and the seat of the Dukes of Marlborough.

Labrador, a compact but strong retriever with a yellowish or black coat. The breed was developed in England at the beginning of the 20th century from stock originating from *Labrador* in Newfoundland, Canada.

Newfoundland, a very large heavy dog, usually black. They were developed in *Newfoundland* in Canada and the name has been used from the late 18th century.

Pekingese, a small dog with short legs, a flat face, and a long soft coat. They have been bred in China for many years and the name comes from the capital *Peking* (now known as Beijing). The breed has been known in Britain from the mid-19th century.

Pomeranian, a very small long-haired dog. *Pomerania* was formerly in northern Prussia, an area that is now part of Poland. The breed has been known in Britain from the mid-18th century.

Further fauna . . .

Arab horse, a horse noted for its beauty, intelligence, strength, and spirit. They were bred in the *Arabian* peninsula in ancient times but were not introduced into Britain until the beginning of the 18th century.

Camberwell beauty, a large blackish-brown butterfly with a broad yellow border on the wing. It is found in temperate parts of Europe, Asia, and North America. It was first seen in Britain in the mid-18th century in *Camberwell*, then a village, but now part of south London.

Guinea pig, a small short-eared tailless rodent, kept as a pet and often used in biological research. Guinea pigs are not from Guinea but from South America. They acquired their name in the mid-17th century, having been introduced to Britain by the ships called *Guineamen* because they usually traded with West Africa.

Manx cat, a short-haired tailless domestic cat. *Manx* means 'from the Isle of Man' and the cats have had this name from the mid-19th century.

Shetland pony, a very small but hardy long-haired pony. They were originally bred in the *Shetland* Islands and have been known since the early 19th century.

Siamese cat, a slender, short-haired domestic cat with blue eyes and a pale fawn body. *Siam* is the former name of Thailand, where the cats originated. They have been known in Britain from the beginning of the 20th century.

Home from home

Is your home a toponym? It is if you live in a 'bungalow', for this name for a single-storey house comes from the Hindi *bangla*, meaning '*of Bengal*'; or if you live in a 'palace', which derives from the *Palatine* Hill in Rome where the emperors had their residences. Your house probably has an 'attic' under the roof, which means it conforms to the Attic order of architecture; *attic* means '*from Attica*', which is the region now called Athens. The walls may be decorated with a painted or sculptured 'frieze', a word deriving ultimately from the ancient country of *Phrygia* in Asia Minor, now part of Turkey. Whatever kind of house you live in, you will hope it is not 'jerry-built'. This expression meaning 'cheaply or insubstantially built' is of uncertain origin, but the most attractive theory is that it refers to *Jericho*, whose walls collapsed when the people of Israel shouted (Joshua 6:1–21).

BIRD WATCHING
Domestic fowl in particular, as well as some other birds, are often named after places.

Aylesbury duck, a breed of large white domestic duck. They were traditionally reared in the market town of *Aylesbury* in Buckinghamshire.

Bantam, a small domestic fowl, often the miniature of standard breeds. *Bantam* (now Banten) is a town in west Java, west of Jakarta. The Dutch introduced the breed in the early 17th century and the name has been used in Britain since the mid-18th century.

Canary, a small yellow finch, kept as a cagebird. They came originally from the *Canary* Islands and have been known in Britain from the late 16th century.

Leghorn, a small hardy domestic fowl. They are a common Mediterranean breed but were probably exported in the mid-18th century from the Italian port of *Livorno*, known to British sailors as Leghorn. A leghorn is also a straw hat.

Orpington, a breed of large, deep-chested poultry. They were bred in the late 19th century by a poultry farmer living in *Orpington*, then a village in Kent, now part of the Greater London borough of Bromley.

Pheasant, a long-tailed, often brightly-coloured bird, bred as a game bird. The name is a development of the Middle English *fesaunt* which comes from the Latin *phasianus*, itself a transliteration of the Greek word *phasianos* meaning 'bird of *Phasis*'. Phasis is the name of a region and river in Colchis, the district on the Black Sea which is now part of Georgia in the Soviet Union.

Rhode Island, a domestic fowl with a long heavy body. *Rhode Island* is a small state on the east coast of the United States. The famous **Rhode Island Red**, a bird with reddish-brown plumage, was bred there in the late 19th century; the **Rhode Island White**, like the Red but with white plumage, was bred in the 1920s.

To coin a phrase

Well-known phrases using place-names include:

Carry coals to Newcastle, to take something to a place where it is already in plentiful supply. *Newcastle-upon-Tyne*, in north-east England, was the centre of the coalmining industry from the time of the industrial revolution.

Chiltern Hundreds, a nominal office for which an MP applies as a means of resigning his or her seat. The *Chiltern Hundreds* were part of the Chiltern hills in Buckinghamshire and there used to be a crown stewardship over the area. The practice of MPs applying for this nominal stewardship began in the mid-18th century.

Cross the Rubicon, to take an irrevocable step. The *Rubicon* was the river dividing Italy and Cisalpine Gaul, and Julius Caesar's crossing of it was a declaration of war.

Dunkirk spirit, courage in a time of crisis. The reference is to *Dunkerque* (Dunkirk) on the north French coast where, in 1940 in World War II, the British army was in a position where only surrender or evacuation was possible. The evacuation was made possible by the courageous efforts of the Royal Navy and Royal Air Force and large numbers of both professional sailors and private boat owners who sailed to Dunkirk.

Gnomes of Zurich, influential international bankers. *Zürich* in Switzerland is a famous banking

of sending Royalist prisoners captured at Birmingham to be executed at Coventry. An alternative theory describes the extreme dislike that the citizens of Coventry had for soldiers in their city. The alienation was so severe that any woman seen talking to the military was immediately ostracized.

Trojan horse, someone or something intended to subvert or defeat from within. The phrase refers to the story of the Greek's defeat of *Troy* by presenting to the city a large wooden horse which turned out to be full of armed soldiers. Thus a Trojan horse is something that appears harmless enough but in reality is filled with danger.

Work like a Trojan, to work very hard, showing qualities of courage and endurance. The reference is to the inhabitants of the ancient city of *Troy* who defended the city during its long siege, although they were finally defeated by the Greeks.

Peculiar people

These nouns applied to people with interesting derivations from place-names.

Bohemian, a person (often an artist or writer) living an unconventional life. *Bohemia* was a former kingdom of the Austrian empire, in what is now Czechoslovakia, and was thought to be the home of wandering vagabonds and gypsies found throughout Europe.

Cannibal, a person who eats human flesh. The word has been used since the mid-16th century, although at that time it was only used in its plural form. It was adapted from the Spanish *canibal* which referred to the *Caribs*, the people of the *Caribbean* or West Indian islands who had been given the name *carib*, meaning 'strong; valiant', by Columbus. The Caribs were said to eat human flesh. The shift from carib to canib can be explained by the fact that the letters r and n were interchangeable in the West Indies.

Gypsy, one of the Romany people; one who leads a migratory way of life. The word dates from the early 16th century when these dark-skinned Caucasian people first arrived in England. The word is an abbreviation of *Egyptian*, as the Romanies were commonly supposed to have come from *Egypt*; in fact they were of Indian origin.

centre, and the expression is a humorous reference to the banking vaults presided over by these bankers, just as legendary gnomes are thought to guard their underground treasures.

Grinning like a Cheshire cat, grinning broadly. The expression is familiar from Lewis Carroll's *Alice's Adventures in Wonderland* but was not invented by Carroll. One theory is that it relates to grinning lions on inn signs in *Cheshire*; another is that Cheshire cheeses were once moulded in the shape of grinning cats.

Meet one's Waterloo, to suffer a decisive defeat. *Waterloo* in Belgium was the scene of Napoleon's final defeat by Wellington's army in 1815 and the phrase was in use shortly after that date.

Not set the Thames on fire, to fail to do anything remarkable or distinguished. There is no particular connection with the *Thames*; similar expressions are used of other rivers.

Pale, beyond the pale, outside the limits of socially accepted practice. *Pale* here comes from the Latin word *palus* 'a stake', stakes being used to mark boundaries, but there was an actual *Pale* in Ireland which was where the English settled when they conquered Ireland in the 12th century. English law operated within this area for centuries and those 'beyond the Pale' were regarded as uncivilized.

Send to Coventry, to ostracize someone. The connection with the English city of *Coventry* is not clear; it may be from a custom in the Civil War

Lesbian, a female homosexual. The word derives from *Lesbos*, the island in the Aegean which was the home of the poet Sappho. She lived about 600 BC at the centre of a group of female pupils, and her love poems are thought to be homosexual in nature.

Plymouth Brethren, members of a puritanical Christian body with no institutional ministry. They were formed in *Plymouth* in Devon in the early 19th century.

Siamese twins, twins who are born with their bodies joined together. The term dates from the early 19th century and refers to the famous twins Chang and Eng Bunker, born in 1811 in *Siam* (now Thailand).

Sodomite, one who practises sodomy. The word has been used since the 14th century and refers to the ancient Palestinian city of *Sodom*, which was destroyed by God because of the wickedness and depravity of its inhabitants. The homosexual lust of the men of Sodom is described in Genesis 19:1–11.

Sybarite, a sensualist; one who loves luxury. The word means 'native of *Sybaris*' which was in ancient times a Greek colony in southern Italy, whose people were devoted to luxury and pleasure. The word has been used since the late 16th century.

Trappist, a member of the branch of the Cistercian monastic order noted for silence and austerity. They take their name from the monastery of La *Trappe* in Normandy where the branch was established in the mid-17th century.

At the ball

Many dances are named after places.

Boston, a kind of waltz. There is also a Boston two-step; both originated in the cultural and fashionable centre of *Boston*, Massachusetts, USA in the late 19th century.

Charleston, a lively form of foxtrot, characterized by side-kicks from the knees. It was a popular dance of the 1920s and, like most of the popular dance and music of the time, was influenced by the jazz of the Southern States blacks, although it may not actually have originated in the South Carolina city of *Charleston*.

Conga, a dance performed by a line of people, and consisting of three steps forward and a side-kick. It is a dance of the mid-1930s, originating in Latin America. *Conga* is the Spanish feminine of *Congo*, the region and river of central Africa, and the name acknowledged the African influence on the dance.

Habanera, a slow dance to music with two beats to the bar. It is a Cuban dance of the mid-19th century, and the name is Spanish for 'from *Havana*'; it quickly reached Spain and is well-known from Bizet's use of it in *Carmen*.

Mazurka, a dance to music with three beats to the bar. It became popular in Britain in the early 19th century but was originally a Polish folk dance whose name meant 'from *Mazowia*', the Polish area that includes Warsaw.

Pavane, a stately court dance. It was introduced into Britain from Italy in the early 16th century, and the name is an alteration of *danza padovana*, meaning 'dance of *Padua*', the town in northeast Italy.

Polka, a lively dance with two beats to the bar. It became popular in mid-19th century Britain and is of Czech origin, although the name is Polish for '*Polish woman*'.

Polonaise, a stately dance. It was originally a Polish processional dance and was introduced into Britain in the early 19th century. The name is the feminine form of the French *polonais* meaning '*Polish*'.

Tarantella, a lively folk dance with rapid whirling steps. The name has been known in Britain from the late 18th century but it was popular in south-

---

Pardon my French

The large number of English phrases containing the word 'French' is a reflection of the close relationship between England and France over the years, sometimes friendly and sometimes hostile. Some of these phrases are quite straightforward terms for things which do actually come from France: 'French chalk', the soft white talc used by tailors; 'French polish' for furniture; the glazed doors opening onto a garden or patio called 'French windows'; the musical instrument known as the 'French horn'.

ern Italy from the 15th century. The name comes from the southern Italian port of *Taranto*, which also gives its name to *tarantulas*. In the 15th to 17th centuries the region was the scene of a hysterical malady known as *tarantism*, supposedly caused by the bite of a tarantula. One of the symptoms was a craving to dance, and dancing the tarantella was supposed to cure the disease.

Warp and woof

The names of textiles often come from place-names.

American cloth, a waterproof enamelled oilcloth, formerly used for tablecloths. It was a 19th century British invention, and apparently had no genuine *American* connections at all.

Angora, the wool from the long silky hair of the Angora goat or Angora rabbit. *Angora* is the capital of Turkey and is now called Ankara. The wool has been known from the early 19th century.

Astrakhan, a cloth with thickly-curled wool, often used for hats and collars. It comes from very young karakul lambs from the Soviet Union province of *Astrakhan*, on the lower Volga. The name dates from the mid-18th century.

Buckram, a stiffened cotton or linen fabric used for lining clothes, stiffening hats, and in bookbinding. The word derives from *Bukhara*, now in the Uzbeg province of the Soviet Union. The word has been used since the 14th century but was probably applied originally to a richer kind of fabric.

Calico, plain Indian cotton cloth. The name has been used from the mid-16th century and comes from the Indian trading port of *Calicut* (now called Kozhikode).

Cambric, a fine white linen. The cloth was made in the French town of *Cambrai*, near the Belgian border, and the name combines the earlier French name *Cambray* with the Flemish name for the town, *Kamerijk*. The name has been used in Britain from the early 16th century.

Cashmere, a fine wool made from the underhair of the cashmere goat. The goats came from *Kashmir* region of Asia, and the wool has been known by this name from the late 17th century.

INTER-CITY QUIZ

Can you explain the origin of the following words that are derived from place-names? Answers on page 86.

1   *Bedlam*, a scene of disorder and noisy confusion.
2   *Borstal*, a penal institution for young offenders.
3   *Canter*, a horse's pace, smoother and slower than a gallop.
4   *Chivvy*, to harass or annoy with persistent petty attacks.
5   *Clink*, slang for 'prison'.
6   *Cologne*, a light scent made from alcohol and aromatic citrus oils (*cologne water, eau de cologne*).
7   *Doolally*, slang for 'slightly mad'.
8   *Jurassic*, a geological period marked by the presence of dinosaurs and the appearance of birds.
9   *Mafficking*, boisterous and hilarious celebration.
10 *Meander*, to follow a winding course; to wander aimlessly.
11 *Serendipity*, the faculty for making pleasant discoveries by accident.
12 *Shanghai*, to force a person into a ship's service by means of drugs or drink; to put into an unpleasant situation by trickery.
13 *Spa*, a mineral spring; a resort with a mineral spring.
14 *Spartan*, marked by self-discipline, frugality, and lack of comfort.
15 *Vaudeville*, variety entertainment; music hall.

My old china . . .

It is very common for ceramic and porcelain ware to take its name from the place where it is manufactured.

China, porcelain; now widely used for every kind of ceramic tableware. The fine porcelain was imported from *China* to Britain in the late 16th century. It was called *china-ware* or *cheney-ware* at first but had become china by the late 17th century.

Delft, glazed Dutch earthenware, usually patterned in blue and white. It has been manufactured in *Delft* in south-west Netherlands for hundreds of years although the name was first used in Britain in the early 18th century.

Derby, a kind of fine porcelain. It has been manufactured in the English city of *Derby* since the mid-18th century, and the fine ware known as Crown Derby is particularly well-known.

Dresden, an ornate and delicate porcelain. *Dresden* is in Saxony, East Germany, and *Dresden china* was the name applied in 18th-century Britain to the porcelain that actually came from Meissen, 15 miles from Dresden (see *Meissen*).

Majolica, a kind of earthenware covered with an opaque tin glaze. The name comes from the Italian word for the island of *Majorca*, where this earthenware was first made, and has been used from the mid-16th century.

Meissen, a delicate porcelain (see *Dresden*). It was made in *Meissen* in East Germany from the early 18th century but the name was not used in Britain until the mid-19th century.

Sèvres, a fine, elaborately decorated porcelain. It is made in the French town of *Sèvres*, in the département of Seine-et-Oise, and the word has been used in Britain since the mid-18th century.

Staffordshire, figures made of porcelain or earthenware. They were made in the *Staffordshire* potteries in the 19th century and are now collectors' items.

Cordwain, a soft fine leather. It is also sometimes known as *cordovan*, as it came from *Córdoba*, formerly known as Cordova, in Spain. Cordwain is the older word, used from the 14th century—and possibly even earlier—while cordovan was used from the late 16th century.

Damask, a rich patterned silk fabric. The name dates from the 14th century and derives from *Damascus* where the fabric was made.

Denim, a twilled cotton material, usually blue. The word was used in Britain from the late 17th century for a kind of serge fabric made in *Nîmes* in southern France; the name was originally *serge de Nim*. It later became associated with the cotton denim cloth that we know today.

Donegal tweed, a heavy woollen fabric with coloured flecks. It is made in the county of *Donegal* in north-west Ireland.

Gauze, a very thin transparent fabric. It has been used since the mid-16th century, deriving from the French *gaze*, which is thought to relate to *Gaza* in Israel where the cloth originated.

Harris tweed, a trademark for a loosely woven tweed. Famous throughout the world for its strength and fine quality, it is made in the Outer Hebridean island of *Harris*.

Lawn, a fine linen. The name has been used from the 15th century and comes from the French town of *Laon*, near Rheims, where it was first made.

Lisle, a smooth, hard, twisted thread often used to make stockings. The name comes from the town of *Lille* in north-west France, where the thread was first made, and has been used since the mid-19th century.

Lincoln green, a bright green cloth. It was made in the city of *Lincoln* in east central England and probably dates back to medieval times, as it is traditionally associated with the Robin Hood legends.

Muslin, a finely-woven cotton fabric. The name has been used since the early 17th century, and comes from *Mosul*, the city in northern Iraq where the cloth was first made.

Satin, a lustrous silk fabric. The word has been used from the 14th century and comes via the Arabic *zaytūnī*, a name for the Chinese port of *Qingjiang*, where it was made.

Shantung, a soft, slubbed silk. The silk was woven in the province of *Shandong* in north-east China and the name has been used since the late 19th century.

Sisal, a tough white fibre, used for cord and twine. It was made in Yucatán in Mexico and exported from the port of *Sisal*. The name dates from the mid-19th century.

Suede, soft napped leather. *Suède* is the French word for 'Swedish'; the French popularized gloves made of Swedish leather and the name was first used in Britain in the late 19th century as an abbreviation of *gants de suède*—Swedish gloves.

Tweed, a rough woollen fabric. The name has been used since the mid-19th century and associated with the Scottish River *Tweed*. However, this was due to a misunderstanding. The cloth was formerly called *twill*, pronounced and written as *tweel* in Scotland, and the name tweed arose from a misreading of tweel.

Worsted, a smooth yarn made from long wool fibres. The name has been used since the 13th century and comes from the Norfolk village of *Worstead*, where Flemish weavers settled.

In a manner of speaking

These words from place-names are all connected in some way with speech.

Babel, a confusion of voices. The word comes from the story in Genesis 11:1–9 which describes the building of the tower at Babel, a city that may have been identical with *Babylon*. God punished the builders of this tower, which was supposed to reach heaven, by making their speech unintelligible to each other.

Barrack, to jeer; to shout derisively. The word dates from the late 19th century and is of Australian origin. It is possible that the word derives

---

The arms race . . .

Weapons whose names derive from places include:

Bayonet, a steel blade attached to the end of a firearm. The name dates from the late 17th century and comes from *Bayonne* in south-west France where the weapons were first made.

Bren gun, a light machine-gun. It was introduced before World War II and takes its name from the first two letters of the two places with which it was associated: *Br*no in Czechoslovakia where it was designed, and *En*field, London where the British version was manufactured.

Dumdum, an expanding bullet. The name dates from the late 19th century and comes from the arsenal at *Dum-Dum* near Calcutta, where the bullets were first used.

Pistol, a small handgun. The word dates from the late 16th century. Some authorities claim that it derives from a Czech word meaning 'pipe', while others believe that its origin is in the Italian *pistolese* meaning 'of *Pistoia*', a town in Tuscany that was noted for metalwork and gun-making.

Shillelagh, an oak cudgel. *Shillelagh* is a village in County Wicklow in Ireland and the first cudgels of this kind were made from oak trees growing near there. The word dates back to the late 18th century.

Toledo, a finely tempered sword. The word applies to swords made in *Toledo* in Spain.

from Victoria *Barracks* in Melbourne, near which rough games of football were played. An alternative theory suggests that the origin is *borak* banter, in a native Australian language.

Billingsgate, coarse, abusive language. The word was first used in this sense in the mid-17th century and referred to the sort of language common to the workers at *Billingsgate* fish market in London.

Blarney, smooth, flattering, but not necessarily sincere, speech. The word has been used from the late 18th century and it comes from the legend that anyone who kisses a particular large stone, the Blarney Stone, in *Blarney* Castle, near Cork in the Irish Republic, becomes endowed with 'the gift of the gab' or skill in flattering speech.

Bunkum, nonsense; foolish talk. In 1820 Felix Walker, the congressional representative for *Buncombe* County in North Carolina, insisted on making a lengthy and irrelevant speech, defending his action by saying he was 'making a speech for Buncombe'. The altered spelling was popular by the mid-19th century, and the abbreviation *bunk* by the end of the century.

Laconic, terse; sparing of words. *Laconicus* was Latin for 'from *Laconia*', the Greek district of which Sparta was the capital. As well as their general austerity, the Spartans were noted for their brevity of speech. The word dates from the late 16th century.

Oxford accent, a slightly exaggerated form of received pronunciation. The accent relates to *Oxford* University rather than to the city of Oxford. The expression is sometimes used merely as a synonym for *educated accent*, *BBC accent*, or *received pronunciation*.

Sardonic, bitterly or cynically humorous. It de-

Answers to toponym Inter-city quiz

1   **Bedlam** is an alteration of *Bethlehem*; the Hospital of St Mary of *Bethlehem* in London became a lunatic asylum in the 16th century. The word *bedlam* was first applied to such asylums in general, and later to the sort of confusion that might be seen in them.

2   The first **borstal** institution was built in the village of **Borstal** in Kent at the beginning of the 20th century.

3   **Canter** was originally *Canterbury gallop*, and referred to the supposed pace of pilgrims travelling to the tomb of Thomas à Becket in *Canterbury*.

4   **Chivvy** derives from the *Cheviot* Hills, on the border between England and Scotland and the scene of many border battles. One such battle was described in the late 14th century ballad *The Battle of Chevy Chase*, from which the word chivvy came, at first meaning 'a chase'.

5   **Clink** comes from a former prison in *Clink* Street in Southwark, London.

6   **Cologne** was invented in the 18th century by an Italian chemist who lived in the West German city of *Cologne* (Köln).

7   *Deolali* in India was the site of a transit camp where soldiers arriving from Bombay encountered military mental patients who were assembled there before being sent back to England. *Deolali* or *deolali-tap* thus came to mean 'a bit crazy' to British soldiers in India, and the form **doolally** returned with them to England in the late 19th century.

8   **Jurassic** comes from the *Jura* mountain range which separates France from Switzerland and contains large quantities of granular limestone.

9   The word **mafficking** was coined by a journalist during the Boer War to describe the enthusiastic celebrations in London on the news of the relief of the besieged town of Mafeking in Cape Province in 1900.

10   The word **meander** was originally referred to the winding river known in Greek as *Maiandros* (now Menderes in western Turkey).

11   *Serendip* is an old name for Sri Lanka. The word **serendipity** was invented in the mid-18th century from the title of a fairy tale *The Three Princes of Serendip*, the heroes of which possessed the faculty in question.

12   The word **shanghai** was first used in the USA in the late 19th century and related to journeys to the Orient and to such ports as *Shanghai*, when unwary seamen were press-ganged into service.

13   The word **spa** comes from the first such resort, the town of *Spa*, near Liège in Belgium.

14   The adjective **spartan** relates to the ancient Greek state of *Sparta*, famed for the toughness and self-discipline of its army and inhabitants.

15   The word **vaudeville** was first used in the mid-18th century to apply to popular satirical songs and was an alteration of *chansons vaudevire* or songs from the *vau* (valley) of the river *Vire* in Normandy.

rives ultimately from the Latin *sardonian*, meaning 'of *Sardinia*'. There was a herb on the island of Sardinia which, the Greeks believed, was so bitter that anyone who ate it would make grimaces of disdainful laughter. Its use dates from the early 17th century.

Solecism, a mistake in speech; a violation of accepted grammar or behaviour. The Greek word *soloikos* from which it is derived means 'speaking incorrectly', but literally 'inhabitant of *Soloi*'. Soloi was a port in the ancient district of Cilicia in Asia Minor, and the Attic spoken there was thought to be substandard. The word has been used from the late 16th century.

Playing the game

Words connected with games and sports that derive from place-names include:

Badminton, a game where shuttlecocks are volleyed over a net with rackets. It was invented in the late 19th century at *Badminton* House in Avon, the seat of the Dukes of Beaufort.

Boston, a kind of whist played with two decks of cards. It has been known from the beginning of the 19th century and originated in *Boston*, Massachusetts.

Marathon, a running race of roughly 42.2

kilometres; any event of great length or needing powers of endurance. The word has been used from the late 19th century and derives from *Marathon* in Greece, the site of a battle where the Greeks were victorious over the Persians. A messenger called Pheidippides ran from Marathon to Athens to relate news of the victory.

Newmarket, a card game where the stakes go to the player whose cards duplicate those lying on the table. It is not known what connection it has with *Newmarket*, Suffolk, but *Newmarket* is the home of a famous racecourse and newmarket is a gambling game.

Olympic Games, a four-yearly festival of international athletic contests. Games were held every four years in the ancient Greek region of *Olympia*; these included music and literature as well as athletics. The original games ended in the 4th century and the modern revivals started in the late 19th century.

Rugby, a football game played with an oval ball, and featuring hand-to-hand sideways passing, kicking and tackling. It was invented at *Rugby* School in Warwickshire in the early 19th century.

Yorker, in cricket a ball aimed so as to bounce and pass under the bat. It is said to have been introduced by cricketers from *Yorkshire* in the late 19th century.

Local colour

Some colour words that derive from places:

Cambridge, a light blue. It is associated with those who represent *Cambridge* University in sporting contests, who are known as 'blues'. Light blue favours used to be worn by supporters of Cambridge in the annual inter-varsity boat race.

Indigo, a dark, greyish blue. The word has been used since the mid-16th century and comes from the Latin *indicus* meaning 'Indian', for the blue dye that gives the colour its name was originally imported from *India*.

Lovat, a dull green. *Lovat* is in the Scottish Highland region and the name, used since the early 20th century, is applied to tweed fabrics of this colour.

Magenta, a deep purplish red. The defeat of the Austrians by French and Sardinian troops at the battle of *Magenta*, near Milan, took place in

1859. Shortly after, the red dye was discovered and named after the battle.

Oxford, a dark blue. See *Cambridge* above; *Oxford blue* relates to Oxford University in exactly the same way.

Prussian blue, a strong greenish blue. It is so named because the pigment was discovered in Berlin, then in *Prussia*, at the beginning of the 18th century.

Sienna, a range of colours from yellowish brown to reddish brown. Pigments of this colour were derived from an earthy substance found in *Sienna* (or Siena) in northern Italy. The name was first used in Britain in the late 18th century.

Turquoise, a range of blue-green colours. The name comes from the colour of the precious stone, known from the 14th century, and whose name derives from the Middle English word meaning '*Turkish*', as the stones were imported from *Turkey*.

Umber, a medium yellowish brown. The pigments **raw umber** and **burnt umber** come from the brown earth found in the Italian province of *Umbria*, and the word has been used from the late 16th century. An alternative theory suggests that the ultimate origin lies in the Latin word *umbra*, 'shade'.

Verdigris, a green or bluish-green. The word has been used from the 14th century and is derived from the Old French *vert de Grice*, or 'green of *Greece*'.

5 *You can say that again!*

'I wish I had said that,' declared Oscar Wilde in response to a witty remark made by Whistler. 'You will, Oscar, you will,' replied the artist. In everyday language most of us make regular use of phrases and sayings originated by others, from the wisdom of the Bible to the catchphrases of the world of entertainment, from the immortal words of Shakespeare to the advertising slogans of the 20th century. This is sometimes done consciously, for effect, but is more frequently unconscious—how many people are aware of the source of such expressions as *all hell broke loose*, *six of one and half a dozen of the other*, and *not to be sneezed at*, for example? These and many more are discussed in this chapter, together with well-known misquotations, graffiti, proverbs, and the dying words of the famous.

Quotations from Shakespeare

The plays of William Shakespeare (1564–1616) have enriched the English language with a wide range of colourful sayings and familiar phrases, such as 'a ministering angel' (*Hamlet*), 'a charmed life' (*Macbeth*), 'small beer' (*Othello*), 'be made of sterner stuff' (*Julius Caesar*), and many more . . .

Salad days means 'a time of youth or inexperience'. The phrase was also used as the title of a musical by Dorothy Reynolds and Julian Slade. It comes from *Antony and Cleopatra* (Act 1, Scene 5):

My salad days,
When I was green in judgment, cold in blood,
To say as I said then!

The phrase **beggar all description** means 'to be difficult or impossible to describe', and was first used of Cleopatra's beauty in *Antony and Cleopatra* (Act 2, Scene 2):

For her own person,
It beggar'd all description.

The use of the phrase **thereby hangs a tale** in contemporary English indicates that there is an interesting story associated with something that has been mentioned. The expression occurs in *As You Like It* (Act 2, Scene 7) and in *Othello* (Act 3, Scene 1), with a play on the words *tale* and *tail*.

To the manner born means 'naturally accustomed to behaving in a specified way'. With a pun on the word *manner* it was used as the title of a television comedy series, *To the Manor Born*. The expression comes from *Hamlet* (Act 1, Scene 4):

But to my mind,—though I am native here,
And to the manner born,—it is a custom
More honour'd in the breach than the
    observance.

The latter half of this quotation also occurs in modern usage.

Caviare to the general is something that is beyond the appreciation or understanding of the majority: the word *general* refers to the general public, not the military rank. The phrase was adopted from *Hamlet* (Act 2, Scene 2):

The play, I remember, pleased not the million;
'twas caviare to the general.

In the expression **there's the rub** the word *rub* refers to an obstacle or difficulty. It occurs in *Hamlet* (Act 3, Scene 1):

To die, to sleep;
To sleep: perchance to dream: ay, there's the
    rub.

This quotation comes from Hamlet's most famous soliloquy, which opens with the line 'To be, or not to be: that is the question' and contains a number of other memorable phrases, such as **'The slings and arrows of outrageous fortune'**, **'When we have** shuffled off this mortal coil', and '**Thus conscience doth make cowards of us all**'. The phrase **perchance to dream** was used as the title of a musical by Ivor Novello.

To **out-herod Herod** is to be unimaginably cruel or evil. The name *Herod* is sometimes replaced by another. The phrase was originally used as a criticism of overacting in *Hamlet* (Act 3, Scene 2):

I would have such a fellow whipped for o'erdoing Termagant; it out-herods Herod: pray you, avoid it.

The expression **hoist with his own petard** is applied to people who are the victims of their own plans to harm others. The word *petard*, meaning

All's Well That Ends Well

Many famous phrases and sayings originate not in the text of a book but in its title, from Shakespeare's *All's Well that Ends Well* to E. F. Schumacher's *Small is Beautiful* (1973). Other notable examples include:

Catch-22 (1961), by Joseph Heller, describing a situation in which mutually exclusive conditions lead to deadlock

Chips with Everything (1962), by Arnold Wesker, which popularized this stereotype of the British diet

The Corridors of Power (1963), by C. P. Snow

French Without Tears (1937), by Terence Rattigan

The Greeks Had a Word for It (1929), by Zoë Atkins

The Hidden Persuaders (1957), by Vance Packard, used with reference to advertisers

How to Win Friends and Influence People (1938), by Dale Carnegie

Life Begins at Forty (1932), by William B. Pitkin

The Power of Positive Thinking (1954), by N. V. Peale

The Shape of Things to Come (1933), by H. G. Wells

'an explosive device', is spelt without a *d* in the original quotation from *Hamlet* (Act 3, Scene 4):

For 'tis the sport to have the enginer
Hoist with his own petar.

The rallying cry, **once more unto the breach**, is sometimes used in modern English when people are returning to a difficult task or troublesome situation. It is based on a quotation from *Henry V* (Act 3, Scene 1):

Once more unto the breach, dear friends, once more;
Or close the wall up with our English dead!

To **be all Greek to someone** is to be utterly incomprehensible. In modern usage the expression may be applied to technical language or any form of speech or writing that is unintelligible to some people. The phrase was used in a more literal sense in *Julius Caesar* (Act 1, Scene 2):

for mine own part, it was Greek to me.

Cry havoc means 'to cause destruction', *havoc* being a former military signal for indiscriminate slaughter and pillage. The phrase comes from *Julius Caesar* (Act 3, Scene 1):

Cry, 'Havoc!' and let slip the dogs of war.

When the line is quoted in full the words *let slip* are sometimes replaced by *let loose* or *unleash*. The phrase **the dogs of war** was used as the title of a novel by Frederick Forsyth.

The expression, **the milk of human kindness**, which is used in modern English to mean 'benevolence' or 'goodwill', originated in *Macbeth* (Act 1, Scene 5):

Yet I do fear thy nature;
It is too full o' the milk of human kindness
To catch the nearest way.

The phrase **the be-all and end-all** means 'the ultimate aim' or 'the most important element'. The expression was first used more literally in *Macbeth* (Act 1, Scene 7):

that but this blow
Might be the be-all and the end-all here.

The expression **at one fell swoop**, meaning 'in a single action' or 'all at once', comes from *Macbeth* (Act 4, Scene 3):

What! all my pretty chickens and their dam,
At one fell swoop?

QUIZ

In which of Shakespeare's plays do the following memorable lines appear? Answers on page 93.

1   *Neither a borrower nor a lender be.*
2   *The course of true love never did run smooth.*
3   *All the world's a stage.*
4   *Is this a dagger which I see before me?*
5   *Brevity is the soul of wit.*
6   (stage direction) **Exit, pursued by a bear.**
7   *Parting is such sweet sorrow.*
8   *Some men are born great, some achieve greatness, and some have greatness thrust upon them.*
9   *Out, damned spot!*
10 *Uneasy lies the head that wears a crown.*
11 *If music be the food of love, play on.*
12 *A horse! a horse! my kingdom for a horse!*
13 *I am a man more sinned against than sinning.*
14 *This royal throne of kings, this scepter'd isle.*
15 *We are such stuff as dreams are made on.*

---

green is the colour that is usually associated with these emotions. The term occurs in *Othello* (Act 3, Scene 3):

O! beware, my lord, of jealousy;
It is the green-ey'd monster which doth mock
The meat it feeds on.

The quotation **the winter of our discontent** comes from the opening lines of *Richard III* (Act 1, Scene 1):

Now is the winter of our discontent
Made glorious summer by this sun of York.

The catchphrase *winter of discontent* was adopted in the winter of 1978/9 to describe the industrial unrest in Britain at that time and the resulting strikes and shortages.

Popularized by the Queen in Lewis Carroll's *Alice's Adventures in Wonderland*, **off with his head** was used by Shakespeare more than 250 years earlier in *Richard III* (Act 3, Scene 4):

Thou art a traitor:
Off with his head!

This is a reference to the massacre of Macduff's wife and children.

To **have one's pound of flesh** is to take what is legally due, regardless of the distress that this may cause. It is an illusion to the bond between the usurer Shylock and the merchant Antonio in *The Merchant of Venice*, in which Shylock tries to enforce an agreement that would allow him to remove a pound of Antonio's flesh.

The saying, **the world's my oyster**, indicates that the person in question has a wide range of opportunities in life. The expression originated in *The Merry Wives of Windsor* (Act 2, Scene 2):

Why, then the world's mine oyster,
Which I with sword will open.

The green-eyed monster is jealousy or envy:

The question, **what's in a name?** from *Romeo and Juliet* (Act 2, Scene 2), suggests that the name borne by a person or thing is of little significance, a proposition that is supported by what follows:

What's in a name? that which we call a rose
By any other name would smell as sweet.

The title of a novel by Aldous Huxley, **brave new world** has entered the English language as a catchphrase, applied to any social change or technological advance that is reminiscent of Huxley's vision of the future. It originated, however, in *The Tempest* (Act 5, Scene 1):

How beauteous mankind is! O brave new world, That has such people in't.

Over the years some of Shakespeare's expressions have changed in form or meaning; others are frequently misquoted or misinterpreted:

The catchphrase, **a poor thing but my own**, applied to something that is of value to its possessor or creator, is based on a quotation from *As You Like It* (Act 5, Scene 4):

A poor virgin, sir, an ill-favoured thing, sir, but mine own.

The expression, **there is method in his madness**, suggests that the irrational behaviour of the person in question is not without purpose. It is derived from a quotation from *Hamlet* (Act 2, Scene 2):

Though this be madness, yet there is method in it.

The witching hour is the time when witches are believed to be active. This phrase, which usually refers to midnight, occurs in the less common form *the witching time* in its source, a line from *Hamlet* (Act 3, Scene 2):

'Tis now the very witching time of night.

The word *well*, from **alas, poor Yorick. I knew him well**, which is invariably inserted when this line is quoted, does not appear in the original quotation from *Hamlet* (Act 5, Scene 1):

Alas, poor Yorick. I knew him, Horatio.

The expression **gild the lily**, which means 'to add unnecessary decoration to something that is already attractive', is a misquotation from *King John* (Act 4, Scene 2):

To gild refined gold, to paint the lily.

The familiar phrase **lead on, Macduff**, often used jocularly to invite someone to go on in front, supposedly spoken by Macbeth in the play of that name (Act 5, Scene 7) is, in its correct form, an invitation to fight:

Lay on, Macduff;
And damn'd be him that first cries, 'Hold, enough!'

The line **Romeo, Romeo! wherefore art thou Romeo?** from *Romeo and Juliet* (Act 2, Scene 2) is frequently misinterpreted. The word *wherefore* means 'why', not 'where': Juliet is lamenting the fact that Romeo belongs to a family that is the enemy of her own.

Quotations from the Bible

A great deal of use is made in modern English of phrases and sayings taken from the Authorized (King James) Version of the Bible. Some of these, such as '**let not the sun go down upon your wrath**' (*Ephesians 4:26*), have a distinctive biblical ring; others, such as '**in the twinkling of an eye**' (*1 Corinthians 15:52*) and '**how are the mighty fallen**' (*2 Samuel 1:19*), are less easily recognizable.

The fat of the land means 'the best of everything'. The phrase comes from *Genesis 45:18*.

I will give you the good of the land of Egypt, and ye shall eat the fat of the land.

The expression, **an eye for an eye**, which means 'retaliation in kind', occurs in *Matthew 5:38*, 'Ye have heard that it hath been said, An eye for an eye, and a tooth for a tooth', a reference to Exodus 21:24.

Eye for eye, tooth for tooth, hand for hand, foot for foot.

The colourful phrase, **by the skin of my teeth**, means 'narrowly' or 'only just'. The original quota-

tion, from *Job 19:20*, has the word *with* in place of *by*:

My bone cleaveth to my skin and to my flesh, and I am escaped with the skin of my teeth.

Used in modern English when a young child makes a perceptive remark, **out of the mouths of babes and sucklings** comes from *Psalm 8:2*:

Out of the mouth of babes and sucklings hast thou ordained strength because of thine enemies.

The expression **like a lamb to the slaughter**, meaning 'without resistance', originated in *Isaiah 53:7*:

... he is brought as a lamb to the slaughter.

The saying, **there's no peace for the wicked**, in which the word *peace* is often replaced by *rest*, is often used ironically in modern English. It comes from *Isaiah 57:21*:

There is no peace, saith my God, to the wicked.

Holier than thou, meaning 'self-righteous' or 'smug', originated in *Isaiah 65:5*:

Stand by thyself, come not near to me; for I am holier than thou.

The expression **the salt of the earth** is used to describe people who are considered to be of admirable character and of great value. It comes from *Matthew 5:13*:

Ye are the salt of the earth: but if the salt have lost his savour, wherewith shall it be salted?

To **cast pearls before swine** is to waste something of quality or value on those who are unable to appreciate it. The phrase occurs in *Matthew 7:6*:

Give not that which is holy unto the dogs, neither cast ye your pearls before swine.

The saying **the blind leading the blind**, which refers to inexperienced people who attempt to guide others, originated in *Matthew 15:14*:

If the blind lead the blind, both shall fall into the ditch.

A direct quotation from *Matthew 16:23*, **get thee behind me, Satan** is an expression used in modern English to rebuff or rebuke a tempter. In its original context the remark is addressed by Jesus to Peter.

The English Bible, a book which, if everything else in our language should perish, would alone suffice to show the whole extent of its beauty and power.

T. B. Macaulay

The saying **the spirit is willing but the flesh is weak** indicates that a person lacks the ability, energy, or willpower to put his or her intentions into practice. It comes from *Matthew 26:41*:

Watch and pray, that ye enter not into temptation: the spirit indeed is willing, but the flesh is weak.

The phrase **no respecter of persons** refers to an egalitarian attitude, disregarding class, rank, wealth, power, fame, etc. It was first applied to God, in *Acts 10:34–5*:

I perceive that God is no respecter of persons: But in every nation he that feareth him, and worketh righteousness, is accepted with him.

The powers that be means 'the Establishment', 'the controlling authority', or 'the governing body'. The phrase originated in *Romans 13:1*:

There is no power but of God: the powers that be are ordained of God.

Those who seek to be **all things to all men** try to please everyone, adapting their behaviour according to the people they are with. The expression comes from *1 Corinthians 9:22*:

I am made all things to all men, that I might by all means save some.

Answers to Shakespeare quiz

1 *Hamlet*, Act 1, Scene 3
2 *A Midsummer Night's Dream*, Act 1, Scene 1
3 *As You Like It*, Act 2, Scene 7
4 *Macbeth*, Act 2, Scene 1
5 *Hamlet*, Act 2, Scene 2
6 *The Winter's Tale*, Act 3, Scene 3
7 *Romeo and Juliet*, Act 2, Scene 2
8 *Twelfth Night*, Act 2, Scene 5
9 *Macbeth*, Act 5, Scene 1
10 *Henry IV, Part II*, Act 3, Scene 1
11 *Twelfth Night*, Act 1, Scene 1
12 *Richard III*, Act 5, Scene 4
13 *King Lear*, Act 3, Scene 2
14 *Richard II*, Act 2, Scene 1
15 *The Tempest*, Act 4, Scene 1

Christian words

The arrival of Christianity in Britain under St Augustine in 597 had a great impact on the English language. Words of Latin and Greek origins became used to express concepts and ideas that were new to the Anglo-Saxons. Examples of such terms are: *altar*, *angel*, *apostle*, *candle*, *disciple*, *martyr*, *mass*, *monk*, *pope*, *priest*, *psalm*, and *shrine*. Non-religious terms of Latin and Greek origin that entered the language at this time include: *cook*, *school*, and *fever*.

Someone who does not **suffer fools gladly** is impatient with or intolerant of foolish people. In modern English the expression is rarely used in the positive sense of its source, *2 Corinthians 11:19*:

For ye suffer fools gladly, seeing ye yourselves are wise.

A thorn in the flesh is a person or thing that constantly annoys or irritates another. The word flesh is sometimes replaced by side. The phrase was first used in *2 Corinthians 12:7*:

There was given to me a thorn in the flesh, the messenger of Satan to buffet me, lest I should be exalted above measure.

To **cover a multitude of sins** is to conceal or compensate for many faults or weaknesses. The expression comes from *1 Peter 4:8*:

... charity shall cover the multitude of sins.

Many phrases and sayings of biblical origin bear a more distant resemblance to their source, while some remain close to the original text but have had their meaning distorted by misquotation or misinterpretation.

The saying **pride goes before a fall** is a misquotation from *Proverbs 16:18*. The original contains a stronger warning:

Pride goeth before destruction, and an haughty spirit before a fall.

The proverb, **there is nothing new under the sun**, is applied to spurious innovations and is an adaptation of *Ecclesiastes 1:8*:

... there is no new thing under the sun.

A fly in the ointment is a person or thing that spoils an otherwise perfect situation. The expression is derived from *Ecclesiastes 10:1*:

Dead flies cause the ointment of the apothecary to send forth a stinking savour.

The proverb **the leopard cannot change his spots** suggests that the fundamental character or nature of a person or institution cannot be changed. It is derived from *Jeremiah 13:23*:

Can the Ethiopian change his skin, or the leopard his spots?

The phrase **wheels within wheels** refers to a complicated situation or a complex series of interconnected issues or influences. It originated in *Ezekiel 1:16*:

Their appearance and their work was as it were a wheel in the middle of a wheel.

To **hide one's light under a bushel** is to conceal or be modest about one's talents or abilities. This saying comes from *Matthew 5:15*:

Neither do men light a candle, and put it under a bushel, but on a candlestick.

The word *bushel* denotes a container used to measure capacity.

To **turn the other cheek** means to refuse to retaliate when provoked. The expression is derived from *Matthew 5:39*:

But I say unto you, That ye resist not evil: but whosoever shall smite thee on thy right cheek, turn to him the other also.

In modern English the saying **the left hand doesn't know what the right hand is doing** is most frequently applied to a lack of communication between departments in large organizations. In the original quotation, from *Matthew 6:3*, it refers to secrecy in giving:

But when thou doest alms, let not thy left hand know what thy right hand doeth.

The straight and narrow is the virtuous, moral, or correct way to behave. The phrase is derived from *Matthew 7:14*:

Strait is the gate, and narrow is the way, which leadeth unto life, and few there be that find it.

The saying **money is the root of all evil** is a misquotation from *1 Timothy 6:10*. It is not money itself, but the love of money, that is condemned by Paul in the original:

For the love of money is the root of all evil: which while some coveted after, they have erred from the faith.

A number of well-known expressions are derived from biblical stories or characters rather than from specific quotations. **The writing on the wall**, for example, is an allusion to the mysterious inscription that appeared on the wall of Belshazzar's palace (*Daniel 5:5–29*) and was interpreted by Daniel as a warning of the king's downfall. **At the eleventh hour**, which means 'at the last minute', refers to the parable recounted in *Matthew 20:1–16*. The terms **good Samaritan**, denoting someone who unselfishly helps those in distress, and **prodigal son**, meaning 'a reformed spendthrift', also allude to New Testament parables (*Luke 10:25–37* and *Luke 15:11–32*).

Other quotations from literature

Many other famous phrases and expressions come from the written word—from plays, poems and prose, and even book titles and cartoon captions.

To **add insult to injury** means 'to make matters worse'. The expression comes from Edward Moore's play *The Foundling* (1748):

This is adding insult to injuries.

When **all hell breaks loose** there is considerable uproar, protest, riot, disorder, etc. The phrase occurs in John Milton's *Paradise Lost* (1667):

But wherefore thou alone? Wherefore with thee Came not all hell broke loose?

The memorable phrase **all human life is there** popularized as an advertising slogan for the *News of the World*, originated in Henry James' novel *Madonna of the Future* (1879):

Cats and monkeys, monkeys and cats—all human life is there.

The expression **all quiet on the western front**, which dates back to World War I, was adopted as the title of the English translation of Erich Maria Remarque's novel *Im Westen Nichts Neues* (1929), filmed in 1930. This popularized the catchphrase, which is now used with reference to any lull in fighting or quarrelling.

The saying **the best-laid schemes of mice and men** is used when something that has been carefully planned goes wrong. It is a quotation from Robert Burns' poem *To a Mouse*:

The best laid schemes o' mice an' men Gang aft a-gley.

The US writer John Steinbeck used the phrase **of mice and men** as the title of a novel, published in 1937.

To **damn with faint praise** is to imply criticism by praising qualities of little importance. The expression comes from Alexander Pope's *Epistle to Dr Arbuthnot* (1735):

Damn with faint praise, assent with civil leer, And, without sneering, teach the rest to sneer.

More than 50 years earlier, however, William Wycherley had used a similar phrase in the prologue to *The Plain Dealer* (1677): 'with faint praises one another damn'.

The expression **do as I say, not as I do** is applied to those who do not practise what they preach, another famous phrase. The former comes from John Selden's *Table Talk* (1689):

Preachers say, Do as I say, not as I do.

The moral saying **do as you would be done by**, which means 'treat others as you would like them to treat you', originated in a letter from Lord Chesterfield to his son, 16 October 1747:

Do as you would be done by is the surest method that I know of pleasing.

It was popularized in Charles Kingsley's *The Water Babies* (1863) by the character Mrs Doasyouwouldbedoneby and her counterpart Mrs Bedonebyasyoudid.

The saying **don't shoot the pianist, he's doing his best**, in which the word *pianist* may be replaced by any appropriate noun, means 'to be tolerant' or 'do not criticize'. It originated in the 19th century as a notice in an American bar, mentioned in Oscar Wilde's *Impressions of America*:

Please do not shoot the pianist. He is doing his best.

The expression **far from the madding crowd**, popularized as the title of a novel by Thomas Hardy, comes from Thomas Gray's *Elegy Written in a Country Churchyard* (1751):

Far from the madding crowd's ignoble strife.

In modern usage the phrase **the female of the species is more deadly than the male** usually refers to women but was originally used to describe a she-bear. *The Female Of The Species* is the title of a poem by Rudyard Kipling, which is the source of the well-known saying:

But the she-bear thus accosted rends the peasant tooth and nail
For the female of the species is more deadly than the male.

The expression **funny peculiar or funny ha-ha** is used to distinguish between the two meanings of

Big Brother is watching you

The novel *Nineteen Eighty-Four* (published 1949), by George Orwell, provided the English language with such words and phrases as 'newspeak', 'doublethink', and 'Big Brother'. *Newspeak*, according to Orwell, is a language 'designed not to extend but to diminish the range of thought'; *doublethink* 'means the power of holding two contradictory beliefs in one's mind simultaneously, and accepting both of them'; *Big Brother* is the omnipotent head of Orwell's fictional totalitarian state. The catchphrase 'Big Brother is watching you' is widely used in modern English, with particular reference to the apparent invasion of privacy by data banks and computer technology. The memorable slogan 'All animals are equal, but some animals are more equal than others' comes from another of Orwell's novels, *Animal Farm* (published 1945).

the word funny—'odd' or 'amusing'. It occurs in Ian Hay's play *The Housemaster* (1936), 'What do you mean, funny? Funny peculiar or funny ha-ha?', but may be of earlier origin.

The saying, **gather ye rosebuds while ye may**, means 'to make the most of the present time' and comes from Robert Herrick's poem *To the Virgins, to Make Much of Time*:

Gather ye rosebuds while ye may,
Old Time is still a-flying.

The expression **God moves in a mysterious way** is from a hymn by William Cowper which opens with the lines:

God moves in a mysterious way
His wonders to perform.

This saying is applied in modern English, sometimes with a different word in place of *God*, to any action or event that cannot be explained or understood.

Hanging is too good for them, an expression of disgust used of people for whom no punishment is harsh enough, originated in John Bunyan's *The Pilgrim's Progress* (1678):

Hanging is too good for him, said Mr Cruelty.

Hope springs eternal, a reference to the optimism of mankind, comes from Alexander Pope's *Essay on Man* (1732–4):

Hope springs eternal in the human breast
Man never is, but always to be blest.

The proverb **if at first you don't succeed, try, try again**, advocating perseverance, was probably coined in the 19th century by the educational writer W. E. Hickson:

'Tis a lesson you should heed,
Try, try again.
If at first you don't succeed,
Try, try again.

The saying **if God did not exist, it would be necessary to invent him**, from Voltaire's *Épîtres*, is often adapted in modern usage to refer to anyone or anything that is considered to be indispensable.

The saying **ignorance is bliss** is often used in modern English as an apology, excuse, or justification for ignorance or folly. In its original context,

Thomas Gray's *Ode on a Distant Prospect of Eton College*, the phrase is a wistful observation on carefree youth:

> Where ignorance is bliss
> 'Tis folly to be wise.

The words **I'll make him an offer he can't refuse** come from Mario Puzo's novel *The Godfather* (1969), filmed in 1972. The expression is widely used with reference to irresistible offers.

Jam tomorrow is a promise of something better in the future—a promise that may never be fulfilled. It comes from Lewis Carroll's *Through the Looking-Glass* (1872):

> The rule is, jam tomorrow and jam yesterday—but never jam today.

The saying **the law is an ass** is used to condemn any example of legislation that seems unfair, illogical, or unnecessary. In the quotation on which it is based, from Charles Dickens' novel *Oliver Twist* (1837–8), *a* is used in place of *an*:

> 'If the law supposes that,' said Mr Bumble ... 'the law is a ass—a idiot.'

(Mr Bumble was referring to the assumption that a wife's behaviour is directed by her husband.)

The proverb **a little learning is a dangerous thing** comes from Alexander Pope's *Essay on Criticism* (1711). It suggests that partial knowledge or understanding may lead to overconfidence and error, with serious consequences. The word *knowledge* is sometimes substituted for *learning* in modern usage. Pope's *Essay on Criticism* is the source of several other famous sayings, such as **to err is human, to forgive, divine**, which is usually quoted as an excuse for making a mistake, and **fools rush in where angels fear to tread**.

The Scottish poet Robert Burns coined the phrase **man's inhumanity to man**, a description of human cruelty in the poem *Man was made to Mourn*:

> Man's inhumanity to man
> Makes countless thousands mourn!

The phrase **the monstrous regiment of women** refers to the formidable aspects of womankind, especially women in positions of power or women united in a common cause. It comes from the title of a pamphlet by John Knox:

The First Blast of the Trumpet Against the Monstrous Regiment of Women.

Nature, red in tooth and claw is a vivid image of the savagery of nature and comes from Tennyson's *In Memoriam*:

> Tho' Nature, red in tooth and claw
> With ravine, shrieked against his creed.

The poem is also the source of the expression **so near and yet so far** and contains many other memorable lines, such as

> 'Tis better to have loved and lost
> Than never to have loved at all.

A necessary evil is something that is undesirable but indispensable. The phrase was used by Samuel Johnson in his preface to the works of Shakespeare (1765)—'Notes are often necessary, but they are necessary evils'—and by Thomas Paine in the pamphlet *Common Sense* (1776): 'Government, even in its best states is but a necessary evil.'

The expression **never the twain shall meet** refers to the fundamental differences that separate certain people, institutions, attitudes, ideas, etc. It comes from *The Ballad of East and West*, by Rudyard Kipling:

> Oh, East is East, and West is West, and never
>   the twain shall meet.

No man is an island means 'nobody is completely independent'. The saying originated in John Donne's *Devotions*:

> No man is an Island, entire of it self.

This passage contains another memorable quotation:

> And therefore never send to know for whom the bell tolls; It tolls for thee.

Ernest Hemingway used the phrase **for whom the bell tolls** as the title for one of his novels.

Not to be sneezed at means 'to be worth consideration' or 'not to be rejected with contempt'. The expression comes from the play *The Heir-at-Law* (1797) by George Colman the Younger.

The phrase **the opium of the people** may be applied to anything that compensates for, or helps people to bear or forget the harsh realities of life. Karl Marx coined the expression, with reference to religion, in his *Critique of Hegel's Philosophy of Right*:

> Religion is the sigh of the oppressed creature, the feeling of a heartless world, and the soul of soulless circumstances. It is the opium of the people.

Pie in the sky is the prospect of something better in the future—something that is unlikely to happen. The phrase comes from Joe Hill's *The Preacher and the Slave*:

> You'll get pie in the sky when you die.
> (That's a lie.)

The expression **the plot thickens** comes from *The Rehearsal* (1672), a play by George Villiers, Duke of Buckingham:

> Ay, now the plot thickens very much upon us.

It is used in modern English when a situation, in fact or fiction, becomes more complicated.

The famous proverb **procrastination is the thief of time** is a warning against putting off until tomorrow what can be done today and comes from Edward Young's poem *Night Thoughts* (1742–5):

> Procrastination is the thief of time
> Year after year it steals, till all are fled.

Roses all the way means 'always pleasant' or 'always easy'. The phrase originated in Robert Browning's poem *The Patriot*:

> It was roses, roses, all the way.

The expression **a sadder and wiser man** refers to someone who has learnt the hard way from misfortune, error, or failure. It comes from *The Rime of the Ancient Mariner* (1798), by S. T. Coleridge:

> A sadder and a wiser man
> He rose the morrow morn.

The poem contains a number of other well-known quotations, such as

> Water, water, everywhere
> Nor any drop to drink.

(The second line is often misquoted as 'and not a drop to drink.')

The phrase **ships that pass in the night** refers to people who meet only briefly. This image originated in Longfellow's *Tales of a Wayside Inn* (1874):

> Ships that pass in the night, and speak each
>   other in passing . . .
> So on the ocean of life we pass and speak one
>   another.

The expression **six of one and half a dozen of the other**, which refers to two people, things, or options of equal worth, comes from Frederick Marryat's novel *The Pirate* (1836):

> I never knows the children. It's just six of one and half-a-dozen of the other.

Based on the wisdom of the Bible (Proverbs 13: 24), the saying **spare the rod and spoil the child** emphasizes the importance of corporal punishment in a child's upbringing. It is a quotation from Samuel Butler's poem *Hudibras* (1663):

> Love is a boy, by poets styl'd,
> Then spare the rod, and spoil the child.

The phrase **things that go bump in the night**, used

humorously in modern English with reference to the supernatural, comes from an anonymous rhyme or prayer:

From ghoulies and ghosties and long-leggety beasties
And things that go bump in the night,
Good Lord, deliver us.

A **tin god** is a self-important person or an object of misplaced veneration. The expression originated in Rudyard Kipling's *Public Waste*:

Wherefore the Little Tin Gods harried their little tin souls
For the billet of 'Railway Instructor to Little Tin Gods on Wheels'.

Spoken quotations

Some well-known sayings are based on the spoken word, originating in political speeches, songs, or the words of the famous.

When the Model T Ford car was first produced, customers were told that they could have '**any colour, so long as it's black**'. The quotation is attributed to the US car manufacturer Henry Ford. This catchphrase is now applied to any situation in which a limited choice is on offer.

Because it's there was the mountaineer George Mallory's reply, in 1923, when asked why he wanted to climb Mount Everest. Since then the words have been attributed to or used by others, notably Sir Edmund Hillary, who conquered Everest 30 years later. The phrase is often quoted as a motive for a dangerous or foolish venture.

A sign bearing the words **the buck stops here** was displayed on the desk of Harry S. Truman, President of the USA from 1945 to 1953. It is a reference to the well-known phrase *pass the buck*, meaning 'shift the responsibility or blame', which originated in the game of poker.

The die is cast means 'an irrevocable decision has been made'. The saying is attributed to Julius Caesar, in the Latin form *iacta alea est*, when he led his troops across the River Rubicon, precipitating civil war. (This incident gave rise to the expression *cross the Rubicon*, meaning 'to take irreversible action'.)

The famous greeting **Doctor Livingstone, I presume** was uttered by Henry Morton Stanley in 1871, at the end of his search for the missionary David Livingstone in the heart of Africa. It is often used informally or humorously, with the substitution of the appropriate name, when strangers meet for the first time. R. B. Sheridan's comedy *The School for Scandal* written nearly a hundred years earlier, coincidentally contains the line 'Mr Stanley, I presume'.

The catchphrase **I cried all the way to the bank** in which the word *cry* is sometimes replaced by *laugh*, is believed to have originated with the US pianist Liberace. It is used by people who make a great deal of money from something, often something that has received adverse criticism.

Include me out, meaning 'don't include me', is one of many sayings attributed to the US film producer Samuel Goldwyn. This one is genuine; others, such as 'we've all passed a lot of water since then' and 'in two words: im-possible', are of doubtful authenticity.

The originator of the remark, **it's all part of life's rich pageant**, uttered resignedly in the face of adversity, is thought to be Arthur Marshall, in a monologue of the 1930s. It was popularized by Peter Sellers, as Inspector Clouseau, in a 'Pink Panther' film. The word *pageant* is sometimes replaced by *tapestry* or *pattern*.

'There are three kinds of lies: **lies, damned lies, and statistics**.' In his autobiography Mark Twain attributed this quotation to Benjamin Disraeli, but it may be of earlier origin. This catchphrase reflects on the unreliability of statistics.

The declaration of loyalty **my country right or wrong** in which the word *country* is sometimes replaced by a different noun, comes from a toast given by the US naval officer Stephen Decatur in 1816:

Our country! In her intercourse with foreign nations, may she always be in the right; but our country, right or wrong.

Something that has **neither rhyme nor reason** or is **without rhyme or reason** is devoid of logic or meaning. The expression is attributed to Sir Thomas More, who advised an aspiring writer to turn his poor prose into poetry, remarking on the result:

Now it is somewhat, for now it is rhyme;
before, it was neither rhyme nor reason.

A **paper tiger** is someone or something that is not as powerful or dangerous as it seems. The term was popularized by Mao Tse Tung (Mao Ze Dong), who used it on a number of occasions, including his famous statement:

All reactionaries are paper tigers.

The familiar phrase **the pound in your pocket** comes from a television broadcast made by Harold Wilson on 19 November 1967, after the devaluation of the pound:

Like the curate's egg

The saying 'like the curate's egg—good in parts' comes from a cartoon that appeared in *Punch* in 1895. A curate, taking breakfast with the bishop, denies that he has a bad egg: 'Oh no, my lord, I assure you! Parts of it are excellent!' A cartoon in the *New Yorker* is believed to be the source of the expression 'back to the drawing-board', meaning 'let's start again'. In this case the caption is accompanied by a picture of an aircraft designer watching an aeroplane explode. The humorist James Thurber produced many memorable cartoons and captions, notably the famous parody of the flowery language of wine connoisseurs: 'It's a naïve domestic Burgundy, without any breeding, but I think you'll be amused by its presumption.'

That doesn't mean, of course, that the pound here in Britain—in your pocket or purse or in your bank—has been devalued.

The saying **praise the Lord and pass the ammunition**, which became the title of a popular song, originated in 1941 during the Japanese attack on Pearl Harbor in World War II. It is usually attributed to the naval chaplain Howell Forgy.

The Duke of Wellington is alleged to have made the defiant response, **publish and be damned**, to a threat of blackmail concerning the publication of a woman's memoirs. It is used in similar circumstances in modern English.

The phrase **a short, sharp shock** was popularized by the Conservative politician William Whitelaw in 1979, with reference to harsh punishments for young criminals. It originated in Gilbert and Sullivan's *The Mikado* (1885):

Awaiting the sensation of a short, sharp shock,
From a cheap and chippy chopper on a big black block.

The colourful expression **squeezed until the pips squeak** comes from a speech made by the Conservative politician Eric Geddes in Cambridge on 10 December 1918:

The Germans, if this Government is returned, are going to pay every penny; they are going to be squeezed, as a lemon is squeezed—until the pips squeak.

Advised not to join the already overcrowded legal profession, the US statesman Daniel Webster replied: '**There is always room at the top**.' This became a catchphrase, and the expression **room at the top** was further popularized as the title of a novel by John Braine (1957).

To **steal someone's thunder** is to anticipate something that is to be said or done by another, undermining its effect. The expression was first used in a more liberal sense by the critic and playwright John Dennis (1657–1734), who devised a sound effect of thunder for one of his plays. The play itself was a failure, but the successful thunder effect was immediately pirated by others, causing Dennis to complain:

Damn them! They will not let my play run, but they steal my thunder!

A well-known phrase originated in a speech made by Edward Heath in the House of Commons on 15 May 1973:

It is the unpleasant and unacceptable face of capitalism, but one should not suggest that the whole of British industry consists of this kind.

Heath was referring to tax avoidance, but the phrase is now used in a wide range of contexts, sometimes with a different noun substituted for *capitalism*.

The origin of **we was robbed**, a cry of protest against unfair defeat, is usually attributed to Joe Jacobs, manager of the boxer Max Schmeling who lost to Jack Sharkey in 1932. The spelling *wuz* is often used in place of *was*. Jacobs is also credited with the saying **I should of stood in bed** (meaning 'I should have stayed in bed'), used in the face of failure or disappointment.

The phrase **wind of change** was popularized by Harold Macmillan in a speech to the South African parliament in Cape Town on 3 February 1960:

> The wind of change is blowing through this continent.

QUIZ

Who said or wrote these well-known lines? (Answers on page 102)

1 It is a far, far better thing that I do, than I have ever done.
2 A thing of beauty is a joy for ever.
3 Not with a bang but a whimper.
4 Genius is one per cent inspiration and ninety-nine per cent perspiration.
5 Hitch your wagon to a star.
6 O what a tangled web we weave, when first we practise to deceive!
7 Justice should not only be done, but should manifestly and undoubtedly be seen to be done.
8 A week is a long time in politics.
9 Tread softly because you tread on my dreams.
10 They also serve who only stand and wait.
11 I have seen the future, and it works.
12 You're a better man than I am, Gunga Din!
13 Laugh, and the world laughs with you; weep, and you weep alone.
14 The lamps are going out all over Europe; we shall not see them lit again in our lifetime.
15 God's in his heaven—all's right with the world!

Macmillan used the plural form of the phrase as the title for the first volume of his memoirs, *Winds of Change* (1966).

The catchphrase, **you ain't heard nothin' yet**, which suggests that there is something much better or worse to come, was originally uttered by Al Jolson in the first talking film, *The Jazz Singer* (1927). The word *heard* is often replaced by *seen* in modern usage, and the whole phrase is sometimes rendered more grammatically as 'you haven't seen anything yet'.

You can't fool all the people all the time is part of a quotation that has been attributed to Abraham Lincoln and Phineas T. Barnum:

> You can fool all the people some of the time, and some of the people all the time, but you can not fool all the people all of the time.

Barnum is also credited with the saying '**there's a sucker born every minute**'.

In Britain the saying **you've never had it so good** is usually associated with Harold Macmillan, although it originated in the USA (*You Never Had It So Good* being the slogan of the Democratic party in the presidential election of 1952). Macmillan first used the expression, in a slightly different form, on 20 July 1957, in a speech at Bedford:

> Let's be frank about it; most of our people have never had it so good.

Misquotations

Some sayings are frequently misquoted, others have become famous in a form that differs from the original quotation.

The phrase **blood, sweat, and tears** is generally ascribed to Winston Churchill, who told the House of Commons on 13 May 1940, in his first speech as Prime Minister, 'I have nothing to offer but blood, toil, tears and sweat.' The words occur in a number of earlier literary references, notably Byron's poem *The Age of Bronze* (1823):

> Year after year they voted cent per cent,
> Blood, sweat, and tear-wrung millions—
> why? for rent!

The remark **crisis? what crisis?** is associated with James Callaghan, Prime Minister of Britain during the industrial unrest of 1978/9. The phrase was not used by Callaghan himself but appeared as a newspaper headline, prompted by the Prime Minister's denial of the 'mounting chaos' in Britain.

The words **elementary, my dear Watson!** attributed to the fictional detective Sherlock Holmes,

There's no business like show business

The following list is just a small selection of the many sayings that are derived from the lyrics or titles of popular songs:

A little of what you fancy does you good
Anything you can do, I can do better
Diamonds are a girl's best friend
If you want to know the time, ask a policeman
It's been a hard day's night
Keep right on to the end of the road
Keep the home fires burning
Life is just a bowl of cherries
Poor little rich girl
See you later, alligator
Thank heaven for little girls
The best things in life are free
There's no business like show business
There's no place like home
Uncle Tom Cobbleigh and all

---

do not appear in any of Arthur Conan Doyle's stories, although *The Crooked Man*, in *The Memoirs or Sherlock Holmes* (1894), contains the following exchange between Watson and Holmes:

'Excellent!' I cried. 'Elementary,' said he.

The catchphrase was used in its familiar form in the film *The Return of Sherlock Holmes* (1929).

The phrase **fresh fields and pastures new**, used when someone is about to embark on a new venture, is a misquotation from Milton's poem *Lycidas* (1637):

At last he rose, and twitch'd his mantle blue;
To-morrow to fresh woods, and pastures new.

The expression **Greek meets Greek** refers to an encounter between people of equal strength, skill, intelligence, cunning, etc. It is derived from Nathaniel Lee's play *The Rival Queens* (1677):

When Greeks joined Greeks, then was the tug of war!

The catchphrase **inside every fat man there's a thin man trying to get out** is generally considered to be an adaptation of a line from Cyril Connolly's *The Unquiet Grave* (1944):

Imprisoned in every fat man a thin one is wildly signalling to be let out.

Five years earlier, however, George Orwell had written, in *Coming Up for Air*:

I'm fat, but I'm thin inside. Has it ever struck you that there's a thin man inside every fat man, just as they say there's a statue inside every block of stone?

The ungrammatical expression **it just growed** refers to something that appears from an unknown origin or increases without apparent effort. It is based on a passage from Harriet Beecher Stowe's novel *Uncle Tom's Cabin* (1852):

'Do you know who made you?' 'Nobody, as I knows on,' said the child, ... 'I 'spect I grow'd.'

The child is Topsy, the phrase **like Topsy** is sometimes added when the expression is used in modern English.

In 1960 Kingsley Amis wrote an article about education in which he remarked 'more will mean worse'. The frequent misquotation of this phrase as **'more means worse'** is a constant source of irritation to the writer. In its original form the saying warns that without selectiveness, standards will fall.

Answers to quiz

1. Charles Dickens, *A Tale of Two Cities* (said by Sydney Carton)
2. John Keats, *Endymion*
3. T. S. Eliot, *The Hollow Men*
4. Thomas Alva Edison
5. Ralph Waldo Emerson, *Civilization*
6. Walter Scott, *Marmion*
7. Lord Hewart
8. Harold Wilson
9. W. B. Yeats, *He Wishes for the Cloths of Heaven*
10. John Milton, *On His Blindness*
11. Lincoln Steffens
12. Rudyard Kipling, *Gunga Din*
13. Ella Wheeler Wilcox, *Solitude*
14. Lord Grey (referring to World War I)
15. Robert Browning, *Pippa Passes*

We are not amused

A number of well-known sayings are of doubtful authenticity. Nobody knows for certain whether Queen Victoria ever uttered the famous snub 'We are not amused,' quoted in Caroline Holland's *Notebooks of a Spinster Lady*. Authentic or not, it became a popular catchphrase in the 20th century.

Marie Antoinette is traditionally believed to have said, on learning that her people had no bread, 'Let them eat cake.' The saying is, however, of older origin and has been attributed to others in similar circumstances.

'Not tonight, Josephine', used informally or humorously in response to any proposition, with or without sexual connotations, was coined as an apocryphal refusal made by Napoleon Bonaparte to the demands of his wife Josephine. It was popularized in music-hall routines of the early 20th century.

The line **music has charms to soothe a savage breast**, from William Congreve's play *The Mourning Bride* (1697), is often misquoted, the **savage beast** being substituted for a savage breast. The saying **hell has no fury like a woman scorned** is based on a quotation from the same play:

> Heav'n has no rage, like love to hatred turn'd,
> Nor Hell a fury, like a woman scorn'd.

The phrase **my lips are sealed**, meaning 'I will not say anything about that', was popularized by Stanley Baldwin during his final term of office as Prime Minister (1935–7). It originated as a misquotation of Baldwin's statement on the Abyssinian crisis (1935): 'my lips are not yet unsealed'.

The derogatory expression **on your bike** meaning 'go away', had already been in use for some 20 years when it became associated with the British Conservative politician Norman Tebbit in the early 1980s. In a speech on unemployment in 1981 Tebbit said, of his father, 'He got on his bike and looked for work.'

Ours not to reason why is a phrase used by those who obey orders or accept the irrational without question. It is a misquotation from Tennyson's poem *The Charge of the Light Brigade* (1854):

> Their's not to make reply,
> Their's not to reason why,
> Their's but to do and die:
> Into the valley of Death
> Rode the six hundred.

The phrase **peace in our time**, from the *Book of Common Prayer*, is generally associated with the statesman Neville Chamberlain, Prime Minister of Britain at the outbreak of World War II. The actual words of Chamberlain's historic announcement after the signing of the Munich agreement were: 'I believe it is peace for our time.'

The self-explanatory saying **power corrupts** is derived from the quotation 'Power tends to corrupt and absolute power corrupts absolutely', which occurs in a letter from Lord Acton to Mandell Creighton (1887).

The expression **speak now or forever hold your peace** is used to warn people of the last opportunity to make an objection, request, etc. It is a misquotation from the marriage ceremony in the *Book of Common Prayer*.

... let him now speak, or else hereafter for ever hold his peace.

The saying **there, but for the grace of God, go I** originated in the 16th century with the Protestant martyr John Bradford. Watching some criminals being led to their execution, Bradford remarked: 'But for the grace of God there goes John Bradford.' Winston Churchill gave the saying a humorous twist when he said of Stafford Cripps: 'There, but for the grace of God, goes God.'

The disparaging remark **those who can, do; those who cannot, teach** which is sometimes adapted and applied to other professions, is a misquotation from George Bernard Shaw's *Maxims for Revolutionists*:

He who can, does. He who cannot teaches.

The saying **to travel hopefully is better than to arrive** is used when the work involved in a particular enterprise proves to be more rewarding than the final result achieved, or when anticipation is more pleasurable than realization. It is derived from Robert Louis Stevenson's *El Dorado*:

To travel hopefully is a better thing than to arrive, and the true success is to labour.

The expression **warts and all** refers to a full description that does not attempt to conceal any defects. It is based on a remark addressed by Oliver Cromwell to the portrait painter Peter Lely:

Mr Lely, I desire that you would use all your skill to paint my picture truly like me, and not flatter me at all; but remark all these roughnesses, pimples, warts, and everything as you see me.

Sir Philip Sidney, wounded in the thigh at Zutphen in 1586, is believed to have passed a drink of water to a dying soldier with the words:

Thy necessity is yet greater than mine.

The modern catchphrase **your need is greater than mine** is derived from this chivalrous gesture.

Catchphrases

The world of entertainment—radio, television, and cinema—has produced a number of memorable catchphrases, many of which have outlived their source.

Radio comedy programmes are the source of such lines as:

I've arrived, and to prove it, I'm here.
A good idea, son!
Jolly hockey sticks!
Educating Archie, 1950s

He's fallen in the water.
No thanks, I'm trying to give them up.
The Goon Show, 1950s

Can I do you now, sir?
I don't mind if I do.
ITMA, 1940s

It was agony, Ivy.
Ray's a Laugh, 1950s

Other famous radio catchphrases include:

Are you sitting comfortably? Then I'll begin.
Listen with Mother, 1950s/60s

Hi-yo, Silver!
The Lone Ranger, 1930s/40s, subsequently filmed

It's a bird! It's a plane! It's Superman!
Superman, 1940s, subsequently filmed. The catchphrase sometimes occurs in the form 'Is it a bird? Is it a plane? No, it's Superman!'

The 64 dollar question.
The US quiz show *Take It or Leave It*, 1940s. The show was subsequently televised and the prize money raised to 64,000 dollars.

It is to television comedy that we owe the following catchphrases:

Listen very carefully, I will say this only once.
'Allo 'Allo, 1980s

Are you free?—I'm free.
Are You Being Served, 1970s

Stupid boy!
Permission to speak, sir?
Dad's Army, 1960s/70s

I didn't get where I am today . . .
The Fall and Rise of Reginald Perrin, 1970s

Qué?
Fawlty Towers, 1970s; the stock response of the bewildered Spanish waiter, Manuel

And now for something completely different.
Nudge, nudge, wink, wink. Say no more. Know what I mean?
Monty Python's Flying Circus, 1970s

What do you think of the show so far?—Rubbish.
There's no answer to that.
You can't see the join.
Morecambe and Wise, 1960s/70s. The last catchphrase refers to Ernie Wise's toupée.

Everybody out!
The Rag Trade, 1950s/60s

Sock it to me!
Very interesting . . . but stupid.
Rowan and Martin's Laugh-In, 1960s/70s

You dirty old man!
Steptoe and Son, 1960s/70s

You silly old moo!
Till Death Us Do Part, 1960s/70s

It's goodnight from me.—And it's goodnight from him.
The Two Ronnies, 1970/80s

Television quiz and game shows have given us:

Nice to see you, to see you, nice!
Didn't he do well?
The Generation Game, 1970s. These were the catchphrases of the show's original host, Bruce Forsyth.

I've started so I'll finish.
Pass.

Mastermind, 1970s/80s. The word *pass*, used when a contestant does not know the answer to a question, is often heard informally as a humorous substitute for 'I don't know'.

Open the box!
Take Your Pick, 1950s/60s

Here's your starter for ten.
And no conferring.
University Challenge, 1960s/70s/80s

And finally, television drama:

I could do that. Gissa job.
The Boys from the Blackstuff, 1982

Evenin' all.
Dixon of Dock Green, 1950s/60s/70s

Exterminate, exterminate!
Doctor Who, 1960s/70s/80s; the cry of the Daleks

Only the names have been changed to protect the innocent.
Dragnet, 1950s/60s

Who loves ya, baby?
Kojak, 1970s

'Er indoors.
A nice little earner.
Minder, 1980s

To boldly go where no man has gone before.
Star Trek, 1960s

Among the many memorable lines and catchphrases of the cinema are:

Here's looking at you, kid

Four of the best-known catchphrases of the cinema are misquotations. The line 'play it again, Sam', associated with Humphrey Bogart in *Casablanca*, does not occur in the soundtrack. It is derived from several lines spoken by Ingrid Bergman and Bogart in the film: 'Play it once, Sam, for old time's sake . . . Play it, Sam . . . You played it for her, and you can play it for me . . . Play it.' James Cagney's supposed catchphrase 'you dirty rat' is based on a line from *Blonde Crazy* (1931): 'You dirty, double-crossing rat.' In *She Done Him Wrong* (1933) Mae West said, 'Why don't you come up some time and see me? This evolved into the famous invitation 'come up and see me some time'. The first talking film of the Tarzan story contains the line, 'Tarzan . . . Jane', but the memorable introduction 'me Tarzan, you Jane' does not feature in any of the Tarzan films.

Of all the gin joints in all the towns in all the world, she walks into mine!
Casablanca, 1942

Phone home!
ET, 1982

A martini, shaken, not stirred.
Goldfinger, 1964

Frankly, my dear, I don't give a damn.
Gone with the Wind, 1939

I want to be alone.
said by Greta Garbo in *Grand Hotel*, 1932

Beulah, peel me a grape.
said by Mae West in *I'm No Angel*, 1933

Love means never having to say you're sorry.
Love Story, 1970

I must get out of these wet clothes and into a dry martini.
said by Robert Benchley in *The Major and the Minor*, 1942

May the Force be with you.
Star Wars, 1977

Western films have given rise to a number of general catchphrases that cannot be attributed to a particular source. These include:

A man's gotta do what a man's gotta do.

Meanwhile, back at the ranch.

There's gold in them thar hills.

They went thattaway!

This town isn't big enough for both of us.

We'll cut them off at the pass.

White man speak with forked tongue.

Many famous people—comedians, actors, sportsmen, magicians, and even cartoon characters—have their own catchphrases:

Hello, playmates! *Arthur Askey*

She knows, you know! *Hylda Baker*

What's up, Doc? *Bugs Bunny*

I wanna tell you a story. *Max Bygraves*

Not many people know that. *Michael Caine*

It's the way I tell 'em. *Frank Carson*

Just like that. *Tommy Cooper*

Wakey-wakey! *Billy Cotton*

You'll like this. Not a lot, but you'll like it.
  Paul Daniels

By Jove, I needed that. *Ken Dodd*

Hello, my darlings! *Charlie Drake*

Oooh, you are awful . . . but I like you!
  Dick Emery

It's all done in the best possible taste.
  Kenny Everett

Pin back your lugholes. *Cyril Fletcher*

Yabbadabba doo! *Fred Flintstone*

It's turned out nice again. *George Formby*

Hello, good evening, and welcome.
  David Frost

Shut that door! *Larry Grayson*

I mean that most sincerely. *Hughie Green*

Here's another fine mess you've gotten me into. *Oliver Hardy*

You cannot be serious! *John McEnroe*

Can you hear me, mother? *Sandy Powell*

Right, monkey! *Al Read*

As it happens. Jimmy Savile

You lucky people. *Tommy Trinder*

Up and under! *Eddie Waring*

Stop messing about! *Kenneth Williams*

Walkies! *Barbara Woodhouse*

Slogans and graffiti

All advertising slogans should be memorable, but only the most successful find their way into the English language as catchphrases. Here are some of the most famous slogans of the 20th century, with the date (where known) of their first appearance.

FOR BEER

Guinness is good for you. (*c.* 1930)

Heineken refreshes the parts other beers cannot reach. (1974)

What we want is Watneys.

I bet he drinks Carling Black Label.

It's what your right arm's for. (1972; Courage)

I'm only here for the beer.
(1971; Double Diamond)

It looks good, it tastes good, and by golly it does you good. (Mackeson)

FOR OTHER DRINKS

Don't be vague, ask for Haig.

I thought . . . until I discovered Smirnoff. (1970)

Any time, any place, anywhere. (1970s; Martini)

Schhh . . . you know who. (1960s; Schweppes)

Good to the last drop. (Maxwell House)

Typhoo puts the T in Britain.

Drinka pinta milka day.
(1958. This slogan introduced the word *pinta* into the English language.)

FOR FOOD

Nice one, Cyril!
(1972; Wonderloaf. The slogan was adopted by supporters of Tottenham Hotspur Football Club in 1973.)

Beanz meanz Heinz. (1960s)

It's fingerlickin' good.
(1960s; Kentucky Fried Chicken)

Go to work on an egg. (1958)

Can you tell Stork from butter? (1956)

Snap, crackle, pop!
(1928; Kellogg's Rice Krispies)

Stop me and buy one. (1923; Walls ice cream)

FOR SWEETS

Roses grow on you. (1960s; Cadbury's Roses)

Don't forget the fruit gums, mum.
(1958; Rowntree)

A Mars a day helps you work, rest, and play.

FOR CARS

What's yours called? (Renault)

Vorsprung durch Technik. (Audi)

At sixty miles an hour the loudest noise in this new Rolls Royce comes from the electric clock. (1958)

OTHERS:

Does she . . . or doesn't she?
(1955; Clairol hair colour)

You'll wonder where the yellow went, when you brush your teeth with Pepsodent. (1950s)

Nothing acts faster than Anadin.

Put a tiger in your tank. (1964; Esso)

It beats as it sweeps as it cleans. (1919; Hoover)

You too can have a body like mine. (1920s; Charles Atlas body-building courses, which also used the line 'I was a seven stone weakling')

It's for yoo-hoo! (British Telecom)

Someone, somewhere, wants a letter from you.
(1960s; Post Office)

A diamond is forever. (1939)

Say it with flowers. (1917)

That will do nicely, sir.
(1980s; American Express)

No, I'm with the Woolwich.

(1970s; Woolwich Building Society. The slogan is a stock response to the question 'Are you with me?')

A number of other slogans are still remembered and quoted:

FROM WORLD WAR I

Daddy, what did you do in the Great War?

Your country needs you!

FROM WORLD WAR II

Careless talk costs lives.

Is your journey really necessary?

Walls have ears.

FROM PROTEST CAMPAIGNS

Ban the bomb. (1953)

Black is beautiful. (1962)

Burn your bra! (1970)

Make love, not war. (1960s)

Power to the people. (1969)

FROM SAFETY CAMPAIGNS

Clunk, click, every trip.

(1971; referring to the use of seat belts)

Don't ask a man to drink and drive. (1964)

Safety first. (1929)

AND FINALLY, GRAFFITI

Kilroy was here.

(This originated in the USA during World War II. The identity of Kilroy—a shipyard inspector? a sergeant in the air force?—has been the subject of much discussion.)

Bill Stickers is innocent.

(written below the notice 'Bill Stickers Will Be Prosecuted')

. . . rules, OK.

(used with any appropriate name or noun. It has given rise to several humorous variants, such as 'Dyslexia lures, KO', 'Amnesia rules, O . . .', 'Apathy ru . . .', 'Scotland rules, och aye', 'Queen Elizabeth rules UK', 'Town criers rule, okez, okez, okez', and—one for word-buffs— 'Roget's Thesaurus dominates, regulates, rules, OK, all right, agreed'.

Today is the first day of the rest of your life.

(The word *today* is sometimes replaced by *tomorrow*.)

Be alert. Your country needs lerts.

Education kills by degrees.

Nostalgia isn't what it used to be.

You're never alone with schizophrenia.

I used to be conceited, but now I'm perfect.

Proverbs

Proverbs are words of wisdom or advice that have been handed down from generation to generation. Those that can be traced back to specific quotations have been discussed in the earlier part of this chapter, but the majority are of unknown origin. Some are so well-known that they rarely need to be quoted in full—**when the cat's away** (the mice will play), **if the cap fits** (wear it), **talk of the devil** (and he appears), **when in Rome** (do as the Romans do), etc—others are less familiar.

AGE

Children should be seen and not heard.

You're only young once.

You can't teach an old dog new tricks.

There's no fool like an old fool.

ANTICIPATION

Don't count your chickens before they are hatched.

Don't cross a bridge till you come to it.

A stitch in time saves nine.

Prevention is better than cure.

APPEARANCE

Appearances are deceptive.

All that glitters is not gold.

Beauty is only skin deep.

Handsome is as handsome does.

Fair without, false within.

Fine feathers make fine birds.

You can't tell a book by its cover.

Still waters run deep.

CAUTION

Don't put all your eggs in one basket.

Once bitten, twice shy.

Discretion is the better part of valour.

Look before you leap.

Softly, softly, catchee monkey.

CHANGE

A change is as good as a rest.

Variety is the spice of life.

A new broom sweeps clean.

Times change.

Circumstances alter cases.

It's never too late to mend.

DEATH

Death comes to us all.

Whom the gods love dies young.

Dead men tell no tales.

Never speak ill of the dead.

DIFFERENCE

It takes all sorts to make a world.

One man's meat is another man's poison.

Everyone to his taste.

There is no accounting for tastes.

Beauty is in the eye of the beholder.

Oil and water don't mix.

Comparisons are odious.

Yes . . . and no!

The wisdom of proverbs is not always to be trusted, for many contain contradictory advice.

Absence makes the heart grow fonder,
  but *out of sight, out of mind.*
Many hands make light work,
  but *too many cooks spoil the broth.*
More haste, less speed,
  but *he who hesitates is lost.*
Nothing venture nothing gain,
  but *better safe than sorry.*
Travel broadens the mind,
  but *east, west, home's best.*
A penny saved is a penny earned,
  but *you can't take it with you.*

EQUALITY

What's sauce for the goose is sauce for the gander.

A cat may look at a king.

We shall lie all alike in our graves.

All cats are grey in the dark.

FAMILIARITY

Familiarity breeds contempt.

No man is a hero to his valet.

Better the devil you know than the devil you don't.

FAMILY

Charity begins at home.

Blood is thicker than water.

Like father, like son.

Like mother, like daughter.

The hand that rocks the cradle rules the world.

FOOD

An apple a day keeps the doctor away.

Bread is the staff of life.

The way to a man's heart is through his stomach.

Hunger is the best sauce.

FRIENDS

A friend in need is a friend indeed.

A true friend is the best possession.

A man is known by the company he keeps.

Birds of a feather flock together.

Like attracts like.

HELP

Every little helps.

Two heads are better than one.

One good turn deserves another.

Scratch my back and I'll scratch yours.

INTERFERING

Let sleeping dogs lie.

Never trouble trouble till trouble troubles you.

The cobbler should stick to his last.

Mind your own business.

Curiosity killed the cat.

Ask no questions, hear no lies.

LOVE
Love is blind.

Love conquers all.

It's love that makes the world go round.

All is fair in love and war.

When poverty comes in at the door, love flies out of the window.

MARRIAGE
Marry in haste, repent at leisure.

Marriages are made in heaven.

Marriage is a lottery.

Matrimony is a school in which one learns too late.

MISFORTUNE
It never rains but it pours.

These things are sent to try us.

Lightning never strikes in the same place twice.

It's an ill wind that blows nobody any good.

Every cloud has a silver lining.

Worse things happen at sea.

MONEY
Money talks.

He who pays the piper calls the tune.

Money isn't everything.

The streets of London are paved with gold.

Take care of the pennies, and the pounds will take care of themselves.

Penny wise, pound foolish.

Don't spoil the ship for a ha'porth of tar.

Where there's muck there's brass.

If you pay peanuts, you get monkeys.

What you gain on the swings you lose on the roundabouts.

One man's loss is another man's gain.

Two can live as cheaply as one.

There's one law for the rich and another for the poor.

A fool and his money are soon parted.

OPPORTUNITY
Opportunity seldom knocks twice.

Strike while the iron is hot.

Make hay while the sun shines.

Christmas comes but once a year.

PATIENCE
Patience is a virtue.

Everything comes to him who waits.

Rome was not built in a day.

A watched pot never boils.

Don't try to run before you can walk.

POSSESSION
Possession is nine points of the law.

What's yours is mine and what's mine is my own.

Finding is keeping.

A bird in the hand is worth two in the bush.

PROOF
The proof of the pudding is in the eating.

The exception proves the rule.

One swallow does not make a summer.

REGRET
It's no use crying over spilt milk.

What's done cannot be undone.

Past cure, past care.

SATISFACTION
Enough is as good as a feast.

Half a loaf is better than no bread.

Beggars can't be choosers.

The grass is always greener on the other side of the fence.

SELF
Look after number one.

Every man for himself, and the devil take the hindmost.

God helps those who help themselves.

Every man is the architect of his own fortune.

SUPERSTITIONS
Cold hands, warm heart.

Lucky at cards, unlucky in love.

Third time lucky.

See a pin and pick it up, all the day you'll have good luck.

Happy is the bride the sun shines on, and the corpse the rain rains on.

TIME
Time is a great healer.

Time is money.

Time and tide wait for no man.

There's no time like the present.

Never put off till tomorrow what you can do today.

The early bird catches the worm.

Early to bed and early to rise, makes a man healthy, wealthy and wise.

Better late than never.

WORDS

The pen is mightier than the sword.

Fine words butter no parsnips.

Sticks and stones may break my bones, but words will never hurt me.

Least said, soonest mended.

Speech is silver but silence is golden.

Actions speak louder than words.

Easier said than done.

Famous last words

The German philosopher Karl Marx is believed to have said, on his deathbed, 'Last words are for fools who haven't said enough.' The last words of many famous people are fairly unremarkable—the name of a loved one, a line from the Bible, a word of farewell—but others are remembered for their noble sentiments, irony, unintentional humour, or sheer banality.

See in what peace a Christian can die.
Joseph Addison, English writer (1672–1719)

Is it my birthday or am I dying?
Nancy Astor, British politician (1879–1964)

I shall hear in heaven.
Ludwig van Beethoven, German composer (1770–1827). Beethoven was deaf in later life.

Don't let the awkward squad fire over me.
Robert Burns, Scottish poet (1759–96)

Have you brought the chequebook, Alfred?
Samuel Butler, British writer (1835–1902)

Et tu, Brute? (You too, Brutus?)
Julius Caesar, Roman statesman (?101–44 BC). Caesar was surprised to find Brutus among his assassins.

I realize that patriotism is not enough. I must have no hatred or bitterness towards anyone.
Edith Cavell, British nurse (1865–1915). Cavell was executed by the Germans.

Let not poor Nelly starve.
Charles II, King of England (1630–85). The king was referring to his mistress, Nell Gwyn.

Goodnight, my darlings. I'll see you tomorrow.
Noël Coward, British playwright (1899–1973)

My design is to make what haste I can to be gone.
Oliver Cromwell, English statesman (1599–1658)

All my possessions for one moment of time.
Elizabeth I, Queen of England (1533–1603)

I've never felt better.
Douglas Fairbanks Senior, US actor (1883–1939)

We are all going to heaven, and Van Dyck is of the company.
Thomas Gainsborough, English artist (1727–88)

Good heavens, has he hurt himself?
Léon Gambetta, French statesman (1838–82). Gambetta was referring to a visitor who had fainted.

How is the Empire?
George V, King of Britain (1865–1936). Other versions of the king's last words include: 'Gentlemen, I am sorry for keeping you waiting like this: I am unable to concentrate'.

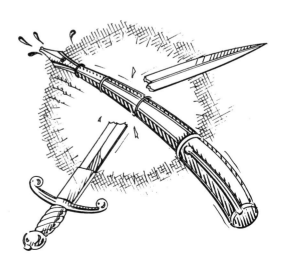

More light!
Johann Wolfgang von Goethe, German writer (1749–1832)

Well, I've had a happy life.
William Hazlitt, English writer (1778–1830)

I am Heinrich Himmler.
Heinrich Himmler, German Nazi leader (1900–45). Himmler committed suicide.

I am about to take my last voyage, a great leap in the dark.
Thomas Hobbes, English philosopher (1588–1679)

On the contrary!
Henrik Ibsen, Norwegian playwright (1828–1906). Ibsen was responding to a remark that he was getting better.

This is it. I'm going, I'm going.
Al Jolson, US singer (1886–1950)

Does nobody understand?
James Joyce, Irish writer (1882–1941)

Such is life.
Ned Kelly, Australian outlaw (1855–80). Kelly was hanged.

Be of good comfort, Master Ridley, and play the men. We shall this day light such a candle by God's grace in England, as I trust shall never be put out.
Hugh Latimer, English Protestant bishop (?1485–1555). Latimer was burnt at the stake.

Why weep you? Did you think I should live for ever? I thought dying had been harder.
Louis XIV, King of France (1638–1715)

I think I'll go to sleep now.
Harold Macmillan, British statesman (1894–1986)

Mozart!
Gustav Mahler, Austrian composer (1860–1911)

When I am dead and opened, you shall find 'Calais' lying in my heart.
Mary I, Queen of England (1516–58). The queen was referring to the loss of Calais to the French.

Dying is a very dull, dreary affair. And my advice to you is to have nothing whatever to do with it.
W. Somerset Maugham, British writer (1874–1965)

This hath not offended the king.
Thomas More, English statesman (1478–1535). More was referring to his beard, which he drew aside as he placed his head on the block. On ascending the scaffold More said, 'See me safe up; for my coming down, let me shift for myself'. To his executioner he offered the following advice: 'Pluck up thy spirits, man, and be not afraid to do thine office. My neck is very short; take heed therefore thou strike not awry, for saving of thine honesty'.

Kiss me, Hardy.
Lord Nelson, British admiral (1758–1805). The authenticity of these words is disputed by some scholars, who prefer: 'Thank God, I have done my duty'. Nelson was killed at the Battle of Trafalgar.

Qualis artifex pereo! (What an artist dies with me!)
Nero, Roman emperor (37–68)

I am just going outside, and I may be some time.
Lawrence Oates, British explorer (1880–1912). With these words Oates, a member of Scott's last expedition, walked out into the blizzard to die.

Die, my dear doctor, that's the last thing I shall do!
Lord Palmerston, British statesman (1784–1865)

Get my swan costume ready.
Anna Pavlova, Russian ballerina (1885–1931)

First words first . . .

The advancement of technology has given rise to a number of memorable *first* lines. On 24 May 1844 the inventor Samuel F. B. Morse sent the first words in Morse Code, 'What hath God wrought?' Alexander Graham Bell transmitted the first telephone message on 10 March 1876: 'Mr Watson, come here; I want you'. The first words uttered on the moon, by the astronaut Neil Armstrong on 21 July 1969, were 'That's one small step for a man, one giant leap for mankind'. (In some versions of the quotation the word *a* is omitted.)

Oh, my country, how I leave my country!
William Pitt the Younger, British statesman (1759–1806). In another version the word *love* is substituted for *leave*. Some believe Pitt to have made the down-to-earth remark, 'I think I could eat one of Bellamy's veal pies'.

I am going to seek the great perhaps. Ring down the curtain, the farce is over.
François Rabelais, French writer (?1494–1553)

So the heart be right, it is no matter which way the head lies.
Walter Raleigh, English courtier (?1552–1618). Raleigh made this remark as he prepared to place his head on the block. With reference to the executioner's axe, he said ''Tis a sharp remedy, but a sure one for all ills'. A third version of Raleigh's last words is: 'I have a long journey to take, and must bid the company farewell'.

So little done, so much to do.
Cecil Rhodes, South African statesman (1853–1902)

I have a terrific headache.
Franklin Delano Roosevelt, US president (1882–1945)

God bless you all, I feel myself again.
Walter Scott, British writer (1771–1832)

They couldn't hit an elephant at this dist—.
John Sedgwick, US general (1813–64). Sedgwick was killed during the American Civil War, disregarding advice not to look over a parapet at the enemy.

What is the answer? ... In that case, what is the question?
Gertrude Stein, US writer (1874–1946)

God bless ... God damn.
James Thurber, US humorist (1894–1961)

The sun is God.
Joseph Mallord William Turner, British artist (1775–1851)

I think I am becoming a god.
Vespasian, Roman emperor (9–79)

Oh, that peace may come.
Victoria, Queen of Britain (1819–1901). The queen was referring to the Boer War.

I die hard, but I am not afraid to go.
George Washington, US president (1732–99)

Go away. I'm all right.
H. G. Wells, British writer (1866–1946)

Either that wallpaper goes, or I do.
Oscar Wilde, Irish writer (1854–1900)

6 Fun with words

What does the child telling 'Knock-knock' jokes in the school playground have in common with the busy executive doing *The Times* crossword on a train or plane? Both are having fun with words, though the executive is probably unaware of the fact and the child unwilling to admit it. Words can be used for so much more than mere communication: they are the basis of many absorbing games and pastimes. Letters can be arranged or changed to form anagrams and doublets. Sounds and meanings can be played upon to create ingenious or atrocious puns. Words can be misused or garbled to humorous effect in malapropisms and spoonerisms, or combined in tongue-twisting sentences that defy pronunciation. Do you know the difference between a pangram and a palindrome? Are you a wordmaster? Read on and find out.

In 1842 a woman advertised herself in *The Times* as:

agreeable, becoming, careful, desirable, English, facetious, generous, honest, industrious, judicious, keen, lively, merry, natty, obedient, philosophic, quiet, regular, sociable, tasteful, useful, vivacious, womanish, xantippish, youthful, zealous, etc.

Acrostics

An acrostic is a poem that spells out one or more words or names using the first letter of each line. In a double acrostic the first and last letters of each line spell out words, and in a triple acrostic the middle letters form a third word.

For hundreds of years, and in many languages, acrostics have been composed as word games, to pay tribute to monarchs, friends, or lovers, or for more mundane purposes, such as a reminder of the order of lines or verses. They were particularly popular in Victorian times, when the following examples were written. The first is an ode to Prince Albert, the second a double acrostic that forms the verb *unite* and its anagram (and antonym) *untie*.

Accomplish'd Prince! from whose aesthetic
mind,
Like Hamlet's, philosophic and refin'd,
Burst the bright vision of that Palace fair,
Enchanging wondering nations gather'd there:
Rare favourite of fortune! well, I ween,
Thou art fit consort, worthy of our Queen.

Unite and untie are the same—so say yoU,
Not in wedlock, I ween, has this unity beeN.
In the drama of marriage each wandering gouT
To a new face would fly—all except you and I—
Each seeking to alter the spell in their scenE.

Lewis Carroll wrote many acrostics, the most famous of which is dedicated to Alice Pleasance Liddell, the inspiration for *Alice's Adventures in Wonderland* and *Through the Looking-Glass*. It opens with the following lines:

A boat, beneath a summer sky
Lingering onward dreamily
In an evening of July—
Children three that nestle near
Eager eye and willing ear, . . .

In an acrostic puzzle the answers to a series of clues form a single, double, or triple acrostic (answer below).

These help you drive safely
When out in the dark.
1   It's worn round the shoulders.
2   This lies near to Sark.
3   One more than a couple.
4   They're found in the park.

Alphabet games

The *comic alphabet*, which makes use of the sounds of letters, exists in many variant forms (and is also known as the *Cockney alphabet*). Here is one example, with some of the less obvious puns explained:

A	for 'orses	L	for leather
	(hay for horses)	M	for sis
B	for mutton	N	for lope
C	for yourself	O	for the rainbow
D	for Mitty	P	for soup
	(deformity)	Q	for the bus
E	for brick	R	for 'mo
	(heave a brick)	S	for you
F	for vescence		(as for you)
G	for police	T	for two
	(chief of police)	U	for mism,
H	for beauty	V	for la différence
	(age before beauty)		(vive la différence)
I	for Novello	W	for a quid
J	for oranges	X	for breakfast
	(Jaffa oranges)	Y	for mistress
K	for teria	Z	for the doctor
	(cafeteria)		(send for the doctor)

Answer to acrostic puzzle above:
CapE   AlderneY   ThreE   SwingS

Another novelty alphabet is made up of words that are prefixed by letters in everyday language (or technical jargon):

A-level   B-movie   C-stream   D-day   E-boat   F-number   G-string   H-bomb   I-beam   J-cloth   K-ration   L-plate   M-way   N-gauge   O-ring   P-type   Q-fever   R-month   S-bend   T-junction   U-turn   V-neck   W-particle   X-ray   Y-fronts   Z-axis

Some alphabet games and pastimes can be tackled either as a solo challenge or in competition with others:

1   Think of words that begin and end with the same letter, working through the alphabet from A to Z:
    arena, blob, colic, dead, edge, fluff, gang, hearth, etc.

2   Think of words that begin and end with consecutive letters of the alphabet:
    Arab, basic, card, date, elf, fishing, growth, etc.

3   Think of words in which the same letter occurs twice, but not at the beginning or end:
    ma*d*am, wo*b*ble, bi*c*ycle, a*d*der, me*t*er, e*f*fort, en*g*age, t*h*ighs, c*i*vil, etc.

4   Think of words of five or more letters that use only half of the alphabet—the letters A to M or N to Z:
    hiked, blade, gleam, rusty, worst, pours, etc.

5   In the words *abstemious* and *facetious* each vowel appears only once, in alphabetical order. Think of other words in which each vowel appears only once, in any order, such as *emulation*, *mendacious*, *favourite*, and *unsociable*, and words in which four consecutive letters appear only once, in alphabetical order, such as *backwardness*, *quadrisect*, *eliminator*, *defying*, and *restful*.

6   Make up a sentence using at least twelve words beginning with the same letter, such as:
    Eleven eager elephants effortlessly eat eighty electric eels each evening, expecting extra energy.

7   Make up a sentence using at least twelve words beginning with consecutive letters of the alphabet, such as:
    Like many nice old places, quaint Redruth sells the usual varied wares.

Sentences that use words beginning with each letter of the alphabet in turn are more difficult to compile without recourse to obscure words or lists.

8   Make up phrases or sentences in which the initial letters spell out words that have some connection with the text:

LAMB   Little Animal Murmuring 'Baa!'
THEATRE   Tasteful High-class Entertainment. All Tickets Really Expensive.

COMPUTER   Can Our Machine Process Useless Trivia, Even Rubbish?

There are many alphabet and letter games that can be played by two or more people—at parties, after dinner, on train journeys, in waiting rooms, etc. Some require a pencil and paper, others require nothing more than an active brain and a good vocabulary!

I LOVE MY LOVE

In this traditional game, which dates back to the 17th century, players work through the alphabet as follows:

Player 1: I love my love with an A because she is Anne from Australia and awfully amorous.
Player 2: I love my love with a B because she is Barbara from Bermuda and breathtakingly bright.
Player 3: I love my love with a C because she is Caroline from Cornwall and completely carefree.

There are many variants of the game, such as 'I love my love with an A because she is an architect, her name is Anne, she comes from Australia, and I gave her an apple', and so on.

In another version the players take turns to name a different quality of their loved one—ambitious, affluent, artistic, amiable, etc.—until someone is unable to think of a new adjective, or repeats one that has already been mentioned, losing a point. The players then move onto the next letter of the alphabet and the game continues.

The same principles are used in the games **Traveller's alphabet** and **A was an apple pie.** In *Traveller's alphabet* each player is asked 'Where are you going?' and 'What will you do there?' The first player might answer 'Austria'—'Admire agile acrobats', the second player 'Bolivia'—'Build big bridges', and so on. In *A was an apple pie* each player has to think of an appropriate verb, working through the alphabet: 'A ate it'; 'B bought it'; 'C cooked it'; 'D dropped it'; 'E examined it'; 'F found it'; etc.

GUGGENHEIM

Players are given a list of categories—animals, flowers, writers, places, food, etc.—and a word, such as TABLE. They must name one item in each category that begins with the individual letters of the chosen word:

	T	A	B	L	E
animals	tiger	anteater	baboon	lemur	elephant
flowers	thistle	aster	bluebell	lupin	edelweiss
writers	Tolstoy	Auden	Browning	Lamb	Eliot
places	Teignmouth	Aylesbury	Birmingham	Liverpool	Edinburgh
food	treacle	apple	bread	lard	egg

HEADS AND TAILS

The first player calls out a word in a chosen category—girls' names, for example—and each player in turn must call out a word in the same category that begins with the last letter of the previous word. The game continues until someone is unable to think of a new word or repeats one that has already been mentioned. For example:

Kate—Elizabeth—Harriet—Teresa—Annabel —Lynn—Nina—Alice—Eunice—Eleanor— Rosalind—Dorothy—Yvonne—Elizabeth.

PYRAMIDS

In this pencil-and-paper game, which is also known as *Word-building* or *Twisting stairway*, each player must build a single letter into the longest possible word, adding one letter at a time and rearranging the letters if necessary. For example:

H

HE

SHE

HERS

SHARE

HEARTS

SHATTER

THEATRES

GHOSTS

The first player chooses a letter (F, for example). The second player thinks of a word that begins with this letter (FELLOW) and calls out a second letter. (The object of the game is not to complete a word.) The next player thinks of a word that begins with these two letters (FEAR) and calls out the third letter. The next player may think of FEATHER and call out T, unwittingly completing the word FEAT. Alternatively, he or she may think of FEAST and call out S. The next player adds I (FEASIBLE), the next B, then L, and the next player is forced to complete the word, so losing the game.

Players must always have a genuine word in mind, and they may be challenged to name it. If the word is acceptable the challenger loses the game; if it is unacceptable the challenged player is the loser.

Some people widen the scope of the game by ignoring completed two-letter words. Others play a variant called *Superghosts*, in which letters can be added at either end of the group.

WORDS WITHIN WORDS

The winner of this well-known game is the player who produces the longest list of words made from the letters of a given word—not necessarily a long word—using each letter only once. Any or all of the following may be excluded: two-letter words, three-letter words, proper nouns, abbreviations, foreign words, plurals, etc. Here is a selection of the words of four or more letters that can be made from MATERIAL, for example:

aerial, alarm, alert, altar, alter, area, earl, irate, item, lair, lame, late, later, liar, lime, mail, male, malt, mare, martial, mate, meat, melt, mile, mire, mite, rail, rate, real, realm, ream, rite, tail, talc, tame, tamer, teal, team, tear, term, tiara, tile, time, trail, trial.

CLUE WORDS

One player, the 'word-maker', thinks of a seven-letter word in which all the letters are different, such as READING, and gives the other players the first clue—a three-letter word made from the letters of the chosen word, such as RID. Each player in turn names a seven-letter word containing these letters in any order (a player who guesses correctly at this stage scores three points and becomes the word-maker, beginning the next round with a new seven-letter word). If the word is not guessed a second clue is given—a four-letter word made from the letters of the chosen word, such as GRIN. A player who guesses correctly at this stage scores two points. The third and final clue is a five-letter word, such as GRADE, and the score for a correct guess is one point. If the word is not guessed at this stage the word-maker scores a point and begins the next round.

It is not necessary to reveal all the letters of the word in the clues, as in the above example. The word-maker might give GIN as the first clue, GRIN as the second, and GRIND as the third, leaving the letters E and A undisclosed.

LAST WORD

In this game, which is also known as *Trackword*, players are given a nine-letter word—GENERALLY, for example—which they write down as follows:

```
G E N
E R A
L L Y
```

They must then make as many words of three or more letters as possible, moving from letter to letter across, up, down, or diagonally, using each letter only once. Here are some of the words that can be made from this example:

ale, all, allergen, are, ear, earl, early, earn, eel, era, gear, green, lane, large, lay, leg, near, nearly, ran, ray, real, renal, yarn.

Anagrams

An anagram is a word or phrase that forms a different word or phrase when the letters are rearranged: *percussion* is an anagram of *supersonic*; *the warm lion* is an anagram of *mother-in-law*. For at least 2000 years the creation and decoding of anagrams has been a popular pastime throughout the world.

One-word anagrams range from two to at least fourteen letters:

on	no
ant	tan
leap	pale
night	thing
solemn	melons
despair	praised
nameless	salesmen
carthorse	orchestra
intoxicate	excitation
legislators	allegorists
conversation	conservation
containerised	inconsiderate
interrogatives	tergiversation

Many words have more than one anagram:

apt—pat—tap
evil—live—veil—vile
aster—rates—resat—stare—tears

More interesting are the words that can be rearranged to form an appropriate phrase:

Can you decipher the following anagrams? The number of words in the solution is shown in brackets. Answers on page 120.

1	it ran (1)	11 seen as mist (1)	22 two plus eleven (3)
2	they see (2)	12 one is apart (1)	23 aim dot in place (3)
3	life's aim (1)	13 has to pilfer (2)	24 mystics in a heap (1)
4	is no meal (1)	14 a rope ends it (1)	25 no city dust here (2)
5	made sure (1)	15 tender names (1)	26 an evil soul's sin (1)
6	a grim era (1)	16 seems put out (1)	27 sit not at ale bars (2)
7	mad policy (1)	17 here come dots (3)	28 faces one at the end (4)
8	his set cry (1)	18 our men earn it (1)	29 calculating rules (2)
9	nine thumps (1)	19 restore plush (1)	30 this is meant as
10	court poser (1)	20 apt is the cure (1)	incentive (6)
		21 is not solaced (1)	

Longest anagrams

The longest scientific anagrams
cholecystoduodenostomy—duodenocholecystostomy—hydropneumopericardium
pneumohydropericardium each of 22 letters.

point—	on tip	Satan—	Santa
twinges—	we sting	united—	untied
waitress—	a stew, sir?	filled—	ill-fed
pittance—	a cent tip	funeral—	real fun
unadorned—	and/or nude	violence—	nice love
uniformity—	I form unity	festival—	evil fast
astronomer—	moon-starer	enormity—	more tiny
revolution—	love to ruin	infection—	fine tonic
misanthrope—	spare him not	militarism—	I limit arms
considerate—	care is noted	misfortune—	it's more fun
saintliness—	least in sins	evangelist—	evil's agent
measurements—	man uses meter	legislation—	is it legal? No
schoolmaster—	the classroom	commendation—	aim to condemn
presbyterian—	best in prayer	the man who laughs—	he's glum, won't ha-ha
alphabetically—	I play all the ABC	a picture of health—	oft pale, I ache, hurt
softheartedness—	often sheds tears		

Similarly, the letters of some phrases can be re-arranged to form a related phrase:

old England—	golden land
the Mona Lisa—	not hat, a smile
HMS Pinafore—	name for ship
slot machines—	cash lost in 'em
silver and gold—	grand old evils
radical reform—	rare mad frolic
a telephone girl—	repeating 'Hello'
the aristocracy—	a rich Tory caste
the nudist colony—	no untidy clothes
French revolution—	violence run forth
police protection—	let cop cope in riot

Rome was not built in a day—
any labour I do wants time

The US Library of Congress
— Its only for research bugs

circumstantial evidence
— actual crime isn't evinced

absence makes the heart grow fonder
— he wants back dearest gone from here

Some words and phrases form antigrams—anagrams that mean the opposite of the original word or phrase:

Anagrams of personal names were once thought to be an indication of character or destiny. Many apt or amusing phrases can be made by rearranging the letters that make up the names of famous people:

Madam Curie—	radium came
Adolf Hitler—	hated for ill
Ronald Reagan—	an oral danger
Indira Gandhi—	had Indian rig
Clint Eastwood—	Old West action
Mary Whitehouse—	I may rue the show
Margaret Thatcher—	that great charmer
Ralph Waldo Emerson—	person whom all read
William Shakespeare—	we all make his praise
Florence Nightingale—	flit on, cheering angel
Oliver Wendell Holmes—	he'll do in mellow verse
Dante Gabriel Rossetti—	greatest idealist born

William Ewart Gladstone—
we want a mild legislator

Henry Wadsworth Longfellow—
won half the New World's glory.

(From *Language on Vocation* by Dmitri A. Borgmann, published by Charles Scribner's Sons 1965.)

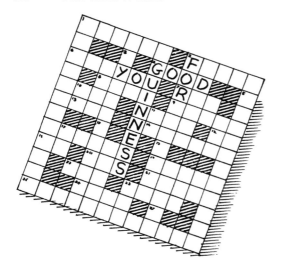

Crosswords

With at least one crossword puzzle in nearly every modern newspaper, not to mention the many specialized magazines and books that are now available, it is hard to believe that this immensely popular pastime is just over 100 years old. The earliest known crossword was a 9 by 9 Double Diamond published in St Nicholas for September 1875 in New York City. This was discovered by Dr Kenneth Miller of Newcastle-upon-Tyne, England, inventor of the colour crossword in 1983. The crossword evolved from the acrostic and word-square puzzles (described elsewhere in this chapter) of the 19th century: in 1913 the British-born journalist Arthur Wynne compiled for the New York *World* a diamond-shaped puzzle made up of interlocking words, with a blank space in the centre. During the following ten years the crossword developed into the now familiar format—a rectangular grid in which numbered interlocking words are separated by black or shaded squares—and became popular throughout the USA. By the mid-1920s the craze had reached Britain: the *Sunday Express* began publishing crosswords in 1924, and the *Sunday Times* and *Daily Telegraph* followed suit in 1925. The first crossword in *The Times*, however, did not appear until 1930.

The world's largest published crossword has been compiled in July 1982 by Robert Turcot of Québec, Canada. It comprised 82,951 squares, contained 12,489 clues across and 13,125 down and covered 38.28ft^2/3.55m^2.

The fastest recorded time for completing *The Times* crossword under test conditions is 3 min 45.0 sec by Roy Dean, 43, of Bromley, London in the BBC *Today* radio studio on 19 December 1970. Dr John Sykes won *The Times* championship 8 times between 1972 and 1985. The longest time obviously knows no bounds: in May 1966 *The Times* received a letter from a woman who had just completed crossword no. 673 in the issue of 4 April 1932.

Adrian Bell (1901–1980) of Barsham, Suffolk contributed a record 4520 crosswords to *The Times* from 2 January 1930 until his death. R. J. Baddock of Plymouth (b. 30 Oct 1894) has been a regular contributor to national newspapers since 13 August 1926. The most prolific compiler is Roger F. Squires of Ironbridge, Shropshire, who compiles

---

Answers to anagram quiz

1 train
2 the eyes
3 families
4 semolina
5 measured
6 marriage
7 diplomacy
8 hysterics
9 punishment
10 prosecutor
11 steaminess
12 separation
13 a shoplifter
14 desperation
15 endearments
16 tempestuous
17 the Morse Code
18 remuneration
19 upholsterers
20 therapeutics
21 disconsolate
22 one plus twelve
23 a decimal point
24 metaphysicians
25 the countryside
26 villainousness
27 total abstainers
28 a sentence of death
29 integral calculus
30 a stitch in time saves nine.

Can you solve the following clues? The number of letters in the answer is shown in brackets. Answers on page 122.

1 Delay departure from Berlin, Germany. (6)
2 Gormless mountain terrier. (5)
3 Rebuke for being concealed in church. (5)
4 Snakes, perhaps, in the vines. (8)
5 This red ghost may be somewhat limited in its outlook. (5-7)
6 The fireplace is enormous, we hear. (5)
7 A minor prize. (5)
8 Popular detectives hold book back. (7)
9 It gives others a right to begin again. (7)
10 Comes to mind at first light. (5)

35 published puzzles single-handedly each week. His total output to August 1987 was over 29,000.

Crossword clues may be straightforward definitions, questions based on general knowledge, or cryptic riddles. Cryptic clues are probably the most popular, the most challenging, and the most satisfying to solve. These usually contain a clue to the whole word together with an anagram or other puzzle from which the letters or syllables of the word can be derived. Individual words within the clue are intended to mislead those who are unfamiliar with crossword-solving conventions: *the French* may mean 'le', 'la', or 'les'; *flower* may mean 'river'; *note* may indicate the letters A, B, C, D, E, F, or G; *round* or *circle* may indicate the letter O. An anagram is usually suggested by such words as *confused*, *upset*, *mixture*, *different*, *reformed*, etc. Abbreviations, such as *Dr*, *St*, *BA*, *US*, etc., are often used.

Here are some examples, with an explanation of the solution where necessary:

No suet needed for this London concoction.
EUSTON (an anagram of *no suet*)

One doesn't have to have them.

NEEDS
Many a pile is not expensive.
CHEAP (*C*, representing 100 (many), and *heap*)

Note on alternative to dat belt—lovers exchange them.
FOND EMBRACES (*F* (note), *on*, and *dem braces*)

Mental exercise not associated with Henry VIII.
THINKING (Henry VIII was not a *thin king*)

I shout in class, without qualification.
CATEGORICALLY (*I call* in *category*)

Sounds as if it goes on and on at the breakfast table.
CEREAL (a pun on *serial*)

A city in Czechoslovakia.
OSLO (hidden in Czechoslovakia)

Look back! Study hours are past.
OLDEN TIMES (*lo* (reversed), *den* (study), and *times*)

Having sampled army life I left and joined up.
SOLDERED (the letter *I* is dropped from *soldiered*)

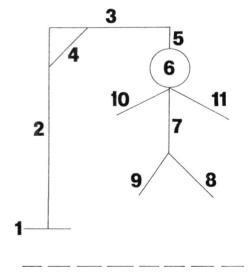

Hangman

Hangman is a popular children's game that can also be enjoyed by adults. The first player, the 'hangman', chooses a word (or a phrase, such as the title of a book, play, film, or television programme, or the name of a famous person) and indicates the number of letters (and spaces, if necessary) with dashes. The other player calls out letters one by one, in any order. Letters that occur in the mystery word or phrase are written over the appropriate dashes; for each incorrect guess a line is added to the gallows, which is usually built up in 11 stages as shown below. The object of the game is to identify the word or phrase before the drawing is completed.

Palindromes

A palindrome is a word, phrase, or sentence that reads the same backwards as forwards. The word **level** is a palindrome, as is Napoleon's apocryphal remark **able was I ere I saw Elba**.

The earliest palindromes were devised by the ancient Greeks: the Greek inscription NIΨON ANOMHMATA MH MONAN OΨIN, a 25-letter palindrome meaning 'wash my sins, not only my face', appears on baptismal fonts in Greece, Turkey, and France, and in a number of English churches, such as St Mary's at Nottingham and St Paul's at Woldingham in Surrey. The first English palindrome was devised by John Taylor in the early 17th century: **Lewd did I live, & evil I did dwel**. This has since been modified in accordance with modern English spelling: **Evil I did dwell; lewd did I live**.

Nun, **ewe**, and **pip** are some of the shortest palindromic words. The longest in the English language is **redivider** (nine letters), the contrived chemical term **detartrated** (eleven letters) being disqualified on the grounds of questionable authenticity. **Kanakanak**, another nine-letter palindrome, is the name of a place in Alaska; **Malayalam** is the language of Kerala in southwest India. The longest known palindromic word in any language is **saippuakivikauppias** (19 letters), which means 'a dealer in lye (caustic soda)' in Finnish. Other English palindromes include **did**, **gag**, **mum**, **deed**, **noon**, **peep**, **minim**, **kayak**, **sexes**, **repaper**, **deified**, and **rotator**.

The creation of palindromic sentences is a more demanding exercise. The longest palindromic composition is one of 66,666 words by Edward Berbow, completed in April 1987. It begins 'Al, sign it, "Lover"! . . .' and hence predictably ends '. . . revolting, Isla.' The longest palindromic novel,

Dr Awkward and Olson in Oslo, contains 31,594 words and was written by Lawrence Levine in 1986. Other less ambitious palindromic compositions include the famous introduction in the Garden of Eden, **Madam, I'm Adam** and **Egad! A base tone denotes a bad age**, attributed to the composer Henry Purcell as well as **Dennis sinned**, which can be expanded to **Dennis and Edna sinned** or **Dennis, Nell, Edna, Leon, Noel, and Ellen sinned** and . . .

God! a dog!

I moan, Naomi.

Sad? I'm Midas.

Draw, O coward!

Step on no pets.

Live not on evil.

Sex at noon taxes.

Never odd or even.

'Tis Ivan, on a visit.

Pull up if I pull up.

No, it is opposition.

Niagara, O roar again!

Yawn a more Roman way.

Deer frisk, sir, freed.

Nurse, I spy gypsies, run!

Was it a car or a cat I saw?

Lew, Otto has a hot towel.

A man, a plan, a canal—Panama.

Was it Eliot's toilet I saw?

Ten animals I slam in a net.

Some men interpret nine memos.

Answers to crossword quiz

1 LINGER (hidden in Ber*lin*, *Ger*many)
2 CAIRN (the syllable *gorm* is dropped from the Cairngorm Mountains)
3 CHIDE (*hid* in *CE*, an abbreviation of Church of England)
4 CREEPERS
5 SHORT-SIGHTED (anagram of *this red ghost*)
6 GRATE (a pun on *great*)
7 AWARD (*a ward* is a minor)
8 DEMOTIC (*tome* in *CID*, reversed)
9 RESTART (*rest* (others), *a*, and *rt* (an abbreviation of *right*))
10 DAWNS

DOUBLETS

In 1878 the writer Lewis Carroll invented the doublet, a puzzle in which a word is changed, letter by letter, into another word of the same length, such as:

HEAD—heal—teal—tell—tall—TAIL

Each link in the chain must be a word in its own right, and the words at either end are usually related, similar, or opposite in meaning. The object is to complete the transformation in as few steps as possible. The game is now known by a variety of other names, such as *Word ladders*, *Word chains*, *Transitions*, *Transformations*, *Laddergrams*, and *Stepwords*.

Here are some more examples:

CAT—cot—dot—DOG
MAT—rat—rut—RUG
MORE—lore—lose—loss—LESS
HATE—have—wave—wove—LOVE
APE—apt—opt—sat—mat—MAN
WORD—woad—road—read—dead—DEED
PITCH—pinch—winch—wench—tench—tenth—TENTS
SLEEP—sheep—cheep—creep—creek—creak—cream—DREAM
ONE—owe—ewe—eye—dye—doe—toe—too—TWO
VERB—herb—hers—hews—sews—sows—sods—nods—nous—NOUN

Can you complete the following doublets in fewer than ten steps? Answers on page 124.

1 PIG → STY
2 FLOUR → BREAD
3 FISH → MEAT
4 HAND → FOOT

5 RICH → POOR
6 COAL → MINE
7 TEARS → SMILE

8 LIVE → DEAD
9 ELM → OAK
10 BLACK → WHITE

Kay, a red nude, peeped under a yak.

Sums are not set as a test on Erasmus.

Satan, oscillate my metallic sonatas.

Marge lets Norah see Sharon's telegram.

Now, Ned, I am a maiden nun; Ned, I am a maiden won.

Straw? No, too stupid a fad. I put soot on warts.

A new order began, a more Roman age bred Rowena.

Are we not drawn onward, we few, drawn onward to new era?

Doc, note. I dissent. A fast never prevents a fatness. I diet on cod.

Variants of the palindrome include words composed of symmetrical letters, such as HOW, MIX, TOMATO, etc., and sentences in which individual words (rather than letters) are symmetrically arranged, such as:

You can cage a swallow, can't you, but you can't swallow a cage, can you?

Bores are people that say that people are bores.

Does milk machinery milk does?

Pangrams

A pangram is a meaningful sentence of minimal length that includes all the letters of the alphabet. Several 26-letter pangrams have been suggested, all of which contain obscure words, abbreviations, initials, or Roman numerals. Michael Jones of Chicago compiled a pangram to describe the situation in which a wryneck woodpecker from the grasslands of Africa climbs up the side of a male bovid which is grazing on sacred Muslim-owned land:

Veldt jynx grimps waqf zho buck.

Other examples include:

Mr Jock, TV quiz PhD, bags few lynx.
J.Q. Schwartz flung D.V. Pike my box.
Blowzy night-frumps vex'd Jack Q.
XV quick nymphs beg fjord waltz.

The shortest pangrams that do not make use of obscure words, initials, etc., are *waltz, nymph, for quick jigs vex Bud* (28 letters) and *quick wafting zephyrs vex bold Jim* (29 letters). The exclusion of proper nouns brings the minimum length to 30 letters: *how quickly daft jumping zebras vex.*
Others in ascending order, include:

Jackdaws love my big sphinx of quartz (31 letters)
Pack my box with five dozen liquor jugs (33 letters)
A quick brown fox jumps over the lazy dog. (33 letters)
Xylophone wizard begets quick jive form. (34 letters)
By Jove, my quick study of lexicography won a prize. (41 letters)
Sexy zebras just prowl and vie for quick hot matings. (43 letters)
Six plump boys guzzled cheap raw vodka quite joyfully. (45 letters)

Pangrams are also found in works of literature. In the following lines from Milton's *Paradise Lost* the passage from *grazed* to *both* is a pangram:

Likening his Maker to the grazed ox,
Jehovah, who, in one night, when he passed
From Egypt marching, equalled with one stroke
Both her first-born and all her bleating gods.

Shakespeare's *Coriolanus* contains an imperfect pangram, lacking the letter *z*:

O! a kiss
Long as my exile, sweet as my revenge!
Now, by the jealous queen of heaven, that kiss
I carried from thee, dear, and my true lip
Hath virgin'd it e'er since.

Another imperfect pangram, in which the letter *j* is missing, occurs in the Authorized Version of the Bible (Ezra 7:21):

And I, even I Artaxerxes the king, do make a decree to all the treasurers which are beyond the river, that whatsoever Ezra the priest, the scribe of the law of the God of heaven, shall require of you, it be done speedily.

Puns

A pun is a play on words, especially words that sound the same (or similar) but have different meanings:

It must be raining cats and dogs—I just stepped on a poodle.
We call our local pub 'The Fiddle' because it's such a vile inn.
A bigamist is one who has loved not wisely but two well.

Often described as the lowest form of wit, puns are usually greeted with groans rather than laughter—the louder the groan, the better the pun. They range from the obscene (and unprintable) to the intellectual: Sir Charles Napier is supposed to have announced his conquest of Sind (in Pakistan) with the Latin word *peccavi*, meaning 'I have sinned'.

Answers to doublets quiz

1 PIG—wig—wag—way—say—STY.
2 FLOUR—floor—flood—blood—brood—broad—BREAD.
3 FISH—fist—list—lest—best—beat—MEAT.
4 HAND—hard—lard—lord—ford—fort—FOOT.
5 RICH—rick—rock—rook—book—boor—POOR.
6 COAL—coat—moat—most—mist—mint—MINE.
7 TEARS—sears—stars—stare—stale—stile—SMILE.
8 LIVE—line—lint—lent—lend—lead—DEAD.
9 ELM—ell—eel—bel—bed—bad—bar—oar—OAK.
10 BLACK—slack—stack—stalk—stale—shale—whale—while—WHITE.

Puns are encountered in the playground, in the pub, at parties, in everyday conversation, and even in works of literature, such as Thomas Hood's poem *Faithless Sally Brown*:

His death, which happen'd in his berth
At forty-odd befell:
They went and told the sexton, and
The sexton toll'd the bell.

Shakespeare made frequent use of puns in his plays, as in the following quotation from *Macbeth* (Act 2, Scene 2):

If he do bleed
I'll gild the faces of the grooms withal
For it must seem their guilt.

Puns are the basis of many question-and-answer jokes:

'What's black, white, and red all over?'
'A newspaper.'

'How does an Eskimo build his house?'
'Igloos it together.'

'What did the grape say when the elephant stepped on it?'
'Nothing. It just gave a little whine.'

'Where is Felixstowe?'
'On Felix's foot.'

'Why are there no aspirins in the jungle?'
'Because the paracetamol.'

'Why is the desert a good place for a picnic?'
'Because of the sand which is there.'

'My wife's gone to the West Indies.'
'Jamaica?'
'No, she went of her own accord.'

'Knock, knock!'
'Who's there?'
'Dave.'
'Dave who?'
'Dave locked me out again.'

There are many variations of the last example, using personal names and other nouns:

'Knock, knock!'
'Who's there?'
'Sarah.'
'Sarah who?'
'Sarah doctor in the house?'

'... Ken ... Ken I come in?'
'... Lydia ... Lydia dustbin's fallen off.'
'... Howard ... Howard you like a punch on the nose?'
'... Sonia ... Sonia shoulder and it's horrible!'
'... Adam ... Adam up and tell me the answer.'
'... Sheila ... Sheila peer in a minute.'
'... Fred ... Fred I can't tell you.'
'... Lettuce ... Lettuce in and you'll find out.'
'... Ammonia ... Ammonia little boy and I can't reach the doorbell.'

A number of games and puzzles are based on puns. One of these involves the invention of adverbial puns:

'I got the first three wrong,' she said forthrightly.
'That's an enormous shark,' said the captain superficially.
'I haven't got any apples,' said Jane fruitlessly.
'I've burnt the sausages,' he said with panache.
'Drop that gun!' said the policeman disarmingly.

Another involves the invention of imaginary authors and the titles of their books:

Continental Breakfast by Roland Coffy.
The White Cliffs by Eileen Dover.
Under Arrest by Watts E. Dunn.
Cutting It Fine by Moses Lawn.
The Boy Soprano by Topsy Sharp.
Philosophy for Beginners by Ivan I. Dear.
Rain on the Carpet by Rufus Quick.
Crime Pays by Robin Banks.
Blood on the Coffin by Horace Tory.
The Dentist at Work by Phil Macavity.
Prehistoric Animals by Dinah Saur and Terry Dactyl.
At the Eleventh Hour by Justin Time.

Another involves the suggestion of appropriate verbs for the dismissal of various people:

A writer is described.
A hairdresser is distressed.
A model is deposed.
A musician is disconcerted.
A tailor is unsuited.
A wine merchant is deported.
A magician is disillusioned.
A chiropodist is defeated.
A salesman is disordered.
A prisoner is excelled.

Rebus

In a rebus letters, numbers, symbols, or pictures are used to represent the sources of missing words or syllables. The well-known abbreviation **IOU**, meaning 'I owe you', is a rebus. Picture rebuses, of which Egyptian hieroglyphics were early examples, are often found in puzzle books for children; they are also used in heraldic devices. Rebuses composed of letters and numbers vary in complexity for the single word (**MT =**

P E	peony
CC ing	seasoning
once 22 7	once upon a time (twenty to seven)
fecItion	eye infection
sta4nce	for instance
what4RU	what are you standing around 4?
paid I'm worked	I'm overworked and underpaid
u n	undivided
ban ana	banana split
gener ation	generation gap
b e d	bedspread
pPPod	two peas in a pod
potOOOOOOOO	potatoes
ehca	backache
geg	scrambled egg
CRea...	vanishing cream
m a n	the descent of man
XQQ	excuse

empty) to phrases (**T42** = tea for two), sentences (**UR2 good 2 me 2B4 got N** = you are too good to me to be forgotten), and rhymes:

YYUR	Too wise you are,
YYUB	Too wise you be,
ICUR	I see you are
YY4 me	Too wise for me.

The following rebus, which dates back to the 19th century, makes use of the punctuation marks:

If the B MT put:
If the B. putting:
If the grate be [great B] empty, put coal on;
If the grate be full, stop putting coal on.

Other single-word rebuses include:

B4	before
DK	decay
FEG	effigy
MN8	emanate
NE1	anyone
NME	enemy
S	largesse
XLNC	excellency

More ingenious are the rebuses in which the position of the letters or words is part of the solution:

Slips of the tongue

MALAPROPISMS

A malapropism is a word that sounds similar to another and is wrongly used in its place: **prostrate** for **prostate**, **facilities** for **faculties**, **computer** for **commuter**, etc. Such confusion usually arises from an attempt to impress others with long words or scientific terminology and often results in unintentional humour. These verbal blunders are named after Mrs Malaprop, a character in Sheridan's play *The Rivals* (1775), who uttered such lines as:

Illiterate him, I say, quite from your memory.

He is the very pineapple of politeness!

If I reprehend any thing in this world, it is the use of my oracular tongue, and a nice derangement of epitaphs!

She's as headstrong as an allegory on the banks of the Nile.

More than 150 years earlier, however, Shakespeare had endowed Dogberry, a character in *Much Ado About Nothing*, with a similar tendency to misuse the English language:

You are thought here to be the most senseless and fit man for the constable of the watch.

You shall comprehend all vagrom men.

For the watch to babble and to talk is most tolerable and not to be endured.

Comparisons are odorous.

Words to show off

At times we all like to display our great knowledge . . . or cover up our lack of such knowledge . . . by using vogue words. Here is the famous 'buzz-phrase' generator devised in the Canadian Defense Department a few years ago. Its aim is to provide 'instant expertise' on defence matters and to impart 'that proper ring of decisive, progressive, knowledgeable authority'. Choose any three-digit number, and take the word from each column to form your own buzz phrase.

Column 1	Column 2	Column 3
0 integrated	0 management	0 options
1 overall	1 organizational	1 flexibility
2 systematized	2 monitored	2 capability
3 parallel	3 reciprocal	3 mobility
4 functional	4 digital	4 programming
5 responsive	5 logistical	5 concept
6 optimal	6 transitional	6 time-phase
7 synchronized	7 incremental	7 projection
8 compatible	8 third-generation	8 hardware
9 balanced	9 policy	9 contingency

Choose 000 and you have *integrated management options*; 491, *functional policy flexibility*; 754, *synchronized logistical programming*. Choose whatever numbers you like and the result will be a phrase that sounds very impressive but in reality means little.

An interesting variant is to include additional new 'buzz words', e.g. in column 1 *ongoing*, *prestigious*, or *viable* and in column 3 *dialogue*, *environment*, *interface*, or *parameter*.

Malapropisms abound in everyday language:

Under the affluence of alcohol.

The answer is in the infirmary.

Are you casting nasturtiums?

They severed his juggler vein.

It's good to be back on terracotta.

Have you met my daughter's fiasco?

He used biceps to deliver the baby.

I'm not enamelled of the colour scheme.

She was riding on the pavilion of her boyfriend's motorbike.

Her husband has had a vivisection.

The government is totally incontinent.

Several villages are now in Afghan hounds.

Let's get down to brass facts.

His father's a wealthy typhoon.

All our efforts have been fertile.

White as the dripping snow.

You could have knocked me over with a fender.

The feeling is neutral.

You have to get things in prospectus.

The agnostics in the church are very poor.

Some malapropisms are the result of mishearing or misunderstanding, such as the taxi driver who was sent to collect **Thor Heyerdahl** and expected to find **four Airedales**, the typist who replaced **triennial balance sheet** with **try any old balance sheet**, the bookshop customer in search of **Spycatcher in the Rye**, and the child who transformed **the Pulitzer prize** into **the pullet surprise**. Lines from songs, hymns, and prayers can also cause confusion:

your walrus hurt the one you love.
you always hurt the one you love.
give our strength to Percy Vere.
give us strength to persevere.

SPOONERISMS

The term *spoonerism* refers to the accidental or deliberate transposition of the initial letters or syllables of words, such as **dressed of chores** for **chest of drawers**, **roaring with pain** for **pouring with rain**, **a homely state** for **a stately home**, and **a tireless tube** for **a tubeless tyre**.

The spoonerism is named after the Reverend

William Archibald Spooner (1844–1930), Warden of New College, Oxford, to whom numerous examples are attributed. Most of these are now believed to be apocryphal:

a half-warmed fish

a well-boiled icicle

a blushing crow

the queer old dean

in a dark, glassly

Kinquering Congs Their Titles Take

The Lord is a shoving leopard

You have hissed my mystery lectures.

You have tasted a whole worm.

You were fighting a liar in the quadrangle.

You will leave by the next town drain.

The cat popped on its drawers.

Is the bean dizzy?

Please sew me to another sheet.

The weight of rages will press harder and harder upon the employer.

Many riddles are based on spoonerisms:

What is the difference between an ornithologist and a bad speller?
One watches birds and the other botches words.

What is the difference between a thin woman and a sherry trifle?
One has a tiny waist and the other has a winy taste.

What is the difference between manhood and deadlock?
One is the male state and the other is a stalemate.

Tongue-twisters

A tongue-twister is a phrase, sentence, or rhyme that is difficult to say because it contains many similar sounds: *the sixth sick sheik's sixth sheep's sick*. The object is to repeat it as many times as possible, as quickly as possible, without mispronunciation. Tongue-twisters are used as an elocution exercise, in speech therapy, as a test of sobriety, and in party games. Here are some of the best-known:

Greek grapes.

Knapsack strap.

Lemon liniment.

Mixed biscuits.

Preshrunk shirts.

Red lorry, yellow lorry.

Six slim slender saplings.

A proper copper coffee pot.

A dozen double damask dinner napkins.

A truly rural frugal ruler's mural.

Some shun sunshine.

The sinking steamer sank.

The Leith police dismisseth us.

Whistle for the thistle sifter.

Freddy thrush flies through thick fog.

Sister Susie's sewing shirts for soldiers.

That bloke's back brake-block broke.

The mink mixed a medicinal mixture.

Around the rugged rocks the ragged rascal ran.

Sinful Caesar sipped his snifter, seized his knees, and sneezed.

How much wood would a woodchuck chuck
If a woodchuck could chuck wood?

Peter Piper picked a peck of pickled pepper;
Where's the peck of pickled pepper Peter Piper picked?

She sells seashells on the seashore;
The shells she sells are seashells, I'm sure.

There's no need to light a night-light
On a light night like tonight.

Three grey geese in the green grass grazing;
Grey were the geese and green was the grazing.

Word squares

A word square is composed of words of equal length that read the same across as down:

```
L A N E     M I L E     O P A L
A R E A     I R I S     P I N E
N E A R     L I M P     A N O N
E A R S     E S P Y     L E N S
```

Word squares containing words of five letters or less are fairly easy to devise:

A	T O	S A D	P A I L	M E R I T
	O N	A L E	A P S E	E V A D E
		D E N	I S L E	R A Z O R
			L E E K	I D O L S
				T E R S E

For six-, seven-, and eight-letter word squares it is sometimes necessary to introduce proper nouns:

C I R C L E	P R E P A R E	C A P I T A T E
I C A R U S	R E M O D E L	A N E M O N E S
R A R E S T	E M U L A T E	P E P P I E S T
C R E A T E	P O L E M I C	I M P O L I T E
L U S T R E	A D A M A N T	T O I L E T T E
E S T E E M	R E T I N U E	A N E I T Y U M*
	E L E C T E D	T E S T T U B E
		E S T E E M E D

Word squares of nine or ten letters cannot be compiled (or deciphered) without recourse to a comprehensive reference library:

Q U A R E L E S T	O R A N G U T A N G
U P P E R E S T E	R A N G A R A N G A
A P P O I N T E R	A N D O L A N D O L
R E O M E T E R S	N G O T A N G O T A
E R I E V I L L E	G A L A N G A L A N
L E N T I L L I N	U R A N G U T A N G
E S T E L L I N E	T A N G A T A N G A
S T E R L I N G S	A N D O L A N D O L
T E R S E N E S S	N G O T A N G O T A
	G A L A N G A L A N

One of the earliest known word squares was inscribed by the Romans at Cirencester and elsewhere. Dating from the 1st century, it is an ingenious combination of acrostic, anagram, palindrome, and word square:

S A T O R
A R E P O
T E N E T
O P E R A
R O T A S

*(An island in the New Hebrides)

The five words make up the palindromic Latin sentence **sator Arepo tenet opera rotas**, which may be translated as 'the sower, Arepo, guides the wheels with care'. The letters of the sentence can be rearranged to form the prayer *oro te, Pater; oro to, Pater; sanas*, meaning 'I pray to thee, Father; I pray to thee, Father; thou healest'.

In the 19th century word-square puzzles became popular:

1	Great happiness	B L I S S
2	A meal	L U N C H
3	To bury	I N T E R
4	Part of a play	S C E N E
5	An animal	S H R E W

The name of an insect my *first*,	G N A T
My *second* no doubt you possess,	N A M E
My *third* is my second transposed,	A M E N
And my *fourth* is a shelter, I guess.	T E N T

There are numerous variants of the simple word square. In a *double word square* the horizontal and vertical words are different:

O R A L
M A R E
E V E N
N E A T

In a *half word square* the words are of decreasing length:

P A R R O T
A L O O F
R O O T
R O T
O F
T

In a *diamond word square* the words form a diamond shape:

L
S E T
S C O R E
L E O P A R D
T R A C E
E R E
D

WORDMASTERY

The words listed below appear in most of the major English dictionaries and occur more or less regularly in speech and writing. But do you know what they mean? Test your wordmastery by deciding which definition, (a), (b), or (c), is closest in sense to the key word. Answers on page 133.

Acclivity (a) a tendency; (b) an upward slope; (c) weather conditions.

Agoraphobia a fear of (a) heights; (b) foreigners; (c) open spaces.

Analogous (a) identical; (b) traditional; (c) corresponding.

Anemometer an instrument for measuring (a) wind; (b) humidity; (c) light.

Archipelago (a) the leader of a tribe; (b) a group of islands; (c) a prehistoric bird.

Armistice (a) a truce; (b) a memorial service; (c) a place where weapons are stored.

Arrogate (a) to claim unduly; (b) to abolish totally; (c) to increase rapidly.

Asinine (a) having a bitter taste; (b) hostile; (c) stupid.

Atrophy (a) idleness; (b) wasting away; (c) a poison.

Attenuate (a) to explain; (b) to develop; (c) to weaken.

Biennial (a) twice a year; (b) every two years; (c) two-hundredth.

Cacography (a) graffiti; (b) bad handwriting; (c) discordant sound.

Campanology (a) stamp-collecting; (b) bell-ringing; (c) flower-arranging.

Catharsis (a) purgation; (b) ecstasy; (c) disappointment.

Caveat (a) a contract; (b) a punishment; (c) a warning.

Complaisant (a) obliging; (b) smug; (c) discontented.

Coruscate (a) to wrinkle; (b) to scold; (c) to sparkle.

Crepuscular (a) stealthy; (b) very ugly; (c) dim.

Culpable (a) obvious; (b) blameworthy; (c) easy to cut.

Desultory (a) unmethodical; (b) impatient; (c) becoming humid.

Discomfit (a) to disconcert; (b) to distract; (c) to distress.

Eclectic (a) intermittent; (b) from various sources; (c) of a religious cult.

Egregious (a) servile; (b) loyal; (c) shocking.

Endemic (a) inevitable; (b) highly contagious; (c) occurring in a particular place.

Enervate (a) to invigorate; (b) to make nervous; (c) to weaken.

Entomology the study of (a) insects; (b) word origins; (c) gastric disorders.

Entrophy (a) cowardice; (b) disorder; (c) motivation.

Esoteric (a) showing a vivid imagination; (b) only for the initiated; (c) of an unusual design.

Eugenics (a) harmonious sounds; (b) physical exercises; (c) selective breeding.

Exiguous (a) scanty; (b) meaningless; (c) urgent.

Extirpate (a) to destroy; (b) to accomplish; (c) to depart.

Farrago (a) a wagon; (b) a mixture; (c) a disaster.

Filibuster (a) delaying tactics; (b) upholstery padding; (c) a medieval weapon.

Fiscal relating to (a) commerce; (b) parliament; (c) taxation.

Friable (a) withstanding heat; (b) easily crumbled; (c) lacking confidence.

Froward (a) temperamental; (c) impertinent; (c) contrary.

Fructify (a) to make productive; (b) to harvest; (c) to nourish.

Fulsome (a) sincere; (b) excessive; (c) attractive.

Garrulous (a) incoherent; (b) friendly; (c) talkative.

Gregarious (a) promiscuous; (b) sociable; (c) disorganized.

Gustatory relating to (a) enthusiasm; (b) taste; (c) wind.

Hedonism (a) a linguistic device; (b) religious discrimination; (c) the pursuit of pleasure.

Heuristic (a) proceeding by trial and error; (b) conducive to happiness; (c) relating to time.

Immolate (a) to praise highly; (b) to fill a dental cavity; (c) to kill as a sacrifice.

Incipient (a) beginning; (b) receiving; (c) unavoidable.

Incumbent (a) awkward; (b) obligatory; (c) twisted.

Indict (a) to object; (b) to reveal; (c) to accuse.

Internecine (a) universal; (b) between families; (c) mutually destructive.

Jejune (a) indigestible; (b) puerile; (c) occult.

Karma (a) destiny; (b) prayer; (c) peace.

Leach (a) to percolate; (b) to steal; (c) to dye.

Lesion (a) relaxation; (b) an injury; (c) a ban.

Lucubration (a) nocturnal study; (b) artificial light; (c) profitable work.

Mandible (a) the handle of a tool; (b) an ecclesiastical vestment; (c) part of the jaw.

Meretricious (a) praiseworthy; (b) tawdry; (c) dishonest.

Mitigate (a) to justify; (b) to alleviate; (c) to protest.

Moratorium (a) a postponement; (b) an investigation; (c) a funeral march.

Mutation (a) agreement; (b) silence; (c) change.

Nadir (a) the highest point; (b) the lowest point; (c) the centre.

Nemesis (a) retribution; (b) reincarnation; (c) decay.

Nodule (a) a hook; (b) a structural part; (c) a small lump.

Noisome (a) boring; (b) harmful; (c) loud.

Nous (a) information; (b) reason; (c) companionship.

Numismatist a person who collects (a) bottles; (b) postcards; (c) coins.

Obsolescent (a) using offensive language; (b) being an overweight teenager; (c) becoming out of date.

Occidental (a) of the west; (b) of the north; (c) of the south.

Occlude (a) to disguise; (b) to obstruct; (c) to subtract.

Oenophile (a) a wine connoisseur; (b) a cat lover; (c) a small bottle.

Ontological relating to (a) the nature of being; (b) extrasensory perception; (c) the behaviour of dolphins.

Panegyric (a) a satirical poem; (b) a musical composition; (c) a speech of praise.

Peripatetic (a) teaching music; (b) travelling from place to place; (c) moving in a circle.

Plenary (a) abundant; (b) administrative; (c) complete.

Polemic (a) controversial; (b) extreme; (c) moderate.

Polyp (a) a rock formation; (b) a small tumour; (c) part of a plant.

Potable (a) not drinkable; (b) drinkable; (c) suitable for cooking.

Pragmatic (a) optimistic; (b) practical; (c) dictatorial.

Prolix (a) long-winded; (b) inclined; (c) favourable.

Putative (a) advisable; (b) accusatory; (c) supposed.

Querulous (a) complaining; (b) inquisitive; (c) disputatious.

Rapacity (a) greed; (b) haste; (c) severity.

Reactionary a person who (a) has radical views; (b) opposes change; (c) is easily angered.

Recalcitrant (a) apologetic; (b) submissive; (c) resisting authority.

Restive (a) restful; (b) restless; (c) resting.

Salubrious (a) obscene; (b) luxurious; (c) healthy.

Scatology the study of (a) excrement; (b) swords; (c) jazz.

Scrofula (a) a flowering plant; (b) an ancient parchment; (c) a glandular disease.

Severance (a) variety; (b) harshness; (c) separation.

Solecism (a) a verbal blunder; (b) sun worship; (c) selfishness.

Sophism (a) civilized behaviour; (b) a misleading argument; (c) a complex system.

Specious (a) deceptively plausible; (b) outstanding; (c) of various kinds.

Stevedore (a) a dock worker; (b) a bullfighter's assistant; (c) a tropical fish.

Suborn (a) to bribe; (b) to undermine; (c) to dominate.

Terpsichorean relating to (a) singing; (b) dancing; (c) acting.

Thespian relating to (a) singing; (b) dancing; (c) acting.

Tintinnabulation (a) endless repetition; (b) a rattling noise; (c) the ringing of bells.

Ubiquitous (a) broad-minded; (b) everywhere at once; (c) omnipotent.

Unexceptionable (a) ordinary; (b) beyond criticism; (c) impartial.

Urbane (a) of the town; (b) of the country; (c) suave.

Usurious (a) exorbitant; (b) lacking authority; (c) difficult to operate.

Uxorial (a) of farm animals; (b) of a manor; (c) of a wife.

Valetudinarian (a) a charity worker; (b) a hypochondriac; (c) a retired officer.

Verdant (a) green; (b) marginal; (c) new.

Vitiate (a) to strengthen; (b) to make ineffective; (c) to authorize.

Votary (a) an idol; (b) an official; (c) an advocate.

Whiffle (a) to smooth; (b) to sell cheaply; (c) to vacillate.

Xenophobia a fear of (a) foreigners; (b) height; (c) open spaces.

Yarmulke (a) a skullcap worn by Jews; (b) an African hunting spear; (c) a cheese made with goats' milk.

Zymotic (a) organically produced; (b) relating to fermentation; (c) of tropical origin.

Answers to wordmastery quiz on page 130.

Acclivity (b) from the Latin *acclivis*, meaning 'ascending'.

Agoraphobia (c) from the Greek *agora*, meaning 'market-place', and *phobos*, meaning 'fear'.

Analogous (c) from the Greek *analogos*, meaning 'proportionate'.

Anemometer (a) from the Greek *anemos*, meaning 'wind', and *metron*, meaning 'measure'.

Archipelago (b) from the Greek *arkhos*, meaning 'chief', and *pelagos*, meaning 'sea'.

Armistice (a) from the Latin *arma*, meaning 'arms', and *sistere*, meaning 'to stop'.

Arrogate (a) from the Latin *rogare*, meaning 'to ask'.

Asinine (c) from the Latin *asininus*, meaning 'like an ass'.

Atrophy (b) from the Greek *atrophos*, meaning 'ill-fed'.

Attenuate (c) from the Latin *attenuare*, meaning 'to make thin'.

Biennial (b) from the Latin *bi-*, meaning 'two', and *annus*, meaning 'year'.

Cacography (b) from the Greek *kakos*, meaning 'bad', and *graphein*, meaning 'to write'.

Campanology (b) from the Latin *campana*, meaning 'bell', and the Greek *logos*, meaning 'word'.

Catharsis (a) from the Greek *kathairein*, meaning 'to purge'.

Caveat (c) from the Latin *cavēre*, meaning 'to beware'.

Complaisant (a) from the Latin *complacēre*, meaning 'to please greatly'.

Coruscate (c) from the Latin *coruscare*, meaning 'to glitter'.

Crepuscular (c) from the Latin *crepusculum*, meaning 'twilight'.

Culpable (b) from the Latin *culpare*, meaning 'to blame'.

Desultory (a) from the Latin *desultorius*, meaning 'superficial'.

Discomfit (a) from the Old French *desconfire*, meaning 'to destroy'.

Eclectic (b) from the Greek *eklegein*, meaning 'to select'.

Egregious (c) from the Latin *egregius*, meaning 'distinguished'.

Endemic (c) from the Greek *endēmos*, meaning 'native'.

Enervate (c) from the Latin *enervare*, meaning 'to remove the sinews'.

Entomology (a) from the Greek *entomon*, meaning 'insect', and *logos*, meaning 'word'.

Entropy (b) from the Greek *tropos*, meaning 'a turn'.

Esoteric (b) from the Greek *esōterō*, meaning 'inner'.

Eugenics (c) from the Greek *eugenēs*, meaning 'wellborn'.

Exiguous (a) from the Latin *exigere*, meaning 'to weigh out'.

Extirpate (a) from the Latin *exstirpare*, meaning 'to root out'.

Farrago (b) from the Latin *farrago*, meaning 'mixed fodder'.

Filibuster (a) from the Spanish *filibustero*, meaning 'freebooter'.

Fiscal (c) from the Latin *fiscus*, meaning 'treasury'.

Friable (b) from the Latin *friare*, meaning 'to crumble'.

Froward (c) from the Middle English *froward*, meaning 'turned away'.

Fructify (a) from the Latin *fructificare*, meaning 'to bear fruit'.

Fulsome (b) from the Middle English *fulsom*, meaning 'copious'.

Garrulous (c) from the Latin *garrire*, meaning 'to chatter'.

Gregarious (b) from the Latin *gregarius*, meaning 'of a flock'.

Gustatory (b) from the Latin *gustare*, meaning 'to taste'.

Hedonism (c) from the Greek *hēdonē*, meaning 'pleasure'.

Heuristic (a) from the Greek *heuriskein*, meaning 'to discover'.

Immolate (c) from the Latin *immolāre*, meaning 'to sacrifice'.

Incipient (a) from the Latin *incipere*, meaning 'to begin'.

Incumbent (b) from the Latin *incumbere*, meaning 'to lie on'.

Indict (c) from the Latin *indicere*, meaning 'to declare'.

Internecine (c) from the Latin *internecinus*, meaning 'deadly'.

Jejune (b) from the Latin *jejunus*, meaning 'empty'.

Karma (a) from the Sanskrit *karma*, meaning 'action'.

Leach (a) from the Old English *leccan*, meaning 'to wet'.

Lesion (b) from the Latin *laedere*, meaning 'to injure'.

Lucubration (a) from the Latin *lucubrare*, meaning 'to work by lamplight'.

Mandible (c) from the Latin *mandere*, meaning 'to chew'.

Meretricious (b) from the Latin *meretrix*, meaning 'a prostitute'.

Mitigate (b) from the Latin *mitigare*, meaning 'to soften'.

Moratorium (a) from the Latin *moratorius*, meaning 'delaying'.

Mutation (c) from the Latin *mutare*, meaning 'to change'.

Nadir (b) from the Arabic *nazīr*, meaning 'opposite'.

Nemesis (a) from the Greek *nemein*, meaning 'to distribute'.

Nodule (c) from the Latin *nodulus*, meaning 'a little knot'.

Noisome (b) from the Middle English *noy*, meaning 'annoyance'.

Nous (b) from the Greek *nous*, meaning 'mind'.

Numismatist (c) from the Greek *nomisma*, meaning 'a coin'.

Obsolescent (c) from the Latin *obsolescere*, meaning 'to become old'.

Occidental (a) from the Latin *occidere*, meaning '(of the sun) to go down'.

Occlude (b) from the Latin *occludere*, meaning 'to shut up'.

Oenophile (a) from the Greek *oinos*, meaning 'wine', and *philos*, meaning 'loving'.

Ontological (a) from the Greek *ōn*, meaning 'being', and *logos*, meaning 'word'.

Panegyric (c) from the Greek *panēgyris*, meaning 'public assembly'.

Peripatetic (b) from the Greek *peripatein*, meaning 'to walk up and down'.

Plenary (c) from the Latin *plenus*, meaning 'full'.

Polemic (a) from the Greek *polemikos*, meaning 'warlike'.

Polyp (b) from the Greek *polypous*, meaning 'having many feet'.

Potable (b) from the Latin *potare*, meaning 'to drink'.

Pragmatic (b) from the Greek *pragma*, meaning 'deed'.

Prolix (a) from the Latin *prolixus*, meaning 'extended'.

Putative (c) from the Latin *putare*, meaning 'to think'.

Querulous (a) from the Latin *queri*, meaning 'to complain'.

Rapacity (a) from the Latin *rapere*, meaning 'to seize'.

Reactionary (b) from the noun *reaction*, in the sense of 'opposition to change'.

Recalcitrant (c) from the Latin *recalcitrare*, meaning 'to kick back'.

Restive (b) from the Middle English *restif*, meaning 'refusing to move'.

Salubrious (c) from the Latin *salus*, meaning 'health'.

Scatology (a) from the Greek *skat-*, meaning 'excrement', and *logos*, meaning 'word'.

Scrofula (c) from the Latin *scrofulae*, meaning 'glandular swellings'.

Severance (c) from the verb *sever*, meaning 'to separate'.

Solecism (a) from the Greek *soloikos*, meaning 'speaking incorrectly'.

Sophism (b) from the Greek *sophos*, meaning 'clever'.

Specious (a) from the Latin *speciosus*, meaning 'beautiful'.

Stevedore (a) from the Spanish *estibador*, meaning 'person who loads ships'.

Suborn (a) from the Latin *subornare*, meaning 'to equip secretly'.

Terpsichorean (b) from *Terpsichore*, the name of the Muse of dancing.

Thespian (c) from *Thespis*, the name of the founder of Greek drama.

Tintinnabulation (c) from the Latin *tintinnabulum*, meaning 'bell'.

Ubiquitous (b) from the Latin *ubique*, meaning 'everywhere'.

Unexceptionable (b) from the adjective *exceptionable*, meaning 'open to objection'.

Urbane (c) from the Latin *urbanus*, meaning sophisticated.

Usurious (a) from the Latin *usura*, meaning 'interest'.

Uxorial (c) from the Latin *uxor*, meaning 'wife'.

Valetudinarian (b) from the Latin *valetudinarius*, meaning 'invalid'.

Verdant (a) from the Old French *verdoier*, meaning 'to be green'.

Vitiate (b) from the Latin *vitium*, meaning 'fault'.

Votary (c) from the Latin *votum*, meaning 'vow'.

Whiffle (c) from the verb *whiff*, meaning 'to puff'.

Xenophobia (a) from the Greek *xenos*, meaning 'stranger', and *phobos*, meaning 'fear'.

Yarmulke (a) from the Yiddish *yarmulke*, meaning 'cap'.

Zymotic (b) from the Greek *zymē*, meaning 'leaven'.

HOW GOOD IS YOUR SPELLING?

1   a *stupefying/stupifying* effect
2   the *forword/forward/foreword* to the book
3   a *forgone/foregone* conclusion
4   the troubled period of *adolesence/adolescence*
5   a stand-up *arguement/argument*
6   and other *miscellaneous/misellanious/miscellanious* items
7   I am very *loath/loathe* to say no.
8   the South African system of *apartheid/aparthied/apartheit*
9   the *yoke/yolk* of slavery
10 an insurance *waver/waiver*
11 the rudimentary *principles/principals* of physics
12 *lackered/laquered/laqueured/lacquered* wood
13 What *impeccible/impeccable* behaviour!
14 Yours *truly/truely*, Freda.
15 They're just good *friends/freinds*.
16 a *hypersensitve/hyposensitive* personality
17 to *canvass/canvas/cannvass* public opinion
18 He suffers from *agoraphobia/agraphobia*.
19 the national *curriculum/curiculum* in education
20 to seek *professional/profesional/proffessional* advice
21 The economy is very *boyant/buoyant* at the moment.
22 She *complemented/complimented* him on his fine appearance.
23 *Clostrophobia/Claustrophobia* is the fear of being in enclosed places.
24 He was severely *censored/censured/censered* for the brutality of the attack.
25 in *ecstacy/ecstasy/exstacy* at the thought
26 a *desprate/desperate/despirate* plea for help
27 the *consensus/concensus* of opinion
28 a long period of *convalesense/convalesence/convalescence/convalescense*
29 This price list *supercedes/supersedes* all others.
30 the local *gimkana/gymkana/gymkhana/gimkhana* on Saturday
31 a drunken *stupor/stupour*
32 degrees *Farenheit/Fahrenheit* and Celsius
33 a *coronory/coronary* thrombosis
34 the *navel/naval* forces of the Western alliance
35 the song's *rythm/rhythm*
36 lay *siege/seige* to
37 an *anonimous/anonymous* donor
38 porters and other *ancillary/ansillary/ancilliary* staff
39 The *lepard/leopard/leperd/lepeard* cannot change his spots.
40 an *irrelivent/irrelivant/irrelevant/irrevelant* argument
41 a shortage of rented *accommodation/acomodation/acommodation/accomodation*
42 on the *threshhold/threshold* of an exciting adventure

43   to *illicit/elicit* the truth from them
44   a *heinous/hienous* crime
45   their *plaintive/plaintiff* cries for help
46   *conscientious/consciensious* workers
47   a matter of careful *pronounciation/pronunciation*
48   an *exilarating/exhilarating* performance
49   *Biege/Beige* is a pale brown colour.
50   *cocooned/coccooned* in a world of his own
51   the small short-haired dog known as the *chhwahwa/chihuahua/chihauwa*
52   seventh, *eigth/eighth*, ninth
53   a *dinghy/dingy/dingey* little corner
54   She managed to *resusitate/resuscitate* the patient.
55   a *supersilious/supercilious* attitude
56   a *garantee/guarantey/guarantee* for twelve months.
57   Where does he *hale/hail* from?
58   the *squalour/squalor* of the basement flat
59   an *exhorbitant/exorbitant* price to pay
60   *committment/comitment/commitment* to a task
61   *mocassin/moccasin/moccassin* slippers
62   a *mantel/mantle* of secrecy
63   The hay had already been *bailed/baled*.
64   *sieze/seize* the opportunity
65   *ante-aircraft/anti-aircraft* fire
66   They *aligned/alligned* themselves with the workers.
67   *liesure/leisure/liezure* activities
68   *indigted/indicted/indited* for murder
69   They *ajdourned/ajourned/ajurned/adjourned* to the sitting-room.
70   not *withhold/withold* any further payment
71   his personal *idiosyncrasies/idiosincracies/idiosyncracies*
72   *harasment/harrassment/harassment* of pupils
73   tins either side of the supermarket *isle/aisle*
74   a *conoisseur/connoiseur/connoisseur* of fine food
75   I *recommend/recomend/reccomend* the steak. It's excellent.
76   the college's inefficient *burocrasy/bureaucracy/bureaucrasy*
77   What a *biautiful/beautiful/beutiful* picture!
78   long *course/coarse* grass
79   *chilblains/chillblains* on his toes
80   He had an *absces/absess/abscess* on his skin.
81   *diarhoea/diarrhoea/diarrhea/diarhoea* and sickness
82   to make a *recconaissance/reconnaisance/reconnaissance* into new territory
83   the aircraft *hanger/hangar*
84   a *parafin/parrafin/paraffin* heater
85   *flaired/flared* trousers
86   Their reply will not *affect/effect* my decision.

87   a *sacreligious/sacriligious/sacrilegious* practice
88   into the next *millenium/millennium*
89   The *lightning/lightening* struck the tree.
90   the *Artic/Arctic* circle
91   *swingeing/swinging* cuts in public expenditure
92   a *veterinary/vetenry/vetinry* surgeon
93   increasing editorial *liason/liaison*
94   their world *itinirary/itinerery/itinerary*
95   the *reign/riegn* of Queen Elizabeth II
96   *vacinnated/vaccinated* against polio
97   *hoardes/hordes* of tourists
98   to tell *humourous/humorous* stories
99   to drain the carrots in the *calendar/colander/callendar/collander*
100   customs *tariffs/tarifs/tarrifs*
101   She *councilled/counselled* him to remain at home.
102   His *physiognomy/physionomy* revealed his true character.
103   a *breach/breech* birth
104   Post Office *commemorative/commemmorative* stamps
105   to eat breakfast *serial/cereal*
106   write in your *exersise/exercise/exersice* books
107   Please be *discrete/discreet*—I don't want everyone to know.
108   *dessicated/desiccated* coconut
109   He got his just *desserts/deserts*.
110   two *parallell/paralel/parallel/paralell* lines
111   painted in a *flourescent/florescent/fluorescent* pink
112   the *assent/ascent* of Everest
113   a *skizophrenic/schizophrenic/schizophreenic* personality
114   *miniskule/minuscule/miniscule* writing
115   drink of *liquor/liqueur* after a meal
116   I *appreciate/apreciate* your kindness.
117   a *woolly/wooly* garment
118   The accusations were *vigorously/vigourously* denied by both parties.
119   This doesn't *altar/alter* the fact that you're wrong.
120   He *preceded/proceeded* to explain in more detail.
121   on the horns of a *dilemma/dilemna*
122   He had a momentary mental *aberration/aberation*.
123   *innoculation/inoculation* against tetanus
124   the *motif/motive* for the crime
125   matters of personal *hygeine/hygiene*
126   the *cannon/canon* of the Cathedral, Peter Duffett
127   a *troop/troupe* of acrobats
128   a bank *currant/current/curant* account
129   the *priviledges/priveleges/priviliges/privileges* given to the higher levels of management
130   No further *buletin/bulletin/bullettin/bulettin* will be issued tonight.

131   The *comitee/commitee/comittee/committee* decided to increase subscriptions by £5.
132   suffer from *cirosis/cirrosis/cirrhosis*, caused by drinking too much alcohol
133   to paint the *cieling/ceiling*
134   highly *embarassed/embarrased/embarrassed* at not being able to spell words
135   *dying/dyeing* cloths a deep red colour

Answers to spelling quiz

1	*stupefying*	46	*conscientious*	91	*swingeing*
2	*foreword*	47	*pronunciation*	92	*veterinary*
3	*foregone*	48	*exhilarating*	93	*liaison*
4	*adolescence*	49	*Beige*	94	*itinerary*
5	*argument*	50	*cocooned*	95	*reign*
6	*miscellaneous*	51	*chihuahua*	96	*vaccinated*
7	*loath*	52	*eighth*	97	*hordes*
8	*apartheid*	53	*dingy*	98	*humorous*
9	*yoke*	54	*resuscitate*	99	*colander*
10	*waiver*	55	*supercilious*	100	*tariffs*
11	*principles*	56	*guarantee*	101	*counselled*
12	*lacquered*	57	*hail*	102	*physiognomy*
13	*impeccable*	58	*squalor*	103	*breech*
14	*truly*	59	*exorbitant*	104	*commemorative*
15	*friends*	60	*commitment*	105	*cereal*
16	*hypersensitive*	61	*moccasin*	106	*exercise*
17	*canvas*	62	*mantle*	107	*discreet*
18	*agoraphobia*	63	*baled*	108	*desiccated*
19	*curriculum*	64	*seize*	109	*deserts*
20	*professional*	65	*anti-aircraft*	110	*parallel*
21	*buoyant*	66	*aligned*	111	*fluorescent*
22	*complimented*	67	*leisure*	112	*ascent*
23	*Claustrophobia*	68	*indicted*	113	*schizophrenic*
24	*censured*	69	*adjourned*	114	*minuscule*
25	*ecstasy*	70	*withhold*	115	*liqueur*
26	*desperate*	71	*idiosyncrasies*	116	*appreciate*
27	*consensus*	72	*harassment*	117	*woolly*
28	*convalescence*	73	*aisle*	118	*vigorously*
29	*supersedes*	74	*connoisseur*	119	*alter*
30	*gymkhana*	75	*recommend*	120	*proceeded*
31	*stupor*	76	*bureaucracy*	121	*dilemma*
32	*Fahrenheit*	77	*beautiful*	122	*aberration*
33	*coronary*	78	*coarse*	123	*inoculation*
34	*naval*	79	*chilblains*	124	*motive*
35	*rhythm*	80	*abscess*	125	*hygiene*
36	*siege*	81	*diarrhoea*	126	*canon*
37	*anonymous*	82	*reconnaissance*	127	*troupe*
38	*ancillary*	83	*hangar*	128	*current*
39	*leopard*	84	*paraffin*	129	*privileges*
40	*irrelevant*	85	*flared*	130	*bulletin*
41	*accommodation*	86	*affect*	131	*committee*
42	*threshold*	87	*sacrilegious*	132	*cirrhosis*
43	*elicit*	88	*millennium*	133	*ceiling*
44	*heinous*	89	*lightning*	134	*embarrassed*
45	*plaintive*	90	*Arctic*	135	*dyeing*

**BIBLIOGRAPHY
INDEX AND
ACKNOWLEDGEMENTS**

BIBLIOGRAPHY

PERIODICALS
English Today
Verbatim

CHAPTER 1
David Crystal, *The Cambridge Encyclopedia of Language*,
Cambridge University Press, 1987
Tom McArthur, *Worlds of Reference*,
Cambridge University Press, 1986

CHAPTER 2
Robert Burchfield, *The English Language*,
Oxford University Press, 1985
Stuart Berg Flexner, *I Hear America Talking*,
Van Nostrand Reinhold, 1976
Kenneth Katzner, *The Languages of the World*,
Routledge & Kegan Paul, revised edition, 1986
Robert McCrum, William Cran, Robert MacNeil, *The Story of English*,
Faber and Faber & BBC Publications, 1986

CHAPTER 3
Martin H. Manser, Nigel D. Turton, *The Penguin Wordmaster Dictionary*,
Penguin Books, 1987
William and Mary Morris, *Morris Dictionary of Word Origins*,
Harper & Row, 1977
Edwin Radford, Alan Smith, *To Coin a Phrase: A Dictionary of Origins*,
Macmillan, 1981
Adrian Room, *Dictionary of True Etymologies*,
Routledge & Kegan Paul, 1986

CHAPTER 4
Cyril Leslie Beeching, *A Dictionary of Eponyms*,
Clive Bingley, 2nd edition, 1983
Rosie Boycott, *Batty, Bloomers and Boycott:
A little etymology of eponymous words*, Hutchinson, 1982
Christopher Smith, *Alabaster, Bikinis and Calvados:
an ABC of toponymous words*, Century Hutchinson, 1985
Nigel Viney, *A Dictionary of Toponyms*,
Library Association, 1986

CHAPTER 5

Oxford Dictionary of Quotations,
Oxford University Press, 3rd edition, 1979

J. M. & M. J. Cohen, *The Penguin Dictionary of Modern Quotations*,
Penguin, 2nd edition, 1980

J. M. & M. J. Cohen, *The Penguin Dictionary of Quotations*,
Penguin 1960

Jonathon Green, *Famous Last Words*, Pan 1980

CHAPTER 6

Tony Augarde, *The Oxford Guide to Word Games*,
Oxford University Press, 1986

Gyles Brandreth, *Everyman's Word Games*,
Dent, 1986

INDEX

ACKNOWLEDGEMENTS

The author wishes to express his gratitude to the following: Rosalind Fergusson, Jenny Roberts, and Sarah Peasley for their help in compiling the typescript; Ania Marzec, Margaret McPhee, and Adrian Room for their advice; Rosalind Desmond and Barbara Newton for their painstaking typing of the manuscript; and Honor Head of the publishers for her editorial guiding skills.